THE BOOK OF
EZEKIEL

The Glory of the Lord Has Departed

By
Kurt Kennedy, M(BS), D.Min.

All scripture references are from the King James Bible

Requests for copies or information should be addressed to:
kennedykt@yahoo.com

ISBN: 978-0692378182

True Word Press

This book is dedicated to Mr. John Knowles,
a soldier of our country and a soldier of the cross.
Thank you for the countless hours.

CONTENTS

SECTION 1 | CHAPTERS 4-24

THE COMING JUDGMENT BY GOD ON JERUSALEM
Given Before the Siege of Jerusalem

SECTION 2 | CHAPTERS 25-32

GOD'S JUDGMENT ON SURROUNDING NATIONS
Given During the Siege of Jerusalem

SECTION 3 | CHAPTERS 33-48

FUTURE RESTORATION OF THE JEWS
Given After the Siege of Jerusalem

Introduction

When one mentions the study of the book of Ezekiel, instantly it is assumed the book is too difficult, that it is a most insurmountable task to comment on. However, it is a book in the Word of God and therefore we are called upon to study it. I am convinced that many who say that the book of Ezekiel is too difficult have not taken the time to thoroughly study it. Possibly they could not get past the first chapter, being overwhelmed by the first vision Ezekiel sees. Had they kept reading they would have found so many beautiful and amazing things on every turn of the page, fulfilled prophecies so accurate they boggle the mind.

As we go through Ezekiel together we will need to remind ourselves to appreciate each little bit of knowledge and insight we get from the Holy Spirit of God and build upon that. Do not fall into the trap of the "I just want it all now" mentality. Bible knowledge is "precept upon precept, line upon line." With that exhortation in mind, let us look into this most amazing book of the Bible.

The Historical Setting:
It is imperative that you understand a little of Ezekiel's historical setting. The house of Israel is divided into two kingdoms, the northern consisting of ten tribes *(often referred to as Israel)* and the southern consisting of two tribes *(often, but not exclusively, referred to as Judah)*. At the time Ezekiel is prophesying the northern tribes had been taken into captivity by the Assyrians more than 100 years prior.

11

The Three Deportations of the Jews:
The northern tribes having been taken away by the Assyrians, God now deals with the judgment on Jerusalem and the southern tribes. Under the leadership of Nebuchadnezzar, the Babylonians complete three sieges against Jerusalem, each time deporting Jews into the region of Babylon.

- 606 B.C. The Babylonians begin the first deportation of the Jews *(Daniel was in this group) under the reign of Jehoiakim.*
- 597 B.C. As a young man Ezekiel was part of the second deportation under the reign of Jehoiachin, being then about the age of 25. He was deported to the Jewish assembly in the region known as Telabib by the river Chebar *(a canal off the Euphrates river.)* (Ezek. 3:15)
- 592 B.C. In the second deportation Ezekiel is taken into captivity. Five years after this deportation he is called to be a prophet of God at the age of 30. **Ezekiel is prophesying prior to, during, and following the final siege on Jerusalem.**
- 586 B.C. Nebuchadnezzar having an oath broken by Judah's last king, Zedekiah, has had enough and comes in and destroys Jerusalem.

It is noteworthy that Jeremiah is preaching at this time in the land of Judah but is considerably older than both Daniel and Ezekiel, who are but young men upon their deportation into Babylon. Daniel is in the court of the king of Babylon while Ezekiel is in a house down south by the river Chebar. All these men are contemporary to one another.

The Man Ezekiel:
- Ezekiel is one of the three that are known as the captivity prophets *(the other two being Daniel and Jeremiah).*

- Ezekiel was a priest but never served in that office because he was taken into captivity to Babylon during the second deportation in the reign of Jehoiachin, also called Jeconiah (I Chron. 3:16.)
- Ezekiel is taken to a Jewish settlement down by the river Chebar, which is a great canal of the Euphrates river, several miles south of Babylon itself.
- Though Ezekiel is in Babylon he is able to see events in Jerusalem through the power of the Spirit of God.
- **Ezekiel is prophesying to the people of Jerusalem before, during and following the final siege on Jerusalem** and deportation of the Jewish people.
- Ezekiel is called upon to be a living parable. He is called upon to do many symbolic acts and similes to get the attention of the people.
- Ezekiel prophesied of coming judgment against Jerusalem while false prophets told the people that God would destroy Babylon and set the captives free.

Outline of the Book of Ezekiel:

1-3   The Call of the Prophet

4-24   God's Judgment on Jerusalem
(Given before the siege of Jerusalem)

25-32   God's Judgment on Surrounding Nations
(Given during the siege of Jerusalem)

33-48   The Future Restoration of the Jews
(Given after the siege on Jerusalem)

CHAPTER 1
The Vision

Ezekiel is down by the river Chebar among a settlement of the Jewish captives from Jerusalem. The Jewish captives were in a state of somberness and depression over their deportation out of the land (Ps. 137!). However, in the midst of this sorrow Ezekiel sees a vision; what mercy and grace.

Now it came to pass in the thirtieth year, in the fourth month, in the fifth day of the month, as I was among the captives by the river of Chebar, that the heavens were opened, and I saw visions of God. In the fifth day of the month, which was the fifth year of king Jehoiachin's captivity, The word of the LORD came expressly unto Ezekiel the priest, the son of Buzi, in the land of the Chaldeans by the river Chebar; and the hand of the LORD was there upon him. (Ezekiel 1:1-3)

The Call of the Prophet (1-3): Ezekiel is in captivity about 5 years (vs. 2) when he receives this first vision. He is about 30 years old (vs. 1) at this time and therefore, though he was a priest (vs. 3), he does not fulfill that role (Num. 4:3) being called at this time (2:1-3) to be a prophet for God.

The Vision of God's Movable Throne: The vision that Ezekiel sees is the movable throne of God. He is not describing an aircraft or a UFO (*in the classic sense of the word*). It is heavenly in nature, and therefore Ezekiel "likens" it to things you and I are familiar with. Note how many times Ezekiel uses the terms "like" "likeness" "as" and "as the appearance of" in describing the things he sees. Thus "likeness of a man..." means similar, not identical with (cf. v. 26), expressing the general form; while "appearance" expresses a general aspect. Thus the prophet senses the inadequacy of human speech to describe the unspeakable.

This chapter needs to be considered with chapters 8 through 11 in which the throne of God moves to the temple in Jerusalem for a specific task. John will see this same throne as well (Rev. 4:6-7).

And I looked, and, behold, a whirlwind came out of the north, a great cloud, and a fire infolding itself, and a brightness was about it, and out of the midst thereof as the colour of amber, out of the midst of the fire. (Ezekiel 1:4)

The Whirlwind of God's Judgment (4): Ezekiel sees a whirlwind out of the north. This is as we mentioned in our introduction, Ezekiel is seeing the vision as though he were in Jerusalem; even though he is in Babylonian captivity. The judgment of God coming from the north is Babylon. The north is also a reference to the place God dwells (Ps 75:6, 7) and therefore the judgment coming against Jerusalem is from God.

Also out of the midst thereof came the likeness of four living creatures. And this was their appearance; they had the likeness of a man. And every one had four faces, and every one had four wings. And their feet

were straight feet; and the sole of their feet was like the sole of a calf's foot: and they sparkled like the colour of burnished brass. And they had the hands of a man under their wings on their four sides; and they four had their faces and their wings. Their wings were joined one to another; they turned not when they went; they went every one straight forward. As for the likeness of their faces, they four had the face of a man, and the face of a lion, on the right side: and they four had the face of an ox on the left side; they four also had the face of an eagle. Thus were their faces: and their wings were stretched upward; two wings of every one were joined one to another, and two covered their bodies. And they went every one straight forward: whither the spirit was to go, they went; and they turned not when they went. As for the likeness of the living creatures, their appearance was like burning coals of fire, and like the appearance of lamps: it went up and down among the living creatures; and the fire was bright, and out of the fire went forth lightning. And the living creatures ran and returned as the appearance of a flash of lightning. (Ezekiel 1:5-14)

The Four Living Creatures (5-14): These four living creatures are called "Cherubim" (see 10:15,22). Cherubim are four-winged creatures each having multiple faces (v.10). They each have a face that is "likened" to a man, lion, ox and eagle. These four faces are associated with the 12 tribes of Israel:
- **Lion** ensign for the tribe of Judah (*East*) (*Issachar and Zebullun*)
- **Ox** ensign for the tribe of Ephraim (*West*) (*Manasseh and Benjamin*)
- **Man** ensign for the tribe of Reuben (*South*) (*Simeon and Gad*)

- **Eagle** ensign for the tribe of Dan (*North*)
  (*Asher and Naphtali*)

These were to be the respective leaders of Israel camped in the four cardinal directions around the Tabernacle.

THE CAMP OF ISRAEL

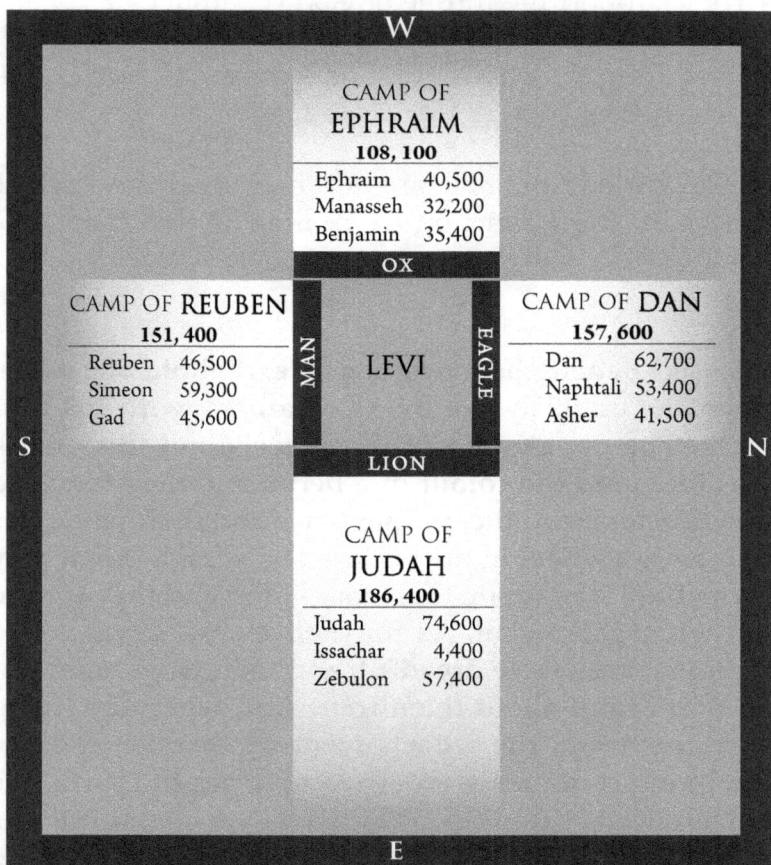

	W	
	CAMP OF **EPHRAIM** 108, 100	

CAMP OF **EPHRAIM**
108, 100

Ephraim	40,500
Manasseh	32,200
Benjamin	35,400

OX

CAMP OF **REUBEN**
151, 400

Reuben	46,500
Simeon	59,300
Gad	45,600

MAN

LEVI

EAGLE

CAMP OF **DAN**
157, 600

Dan	62,700
Naphtali	53,400
Asher	41,500

S

N

LION

CAMP OF
JUDAH
186, 400

Judah	74,600
Issachar	4,400
Zebulon	57,400

E

(Note: when each of these tribes are numbered on their respective sides (Num. Ch. 2) an interesting truth is seen – Judah, Issachar and Zebullun = 186,400; Ruben, Simeon and Gad = 151,450; Ephraim, Manasseh and Benjamin = 108,100; Dan, Asher and Naphtali = 157,600. This arrangement places the people in the shape of a cross surrounding the Tabernacle.)

These Cherubim are Associated with the Throne of God:
- They guard the way to the tree of life (Gen.3:24)
- They covered the mercy seat in the Tabernacle (Ex. 25:18-20; 37:7-9) and Solomon's Temple (I Kings 6:23-28)
- They support the throne of God (I Samuel 4:2; 2 Sam. 6:2; 2 Kings 19:15; Ps. 80:1)
- They form the chariot of God's throne (2 Sam. 22:11; Ps. 104:3; <u>I Chr. 28:18</u>)

These various actions are all presented in Ezekiel, especially their function as bearers of the throne of God.

Now as I beheld the living creatures, behold one wheel upon the earth by the living creatures, with his four faces. The appearance of the wheels and their work was like unto the colour of a beryl: and they four had one likeness: and their appearance and their work was as it were a wheel in the middle of a wheel. When they went, they went upon their four sides: and they turned not when they went. As for their rings, they were so high that they were dreadful; and their rings were full of eyes round about them four. And when the living creatures went, the wheels went by them: and when the living creatures were lifted up from the earth, the wheels were lifted up. Whithersoever the spirit was to go, they went, thither was their spirit to go; and the wheels were lifted up over against them: for the spirit of the living creature was in the wheels. When those went, these went; and when those stood, these stood; and when those were lifted up from the earth, the wheels were lifted up over against them: for the

spirit of the living creature was in the wheels. (Ezekiel 1:15-21)

The Wheels of God's Throne (15-21): Ezekiel now sees the "likeness" of wheels in the middle of wheels (v.16). These wheels were located next to each of the Cherubim moving wherever the spirit (*spirit of the Cherubim*) commanded to go, given direction from the one on the throne, God the Father (v. 17-20,25). Wheels being associated with God's throne is nothing new, see Daniel 7:9.

And the likeness of the firmament upon the heads of the living creature was as the colour of the terrible crystal, stretched forth over their heads above. And under the firmament were their wings straight, the one toward the other: every one had two, which covered on this side, and every one had two, which covered on that side, their bodies. And when they went, I heard the noise of their wings, like the noise of great waters, as the voice of the Almighty, the voice of speech, as the noise of an host: when they stood, they let down their wings. And there was a voice from the firmament that was over their heads, when they stood, and had let down their wings. (Ezekiel 1:22-25)

The Firmament Platform of God's Throne (22-25): The Cherubim and the wheels within the wheels are located under a "firmament," a sea of glass as crystal (v. 22, 23 Ezek. 10:1 cf. Rev. 4:6-7). This is the firmament platform that God's throne sits upon (v. 26).

And above the firmament that was over their heads

19

was the likeness of a throne, as the appearance of a sapphire stone: and upon the likeness of the throne was the likeness as the appearance of a man above upon it. And I saw as the colour of amber, as the appearance of fire round about within it, from the appearance of his loins even upward, and from the appearance of his loins even downward, I saw as it were the appearance of fire, and it had brightness round about. As the appearance of the bow that is in the cloud in the day of rain, so was the appearance of the brightness round about. This was the appearance of the likeness of the glory of the LORD. And when I saw it, I fell upon my face, and I heard a voice of one that spake. (Ezekiel 1:26-28)

God the Father on the Throne (26-28): Now Ezekiel describes what he sees and hears above the Cherubim. He first describes a voice over the firmament (v. 25) The voice is that of God Almighty (v. 1, 28). Ezekiel describes the "likeness" of Him on the throne having the "likeness" of a man (v.26) in the appearance of burning fire, amber. The Glory of the LORD is used throughout the book of Ezekiel for the person of God who is manifested.

Conclusion:
Ezekiel sees God appear in great glory coming out of the north to commission him as prophet (2:3) and lay the final judgment against His people. Ezekiel sees God seated on a throne above a firmament of crystal; under which are wheels and Cherubim which move at His demand. Thus God is moving in judgment against Jerusalem (remember chapters 1-24 are prior to the destruction of the temple).

CHAPTER 2

The Call of Ezekiel

And he said unto me, Son of man, stand upon thy feet, and I will speak unto thee. And the spirit entered into me when he spake unto me, and set me upon my feet, that I heard him that spake unto me. And he said unto me, Son of man, I send thee to the children of Israel, to a rebellious nation that hath rebelled against me: they and their fathers have transgressed against me, even unto this very day. (Ezekiel 2:1-3)

The Glory of the Vision (1-3): Upon seeing the glory of the Lord, Ezekiel "fell to his knees" (1:28), as did Daniel (Dan. 10:9) and John (Rev. 1:17). Ezekiel is now told to "stand" (v. 1) and is placed upon his feet (2). Notice they have rebelled and transgressed against "me." The nation has merited all that has and will come upon them, even the carrying away into Babylon (Lev. 26:33).

For they are impudent children and stiffhearted. I do send thee unto them; and thou shalt say unto them, Thus saith the Lord GOD. And they, whether they will hear, or whether they will forbear, (for they are a rebellious house,) yet shall know that there hath been a prophet among them. And thou, son of man, be not afraid of them, neither be afraid of their words, though briers and thorns be with thee, and thou dost dwell among scorpions: be not afraid of their words, nor be dismayed at their looks, though they be a rebellious house. And thou shalt speak my words unto them, whether they will hear, or whether they will forbear: for they are most rebellious. (Ezekiel 2:4-7)

Thus Saith the Lord (4-7): Ezekiel will speak for God, "...thou shalt say unto them, Thus saith the Lord GOD." By using this phrase, one exposed himself to be charged guilty of a capital crime. The Nation of Israel, even in its idolatry, took the concept of blasphemy very seriously, and if you pretended to be speaking on behalf of God Himself, you took your life in your hands (Deut. 18:20-22; Jer. 28:9). Notice how many times the word "rebellious" comes up in this chapter alone. Ezekiel is to speak to the people regardless of the results!

But thou, son of man, hear what I say unto thee; Be not thou rebellious like that rebellious house: open thy mouth, and eat that I give thee. And when I looked, behold, an hand was sent unto me; and, lo, a roll of a book was therein; And he spread it before me; and it was written within and without: and there was written therein lamentations, and mourning, and woe. (Ezekiel 2:8-10)

Role of a Book Full of Lamentations, Mourning and Woe (8-10): This is representative of chapters 4-32, however in chapter 33 Ezekiel is re-commissioned, thus the rest of the book, chapters 33-48, is a promise of blessing for the "nation." There are only two books described as "written on both the inside and the outside": One is given to Ezekiel to eat (3:1-3), the other is the seven sealed book in Revelation 5 (both of these books bring judgment).

CHAPTER 3

The Preparation of the Prophet

Moreover he said unto me, Son of man, eat that thou findest; eat this roll, and go speak unto the house of Israel. So I opened my mouth, and he caused me to eat that roll. And he said unto me, Son of man, cause thy belly to eat, and fill thy bowels with this roll that I give thee. Then did I eat it; and it was in my mouth as honey for sweetness. And he said unto me, Son of man, go, get thee unto the house of Israel, and speak with my words unto them. (Ezekiel 3:1-4)

Digesting His Words (1-4): The concept of eating the words of God is nothing foreign to Scripture, Jeremiah said, "Thy words were found and I did eat them" (Jer.15:16). John is told to eat a book as well (Rev. 10:8-11). The Lord Himself, when tempted of Satan, quoted Deuteronomy 8:3, **"But he answered and said, It is written, Man shall not live by bread alone, but by every word that proceedeth out of the mouth of God."** (Matthew 4:4)

This eating is both literal (*he really ate*) and symbolic (*he is to fully digest the words given him to speak*); see 3:10.

For thou art not sent to a people of a strange speech and of an hard language, but to the house of Israel; Not to many people of a strange speech and of an hard language, whose words thou canst not understand. Surely, had I sent thee to them, they would have hearkened unto thee. But the house of Israel will not hearken unto thee; for they will not hearken unto me: for all the house of Israel are impudent and hardhearted. Behold, I have made thy face strong against their faces, and thy forehead strong against their foreheads. As an adamant harder than flint have I made thy forehead: fear them not, neither be dismayed at their looks, though they be a rebellious house. (Ezekiel 3:5-9)

Not Sent unto a People of Strange Speech and Hard Language (5-9): Ezekiel is sent unto the "house of Israel," those of his own language. If God sent him unto the Gentiles (*those of strange speech and hard language*) they would have heard! Notice it's the "house of Israel." The 10 northern tribes had been taken over 100 years prior to this, thus in using the expression "house of Israel" God has the entire nation in view. God tells Ezekiel that they will not harken for they are a "hardhearted" people. Not only is the nation a hardhearted people, but they are hard-headed as well, thus Ezekiel is called to be so also.

Moreover he said unto me, Son of man, all my words that I shall speak unto thee receive in thine heart, and hear with thine ears. And go, get thee to them of the captivity, unto the children of thy people, and speak unto them, and tell them, Thus saith the Lord GOD; whether they will hear, or whether they will forbear. Then the spirit took me up, and I heard behind me a voice of a great rushing, saying, Blessed be the glory of the LORD from his place. I heard also the noise of the wings of the living creatures that touched one another, and the noise of the wheels over against them, and a noise of a great rushing. So the spirit lifted me up, and took me away, and I went in bitterness, in the heat of my spirit; but the hand of the LORD was strong upon me. Then I came to them of the captivity at Telabib, that dwelt by the river of Chebar, and I sat where they sat, and remained there astonished among them seven days. (Ezekiel 3:10-15)

The Spirit Lifted me up and Took me Away (10-15): Ezekiel is transported to another Jewish settlement by the river Chebar called Telabib (v. 15). Ezekiel's transportation is associated with the Chariot of God (cf. chapter 1). Thus, you have the "wheels" the "wings of the living creatures" and the noises associated with its movement (vs. 12-13). Notice Ezekiel is *physically* transported, not a second sight type of experience (*"took me up" v. 12 & "took me away" v. 14*).

The whole experience of what he saw in chapter 1, and the Lord talking with him through chapters 2 and 3, left Ezekiel physically overwhelmed for seven days.

And it came to pass at the end of seven days, that the word of the LORD came unto me, saying, Son of man, I have made thee a watchman unto the house of Israel: therefore hear the word at my mouth, and give them warning from me. When I say unto the wicked, Thou shalt surely die; and thou givest him not warning, nor speakest to warn the wicked from his wicked way, to save his life; the same wicked man shall die in his iniquity; but his blood will I require at thine hand. Yet if thou warn the wicked, and he turn not from his wickedness, nor from his wicked way, he shall die in his iniquity; but thou hast delivered thy soul. Again, When a righteous man doth turn from his righteousness, and commit iniquity, and I lay a stumblingblock before him, he shall die: because thou hast not given him warning, he shall die in his sin, and his righteousness which he hath done shall not be remembered; but his blood will I require at thine hand. Nevertheless if thou warn the righteous man, that the righteous sin not, and he doth not sin, he shall surely live, because he is warned; also thou hast delivered thy soul. (Ezekiel 3:16-21)

The Calling of a Watchman (16-21): Following the seven days (16) Ezekiel is made a watchman unto the house of Israel (17). The watchmen of old were to not rest day or night while they fulfilled that role upon the walls of Jerusalem (Isa. 62:2; 2 Sam. 18:24-27; 2 Kings 9:17-20). Thus, Ezekiel is accountable for the faithful deliverance of God's message to the people, not for its success or failure (vs. 17-19). The roll of the watchman is an informational role:

• The people of the nation that are <u>not warned</u> (v. 18) - *Ezekiel accountable*
• The people of the nation that <u>are warned</u> but do not repent (v. 19) - *Ezekiel not accountable*
• The righteous man of the nation who turns from his righteousness and is <u>not warned</u> (v. 20) - *Ezekiel accountable*
• The righteous man who <u>is warned</u> and remains righteous (v. 21) - *Ezekiel not accountable*

When reading this portion note that "die" and "live" are not in the New Testament sense of heaven and hell, but here to "die" is to perish in the destruction of the state, versus "live" by going into Babylonian captivity (*with a far reaching view of the established Millennial Kingdom*).

Then I arose, and went forth into the plain: and, behold, the glory of the LORD stood there, as the glory which I

saw by the river of Chebar: and I fell on my face. Then the spirit entered into me, and set me upon my feet, and spake with me, and said unto me, Go, shut thyself within thine house. But thou, O son of man, behold, they shall put bands upon thee, and shall bind thee with them, and thou shalt not go out among them: And I will make thy tongue cleave to the roof of thy mouth, that thou shalt be dumb, and shalt not be to them a reprover: for they are a rebellious house. But when I speak with thee, I will open thy mouth, and thou shalt say unto them, Thus saith the Lord GOD; He that heareth, let him hear; and he that forbeareth, let him forbear: for they are a rebellious house. (Ezekiel 3:23-27)

Go Shut Thyself in Thy House (23-27): Ezekiel is to go back and shut himself into his house. This does not imply that Ezekiel was never to leave his house (cf. Ezek. 5:2; 12:3). Instead he was to refrain from open fellowship with the people. Often the leaders came to him at his house to receive God's word (cf. Ezek. 8:1; 14:1; 20:1). This intermediate silence prevailed from the beginning of the siege of Jerusalem, until news of the fall of Jerusalem was brought to the prophet by a fugitive (Ezek. 24:1, 27 cf. 33:21-23).

Section 1
CHAPTERS 4-24

———•———

THE COMING JUDGMENT
BY GOD ON JERUSALEM
Given Before the Siege of Jerusalem

CHAPTER 4

Signs Regarding the Judgments on Jerusalem

Ezekiel is going to do a number of symbolic acts representing the coming judgment on Jerusalem. Remember these chapters are **prior to the siege** the final destruction of Jerusalem. Ezekiel's task is to confront Israel with her sin and warn her of impending destruction. Ezekiel employed various means to focus on the people's need for judgment. These included: signs (chapters 4&5); sermons (chapters 6&7), and visions (chapters 8-11). In each case the emphasis was on sin and the ensuing suffering.

Thou also, son of man, take thee a tile, and lay it before thee, and pourtray upon it the city, even Jerusalem: And lay siege against it, and build a fort against it, and cast a mount against it; set the camp also against it, and set battering rams against it round about. Moreover take thou unto thee an iron pan, and set it for a wall of iron between thee and the city: and set thy face against it, and it shall be besieged, and thou shalt lay siege against it. This shall be a sign to the house of Israel. (Ezekiel 4:1-3)

Playing War (1-3): Ezekiel was to take a tile (*clay brick, the main building material used in Babylon- Gen. 11:3)* and inscribe upon it the city of Jerusalem and then "lay siege" against it. Notice the instruments of war, "build a fort" "cast a mount" and "set battering rams." Ezekiel is then to take an iron pan and place it between himself and the city, thus indicating that they will not be able to fight against it; it will come to pass.

Lie thou also upon thy left side, and lay the iniquity of the house of Israel upon it: according to the number of the days that thou shalt lie upon it thou shalt bear their iniquity. For I have laid upon thee the years of their iniquity, according to the number of the days, three hundred and ninety days: so shalt thou bear the iniquity of the house of Israel. And when thou hast accomplished them, lie again on thy right side, and thou shalt bear the iniquity of the house of Judah forty days: I have appointed thee each day for a year. Therefore thou shalt set thy face toward the siege of Jerusalem, and thine arm shall be uncovered, and thou shalt prophesy against it. And, behold, I will lay bands upon thee, and thou shalt not turn thee from one side to another, till thou hast ended the days of thy siege. (Ezekiel 4:4-8)

430 Years of Iniquity (4-8): Ezekiel is now to lie on his left side for the iniquity of the house of Israel (4-5). He is to do this for 390 days, each day representing a year and each year representing the years God bore the iniquity of the house of Israel. This could be reckoning from the first apostasy under Jeroboam to the Assyrian captivity. Be that as it may, the 390 years represented the time in which God bore the iniquity of the Northern tribes, until judgment came. God is able to bear them no more (Jer. 44:22).

Once these days are completed Ezekiel is told to lie on his right side and bear the iniquity of the house of Judah (v.6). He is to lie on his right side 40 days, each day representing a year that God had to bear the iniquity of the house of Judah. The final reckoning for both houses total 430 years of God bearing the iniquity of the whole house of Israel. With each side he laid on his respective arm was uncovered (v.7).

All this was to be done at a certain time of the day (v. 10) while he faced the "siege of Jerusalem" that he had made with the tile (v.7) and while he ate the meager food and drink mentioned in verses 9-11. Ezekiel was to be bound while this took place (v.8).

Take thou also unto thee wheat, and barley, and beans, and lentiles, and millet, and fitches, and put them in one vessel, and make thee bread thereof, according to the number of the days that thou shalt lie upon thy side, three hundred and ninety days shalt thou eat thereof. And thy meat which thou shalt eat shall be by weight, twenty shekels a day: from time to time shalt thou eat it. Thou shalt drink also water by measure, the sixth part of an hin: from time to time shalt thou drink. And thou shalt eat it as barley cakes, and thou shalt bake it with dung that cometh out of man, in their sight. And the LORD said, Even thus shall the children of Israel eat their defiled bread among the Gentiles, whither I will drive them. Then said I, Ah Lord GOD! behold, my soul hath not been polluted: for from my youth up even till now have I not eaten of that which dieth of itself, or is torn in pieces; neither came there abominable flesh into my mouth. Then he said unto me, Lo, I have given thee cow's dung for man's dung, and thou shalt prepare thy bread therewith. Moreover he said unto me, Son of man, behold, I will break the

staff of bread in Jerusalem: and they shall eat bread by weight, and with care; and they shall drink water by measure, and with astonishment: That they may want bread and water, and be astonied one with another, and consume away for their iniquity. (Ezekiel 4:9-17)

Judgment of Famine (9-17): Ezekiel is now to prepare bread in the form of barley cakes (v.9,12). Both the food and the drink was to be only a meager amount (*Meat was twenty shekels weight, or about 8 oz a day, and the water ration was a sixth part of a hin, or about a pint and a half a day*). All this was symbolic that famine was coming!

The meager food was to be prepared (*or baked v.12*) in an unclean manner (v.12-15). It was common in the desert or wilderness where trees would be scarce that cow dung mixed with straw would be used for fuel in baking. In order to put emphasis on the extreme famine coming, God told Ezekiel to use human dung because there would not even be cattle left to fuel their fires (v.12). However, later God conceded to Ezekiel's plea and allowed cow dung to be used instead, for the sake of this symbolic act (vs. 12-15). Thus, he was to eat his defiled bread among the Gentiles (Hos. 9:3,4).

The final siege of Jerusalem is recorded in 2 Kings 25:1-12. The siege lasted about a year and a half before its final destruction. It was during this year and a half that this great famine was experienced by God's people in Jerusalem (Lam. 4; Ezek. 5:10, 12, 16-17) as the Northern tribes had already experienced years earlier (2 Kings 6:24-29).

Ezekiel lying on his side looking toward the besieged city, bound, represents God, who is bound by the iniquity of the sins of Israel and Judah and can no longer bear them (Jer. 44:22). **The iron pan** placed between Ezekiel and the besieged city represents the reality that Israel's time for repenting is over, the heavens are as iron, God is not listening (Ezek. 8:18). The **tile with Jerusalem inscribed on it and the items of war laying siege against it,** represents what God is going to allow to happen to His beloved city (2 Kings 25:1-12). The **eating of the meager food prepared in an unclean manner** represents the severity of the famine that is coming (2 Kings 25:1-3).

CHAPTER 5
The Judgments of Thirds

Cutting Ezekiel's beard in thirds is symbolic of what God was doing with His people in Jerusalem (v. 8). God will judge a third by famine and pestilence, a third by sword, and a third will be scattered to the wind.

And thou, son of man, take thee a sharp knife, take thee a barber's rasor, and cause it to pass upon thine head and upon thy beard: then take thee balances to weigh, and divide the hair. Thou shalt burn with fire a third part in the midst of the city, when the days of the siege are fulfilled: and thou shalt take a third part, and smite about it with a knife: and a third part thou shalt scatter in the wind; and I will draw out a sword after them. Thou shalt also take thereof a few in number, and bind them in thy skirts. Then take of them again, and cast them into the midst of the fire, and burn them in the fire; for thereof shall a fire come forth into all the house of Israel. (Ezekiel 5:1-4)

Shaving of the Head and Beard (1-4): This symbolic act was figurative of wiping the city clean of its inhabitants (Isa. 7:20, 2 Kings 21:13). The weighing of the hair is to show that the judgment is just; it is from God.

A third of the hair is to be burnt with fire. This is the third that will be consumed with famine and pestilence (cf. v. 12). A third part is to be smitten with a knife. This is the third of the people that are to be smitten by the sword (cf. v. 12). And the last third is to be scattered in the wind; the final third that is scattered among the nations (cf. v. 12).

A few in number from the whole of the hairs (people) described above, Ezekiel was to take and hide in his skirt or robe. This symbolic act was to represent the remnant that God would preserve; God is not going to completely obliterate His people (6:8).

Thus saith the Lord GOD; This is Jerusalem: I have set it in the midst of the nations and countries that are round about her. And she hath changed my judgments into wickedness more than the nations, and my statutes more than the countries that are round about her: for they have refused my judgments and my statutes, they have not walked in them. Therefore thus saith the Lord GOD; Because ye multiplied more than the nations that are round about you, and have not walked in my statutes, neither have kept my judgments, neither have done according to the judgments of the nations that are round about you; Therefore thus saith the Lord GOD; Behold, I, even I, am against thee, and will execute judgments in the midst of thee in the sight of the nations. And I will do in thee that which I have not done, and whereunto I will not do any more the like, because of all thine abominations. Therefore the fathers shall eat the sons in the midst of thee, and the sons shall eat their fathers; and I will execute judgments in thee, and the whole remnant of thee will I scatter into all the winds. Wherefore, as I live, saith the Lord GOD; Surely, because thou hast defiled my sanctuary with all thy detestable things, and with all thine abominations, therefore will I also diminish

thee; neither shall mine eye spare, neither will I have any pity. A third part of thee shall die with the pestilence, and with famine shall they be consumed in the midst of thee: and a third part shall fall by the sword round about thee; and I will scatter a third part into all the winds, and I will draw out a sword after them. Thus shall mine anger be accomplished, and I will cause my fury to rest upon them, and I will be comforted: and they shall know that I the LORD have spoken it in my zeal, when I have accomplished my fury in them. Moreover I will make thee waste, and a reproach among the nations that are round about thee, in the sight of all that pass by. So it shall be a reproach and a taunt, an instruction and an astonishment unto the nations that are round about thee, when I shall execute judgments in thee in anger and in fury and in furious rebukes. I the LORD have spoken it. When I shall send upon them the evil arrows of famine, which shall be for their destruction, and which I will send to destroy you: and I will increase the famine upon you, and will break your staff of bread: So will I send upon you famine and evil beasts, and they shall bereave thee; and pestilence and blood shall pass through thee; and I will bring the sword upon thee. I the LORD have spoken it. (Ezekiel 5:5-17)

Vindication for God's Judgment (5-17): God describes the reasons for His fury against His people. They were called to be the salt (Matt. 5:13) and light (Matt. 5:14-16) to the heathen nations around them (See: Deut. 4:4-8), and instead they became more corrupt than those nations. Thus, God is stating that He is going to bring these judgments to pass; their opportunity for repentance is past (5:11).

CHAPTER 6

Judgment Against the Entire Land of Israel

Ezekiel up to this point was using object lessons to convey the truth of coming judgments. Now he will elaborate on these object lessons. Up until this point the judgments were concerning Jerusalem. However, the prophet will now turn his attention to the whole land of Israel; judgment is coming to the entire land.

And the word of the LORD came unto me, saying, Son of man, set thy face toward the mountains of Israel, and prophesy against them, And say, Ye mountains of Israel, hear the word of the Lord GOD; Thus saith the Lord GOD to the mountains, and to the hills, to the rivers, and to the valleys; Behold, I, even I, will bring a sword upon you, and I will destroy your high places. And your altars shall be desolate, and your images shall be broken: and I will cast down your slain men before your idols. And I will lay the dead carcases of the children of Israel before their idols; and I will scatter your bones round about your altars. In all your dwellingplaces the cities shall be laid waste, and the high places shall be desolate; that your altars may be laid waste and made desolate, and your idols may be broken and cease, and your images may be cut down, and your works may be abolished. And the slain shall fall in the midst of you, and ye shall know that I am the LORD. (Ezekiel 6:1-7)

Judgment of the Entire Land of Israel (1-7): Ezekiel is now called upon to prophesy against the land itself. The land had become corrupted by false worship. Temples to pagan gods dotted the landscape. These temples and idols of false worship were erected upon the mountaintops and high places (note the terms "high places" and "groves" in reference to them). The conflict between true worship and false worship centered on these high places. Those who followed God tried to destroy the high places: Hezekiah (2 Kings 18:3-4) and Josiah (2 Kings 23:8-9); kings who did not follow God rebuilt them: Manasseh (2 Kings 21:1-6). In verse six we see the judgment upon these places of false worship that will ensue: **In all your dwellingplaces the cities shall be laid waste, and the <u>high places shall be desolate;</u> that your <u>altars may be laid waste</u> and <u>made desolate,</u> and your <u>idols may be broken and cease,</u> and your <u>images may be cut down,</u> and <u>your works may be abolished.</u> (Ezekiel 6:6)**

Yet will I leave a remnant, that ye may have some that shall escape the sword among the nations, when ye shall be scattered through the countries. And they that escape of you shall remember me among the nations whither they shall be carried captives, because I am broken with their whorish heart, which hath departed from me, and with their eyes, which go a whoring after their idols: and they shall lothe themselves for the evils which they have committed in all their abominations. And they shall know that I am the LORD, and that I have not said in vain that I would do this evil unto them. (Ezekiel 6:8-10)

The Continual Mercy of God (8-10): God's continual

mercy is seen in the promised remnant of His people. Israel will not be utterly abolished (Jer. 43:5; Zeph. 2:7; Zech. 10:9, 12:2-3, 12:9-10; Rom. 9:6-13, 11:5-25).

Thus saith the Lord GOD; Smite with thine hand, and stamp with thy foot, and say, Alas for all the evil abominations of the house of Israel! for they shall fall by the sword, by the famine, and by the pestilence. He that is far off shall die of the pestilence; and he that is near shall fall by the sword; and he that remaineth and is besieged shall die by the famine: thus will I accomplish my fury upon them. Then shall ye know that I am the LORD, when their slain men shall be among their idols round about their altars, upon every high hill, in all the tops of the mountains, and under every green tree, and under every thick oak, the place where they did offer sweet savour to all their idols. So will I stretch out my hand upon them, and make the land desolate, yea, more desolate than the wilderness toward Diblath, in all their habitations: and they shall know that I am the LORD. (Ezekiel 6:11-14)

Totality of God's Judgment, the People, the False gods and the Land (11-14): The idols that were worshiped and burnt incense to, would now be covered with the smell of the rotting corpses of God's people. The land will become desolate (vs. 14).

CHAPTER 7

The End is Come

Chapter seven is the climax to chapters 4-6. The final words are, "the end is come." All the hundreds of years of pleading with His people are over; the end is sure, their fate is sealed. This chapter is very appropriate given the next section (chapters 8-11) is concerning *the glory of the Lord departing the temple.*

Moreover the word of the LORD came unto me, saying, Also, thou son of man, thus saith the Lord GOD unto the land of Israel; An end, the end is come upon the four corners of the land. Now is the end come upon thee, and I will send mine anger upon thee, and will judge thee according to thy ways, and will recompense upon thee all thine abominations. And mine eye shall not spare thee, neither will I have pity: but I will recompense thy ways upon thee, and thine abominations shall be in the midst of thee: and ye shall know that I am the LORD. Thus saith the Lord GOD; An evil, an only evil, behold, is come. An end is come, the end is come: it watcheth for thee; behold, it is come. The morning is come unto thee, O thou that dwellest in the land: the time is come, the day of trouble is near, and not the sounding again of the mountains. Now will I shortly pour out my fury upon thee, and accomplish mine anger upon thee: and I will judge thee according to thy ways, and will recompense thee for all thine abominations. And mine eye shall not spare, neither will I have pity: I will recompense thee

according to thy ways and thine abominations that are in the midst of thee; and ye shall know that I am the LORD that smiteth. Behold the day, behold, it is come: the morning is gone forth; the rod hath blossomed, pride hath budded. Violence is risen up into a rod of wickedness: none of them shall remain, nor of their multitude, nor of any of theirs: neither shall there be wailing for them. The time is come, the day draweth near: let not the buyer rejoice, nor the seller mourn: for wrath is upon all the multitude thereof. For the seller shall not return to that which is sold, although they were yet alive: for the vision is touching the whole multitude thereof, which shall not return; neither shall any strengthen himself in the iniquity of his life. (Ezekiel 7:1-13)

God is Bringing the Land and His People to Their End (1-13): Throughout these verses one thing is made perfectly clear, the imminent judgment from God:
- The end is come (vss. 1-6)
- The morning is come (vss. 7-9)
- The day is come (vss. 10-11)
- The time is come (vss. 12-15)

Jerusalem's judgment is looming on the horizon; that is what these verses communicate. They also tell us why God is bringing this sore judgment, *"recompense upon thee all thine abominations"* (vss. 3,4,8,9). The abominations of which Israel partook are a constant theme throughout the prophets. Nebuchadnezzar is going to be the rod God will use to punish His people (Isaiah 10:5). Israel's pride-filled heart hath budded, violence has risen up into a rod of wickedness. Thus, Israel is ripe for God's judgment. Possessions would be confiscated and property owners torn from their land and carried to Babylon. The buyer who normally rejoiced over a good business deal would not be happy because he would not be able to possess the land he had purchased. And, one forced to sell his land should not grieve because he would have lost it anyway. Every 50 years, during the Year of Jubilee, the property reverted to its original owners (Lev. 25:10,13-17). However, God's judgment would prevent original owners from reclaiming their properties; they would be in exile along with the buyers (vs. 13).

They have blown the trumpet, even to make all ready; but none goeth to the battle: for my wrath is upon all the multitude thereof. The sword is without, and the pestilence and the famine within: he that is in the field shall die with the sword; and he that is in the city, famine and pestilence shall devour him. (Ezekiel 7:14-15)

The Watchman (14-15): Ezekiel was commissioned to be a watchman (3:17-21). The watchmen upon the city walls were to blow the trumpet when they saw the enemy approaching, signaling the soldiers to man their posts. However, what little army will be left will find resistance utterly futile.

But they that escape of them shall escape, and shall be on the mountains like doves of the valleys, all of them mourning, every one for his iniquity. All hands shall be feeble, and all knees shall be weak as water. They shall also gird themselves with sackcloth, and horror shall cover them; and shame shall be upon all faces, and baldness upon all their heads. (Ezekiel 7:16-18)

The Doves in the Valley (16-18): Those that escape shall be scattered upon the mountains, mourning like the mourning dove *(named for the mourning sound it makes) Isaiah 59:11.* It is from this group that God will form His Remnant.

They shall cast their silver in the streets, and their gold shall be removed: their silver and their gold shall not be able to deliver them in the day of the wrath of the LORD: they shall not satisfy their souls, neither fill their bowels: because it is the stumblingblock of their iniquity. As for the beauty of his ornament, he set it in majesty: but they made the images of their abominations and of their detestable things therein: therefore have I set it far from them. And I will give it into the hands of the strangers for a prey, and to the wicked of the earth for a spoil; and they shall pollute it. My face will I turn also from them, and they shall pollute my secret place: for the robbers shall enter into it, and defile it. (Ezekiel 7:19-22)

The Casting Away of Riches (19-22): During the final days the rich had become richer and the poor, poorer. However, the refugees could not carry their wealth as they fled Jerusalem, so they treated it like garbage and threw it into the streets. God's payment to Babylon would be the wealth of the Jews.

Make a chain: for the land is full of bloody crimes, and the city is full of violence. Wherefore I will bring the worst of the heathen, and they shall possess their houses: I will also make the pomp of the strong to cease; and their holy places shall be defiled. Destruction cometh; and they shall seek peace, and there shall be

none. Mischief shall come upon mischief, and rumour shall be upon rumour; then shall they seek a vision of the prophet; but the law shall perish from the priest, and counsel from the ancients. The king shall mourn, and the prince shall be clothed with desolation, and the hands of the people of the land shall be troubled: I will do unto them after their way, and according to their deserts will I judge them; and they shall know that I am the LORD. (Ezekiel 7:23-27)

The Leadership Shall Not Escape Judgment (23-27): Judgment is going to be upon the leadership of the people, from the prophet, to the priest, to the king (vss. 23-27). "Make a chain" (23) has the idea of being carried away into captivity. Notice they shall seek peace and "there shall be none." Peace is what all the world wants. The man of sin will use this desire to his advantage (Psalm 83, I Thess. 5:3).

Conclusion: This first section of Scripture ends with this very fitting chapter. The end is come for God's people. They will get their just "deserts" (vs.27).

In the next section, chapters 8-11, we will move to the next logical step, the departing of the glory of the Lord. Prior to Babylonian armies destroying God's temple He must depart from it. We will look at this in detail to gain a further appreciation of the holiness of God.

CHAPTER 8

The Glory of the Lord Departing
Overview

We now come to a major section of prophecy in Ezekiel, chapters 8-11. In these chapters the complete captivity of Jerusalem and Israel will become a reality, and the glory of the Lord will depart from the temple in Jerusalem.

Before we look into these chapters lets remind ourselves of the time under Solomon when the glory of the Lord filled the temple: **And it came to pass, when the priests were come out of the holy place, that the cloud filled the house of the LORD, So that the priests could not stand to minister because of the cloud: for the glory of the LORD had filled the house of the LORD. Then spake Solomon, The LORD said that he would dwell in the thick darkness. (1 Kings 8:10-12)**

What a glorious time under Solomon. However, following Solomon's prayer (I Kings 9:1) the Lord appears unto him and lays before him judgments for his people if they don't walk according to God's statutes and commandments. Among these is the judgment of Israel being cut off out of the land, and becoming an astonishment to the heathen nations around them: **Then will I cut off Israel out of the land which I have given them; and this house, which I have hallowed for my name, will I cast out of my sight; and Israel shall be a proverb and a byword among all people: And at this house, which is high, every one that passeth by it shall** be astonished, and shall hiss; and they shall say, Why hath the LORD done thus unto this land, and to this house? And they shall answer, Because they forsook the LORD their God, who brought forth their fathers out of the land of Egypt, and have taken hold upon other gods, and have worshipped them, and served them: therefore hath the LORD brought upon them all this evil. (1 Kings 9:7-9)

It is this judgment from the Lord that Israel will now be experiencing at the time of Ezekiel (I Kings 9:8, 9 cf. Ezek. 5:14, 15).

The glory of the Lord now appears a second time to Ezekiel. Ezekiel is going to be transported to Jerusalem, the holy city to be shown all the abominations that the leadership of Israel commit in the temple itself.

Four-fold View of the Sins of Judah:

- An image set up at the north gate of the temple (Ezek. 8:5).

- Secret heathen worship in the hidden chambers of the Temple (Ezek. 8:6-12)

- Jewish women weeping for the god Tammuz, who was supposed to die and be raised from the dead each spring (Ezek. 8:13-14)

- The 25 priests and the High Priest worshiping the sun (Ezek. 8:15-16)

It is because of this idolatry that we are going to see the gradual departure of the glory of the Lord from the temple and from Israel. In chapter 8 the glory of the Lord is lifted up from the temple, goes out over the city to the east, and in chapter 11 departs from the mount, east of Jerusalem.

The glory of the Lord will not return into the land and temple until the Millennial temple is established (Ezek. 43:1-6). Thus, during the time that our Lord was on earth He states, "Behold, **your house** is left unto you desolate" (Matthew 23:38), indicating that even at that time the temple (house) was not His but the corrupt religious leaders' (Matt. 21:13 cf. Isa. 56:7).

Abominations in the House of God

And it came to pass in the sixth year, in the sixth month, in the fifth day of the month, as I sat in mine house, and the elders of Judah sat before me, that the hand of the Lord GOD fell there upon me. Then I beheld, and lo a likeness as the appearance of fire: from the appearance of his loins even downward, fire; and from his loins even upward, as the appearance of brightness, as the colour of amber. (Ezekiel 8:1-2)

The Vision of the Glory of the Lord (1-2): The vision is that of God the Father manifested, or the glory of the Lord. It is similar enough to identify it with the first vision in chapter one (26-28). We are emphatically told that it is the glory of the Lord, the vision of God manifested (vs. 3,4). This reappearance of the glory of the Lord marks the next section of Ezekiel, chapters 8-11.

EZEKIEL'S VISION OF SOLOMON'S TEMPLE IN CHAPTER 8

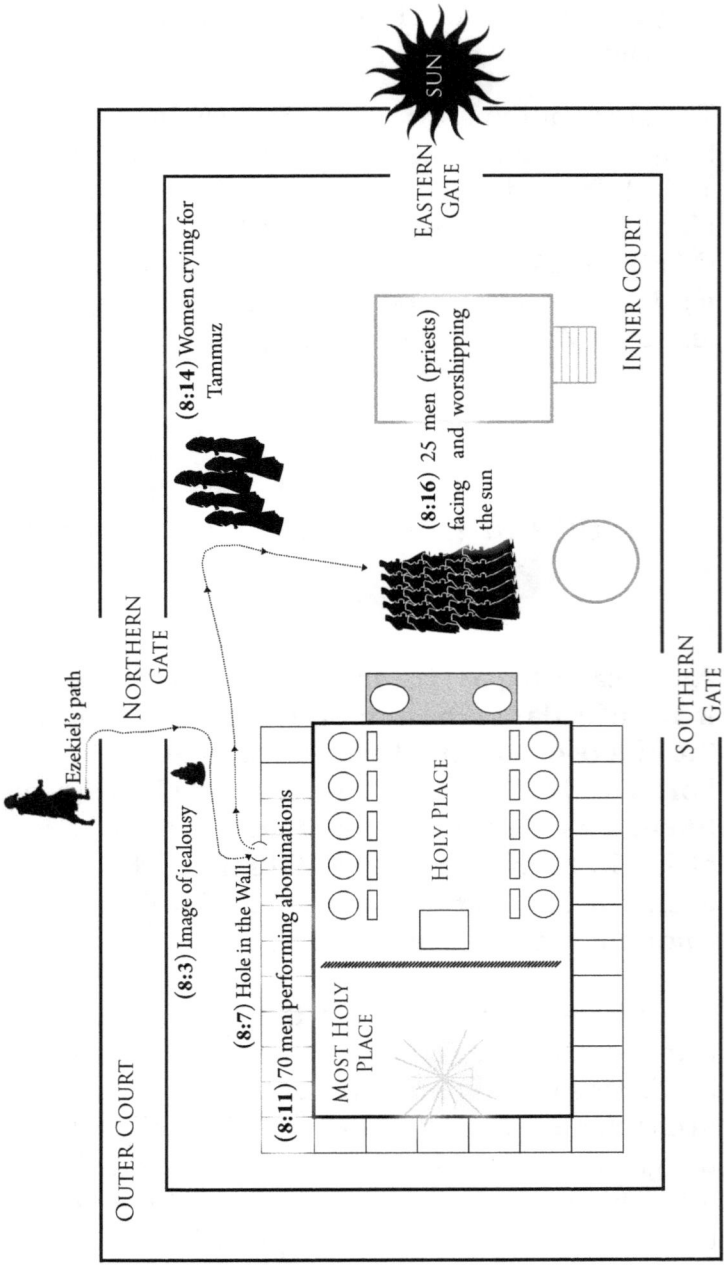

SUN

EASTERN GATE

OUTER COURT

INNER COURT

Ezekiel's path

NORTHERN GATE

SOUTHERN GATE

(8:3) Image of jealousy

(8:7) Hole in the Wall

(8:11) 70 men performing abominations

(8:14) Women crying for Tammuz

(8:16) 25 men (priests) facing and worshipping the sun

MOST HOLY PLACE

HOLY PLACE

Ezekiel is sitting before the elders of Judah when he receives this vision. Notice it is the "hand of the Lord God" falling upon him that puts him into this trance state to see the vision (cf. 1:3; 11:5).

And he put forth the form of an hand, and took me by a lock of mine head; and the spirit lifted me up between the earth and the heaven, and brought me in the visions of God to Jerusalem, to the door of the inner gate that looketh toward the north; where was the seat of the image of jealousy, which provoketh to jealousy. And, behold, the glory of the God of Israel was there, according to the vision that I saw in the plain. Then said he unto me, Son of man, lift up thine eyes now the way toward the north. So I lifted up mine eyes the way toward the north, and behold northward at the gate of the altar this image of jealousy in the entry. He said furthermore unto me, Son of man, seest thou what they do? even the great abominations that the house of Israel committeth here, that I should go far off from my sanctuary? but turn thee yet again, and thou shalt see greater abominations. (Ezekiel 8:3-6)

Ezekiel is Transported to Jerusalem (3-6): There are three possibilities concerning Ezekiel's transportation to Jerusalem: Actually transported to Jerusalem physically, a vision by the river Chebar (second sight) or taken in the spirit while his body remained before the elders in a hypnotic state.

(Ezekiel being physically transported to Jerusalem would not be something new in Scripture, such as Elijah in 2 Kings 2 or Philip in Acts 8:39. However, I believe in this case Ezekiel is taken in the spirit to Jerusalem while his body remained

by the river Chebar before the elders. We are told these were "visions" (vs. 3, 11:24 cf. 3:12) a kind of second sight.)

Ezekiel is standing in the door of the inner court on the north side (3). It is here he is shown the image of jealousy. This image was to arrest the attention of all worshipers as they entered the temple. King Manasseh had set up similar idols (2 Kings 21:3, 7). Each abomination described will end with the phrase "thou shalt see greater abominations," which shows the height of the apostasy the nation had reached.

And he brought me to the door of the court; and when I looked, behold a hole in the wall. Then said he unto me, Son of man, dig now in the wall: and when I had digged in the wall, behold a door. And he said unto me, Go in, and behold the wicked abominations that they do here. So I went in and saw; and behold every form of creeping things, and abominable beasts, and all the idols of the house of Israel, pourtrayed upon the wall round about. And there stood before them seventy men of the ancients of the house of Israel, and in the midst of them stood Jaazaniah the son of Shaphan, with every man his censer in his hand; and a thick cloud of incense went up. Then said he unto me, Son of man, hast thou seen what the ancients of the house of Israel do in the dark, every man in the chambers of his imagery? for they say, The LORD seeth us not; the LORD hath forsaken the earth. (Ezekiel 8:7-12)

The Priests' Chambers and the Seventy Ancients of the House of Israel (7-12): Ezekiel moves to the wall of the priests' chambers. He digs within the wall and sees wicked abominations portrayed upon all the walls (8-10) and 70 men of the house of Israel worshiping them (11-12).

These people are worshiping the creature rather than the creator — this is as low as they could go. Man will turn to this type of thing when he has absolutely repudiated the living and true God (Rom. 1:21, 25).

He said also unto me, Turn thee yet again, and thou shalt see greater abominations that they do. Then he brought me to the door of the gate of the LORD'S house which was toward the north; and, behold, there sat women weeping for Tammuz. (Ezekiel 8:13-14)

Women Weeping for Tammuz Near the Door of the Inner Court (13-14): Tammuz was a deity that supposedly died at the winter solstice and went down to the netherworld to be resurrected again in spring. The women weeping were celebrating the death of this god; his worship was actually the worship of nature.

Then said he unto me, Hast thou seen this, O son of man? turn thee yet again, and thou shalt see greater abominations than these. And he brought me into the inner court of the LORD'S house, and, behold, at the door of the temple of the LORD, between the porch and the altar, were about five and twenty men, with their backs toward the temple of the LORD, and their faces toward the east; and they worshipped the sun toward the east. (Ezekiel 8:15-16)

Worshiping the Sun in the LORD'S House (15-16): These men most likely make up the 24 priests and the high priest himself. A priest was to have his back to the people and face the temple, making prayer and supplications for the people. However these having their back to the temple were worshiping the sun (Deut. 4:19; 2 Chron. 14:5; 2 Kings 23:5; Jer. 44:17; Job 31:26).

Then he said unto me, Hast thou seen this, O son of man? Is it a light thing to the house of Judah that they commit the abominations which they commit here? for they have filled the land with violence, and have returned to provoke me to anger: and, lo, they put the branch to their nose. Therefore will I also deal in fury: mine eye shall not spare, neither will I have pity: and though they cry in mine ears with a loud voice, yet will I not hear them. (Ezekiel 8:17-18)

The Branch to the Nose (17-18): This closing remark is telling, for this expression is similar to today's saying "thumbing the nose." This is the heart of the religious leadership of all Israel (cf. Isaiah 65:5).

CHAPTER 9
The Departure of the Glory of the Lord Begins

He cried also in mine ears with a loud voice, saying, Cause them that have charge over the city to draw near, even every man with his destroying weapon in his hand. And, behold, six men came from the way of the higher gate, which lieth toward the north, and every man a slaughter weapon in his hand; and one man among them was clothed with linen, with a writer's inkhorn by his side: and they went in, and stood beside the brasen altar. (Ezekiel 9:1-2)

The Calling Forth of the Six Men of Slaughter (1-2): The Lord calls forth six men with destroying weapons in their hands.

And the glory of the God of Israel was gone up from the cherub, whereupon he was, to the threshold of the house. And he called to the man clothed with linen, which had the writer's inkhorn by his side; And the LORD said unto him, Go through the midst of the city, through the midst of Jerusalem, and set a mark upon the foreheads of the men that sigh and that cry for all the abominations that be done in the midst thereof. (Ezekiel 9:3-4)

The Glory of the Lord Departs to the Threshold of the Temple and Commissions the Man Clothed with Linen (3-4): The Lord now moves to the threshold of the temple door, and there commissions one man among the six (2) that is clothed in linen to go throughout the city with a writer's ink horn and place a mark on the forehead of those that "sigh and that cry for all the abominations."

And to the others he said in mine hearing, Go ye after him through the city, and smite: let not your eye spare, neither have ye pity: Slay utterly old and young, both maids, and little children, and women: but come not near any man upon whom is the mark; and begin at my sanctuary. Then they began at the ancient men which were before the house. And he said unto them, Defile the house, and fill the courts with the slain: go ye forth. And they went forth, and slew in the city. (Ezekiel 9:5-7)

The Commissioning of the Men of Slaughter (5-7): Following the marking of the righteous, they are commissioned to go throughout the city and "slay utterly old and young both maids and little children and women" beginning with the temple. (*Notice all the people from old to young had corrupted themselves cf. Gen. 19:4*). This event had to transpire prior to the departing of the Lord's glory from the temple. Our Lord is a holy and righteous God and cannot depart while there is sin within the temple, thus the slaughter begins in the temple (6).

And it came to pass, while they were slaying them, and I was left, that I fell upon my face, and cried, and said, Ah Lord GOD! wilt thou destroy all the residue of Israel in thy pouring out of thy fury upon Jerusalem? Then said he unto me, The iniquity of the house of

EZEKIEL'S VISION OF SOLOMON'S TEMPLE IN CHAPTER 9

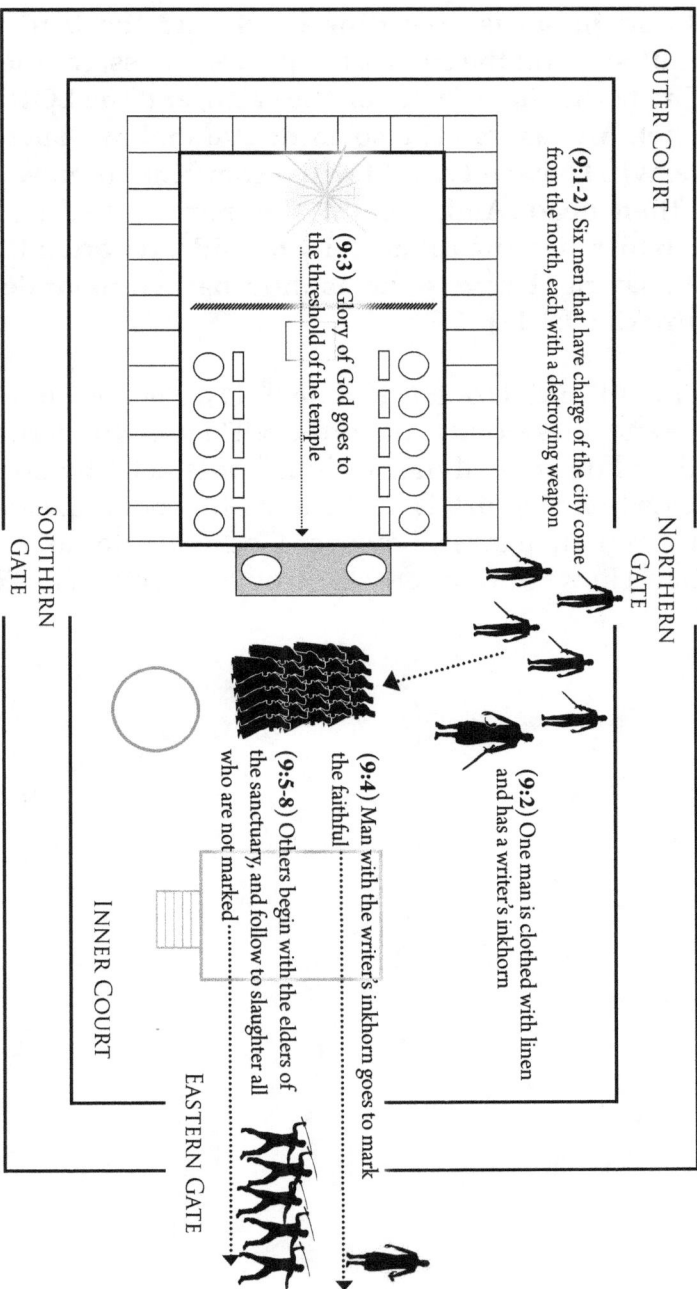

OUTER COURT

(9:1-2) Six men that have charge of the city come from the north, each with a destroying weapon

NORTHERN GATE

(9:3) Glory of God goes to the threshold of the temple

(9:2) One man is clothed with linen and has a writer's inkhorn

(9:4) Man with the writer's inkhorn goes to mark the faithful

(9:5-8) Others begin with the elders of the sanctuary, and follow to slaughter all who are not marked

SOUTHERN GATE

INNER COURT

EASTERN GATE

Israel and Judah is exceeding great, and the land is full of blood, and the city full of perverseness: for they say, The LORD hath forsaken the earth, and the LORD seeth not. And as for me also, mine eye shall not spare, neither will I have pity, but I will recompense their way upon their head. And, behold, the man clothed with linen, which had the inkhorn by his side, reported the matter, saying, I have done as thou hast commanded me. (Ezekiel 9:8-11)

The Cry of Ezekiel for His People (8-11): Ezekiel falls on his face and cries aloud "Ah Lord God!" He is wondering if God will destroy all the "residue" of Israel. The Lord responds that His fury is justified. At this point Ezekiel is not given an answer, however God will later assure him that He will not utterly destroy the people (11:13-23).

CHAPTER 10

The Departure of the Glory of the Lord from the Temple

Then I looked, and, behold, in the firmament that was above the head of the cherubims there appeared over them as it were a sapphire stone, as the appearance of the likeness of a throne. And he spake unto the man clothed with linen, and said, Go in between the wheels, even under the cherub, and fill thine hand with coals of fire from between the cherubims, and scatter them over the city. And he went in in my sight. Now the cherubims stood on the right side of the house, when the man went in; and the cloud filled the inner court. Then the glory of the LORD went up from the cherub, and stood over the threshold of the house; and the house was filled with the cloud, and the court was full of the brightness of the LORD'S glory. And the sound of the cherubims' wings was heard even to the outer court, as the voice of the Almighty God when he speaketh. And it came to pass, that when he had commanded the man clothed with linen, saying, Take fire from between the wheels, from between the cherubims; then he went in, and stood beside the wheels. And one cherub stretched forth his hand from between the cherubims unto the fire that was between the cherubims, and took thereof, and put it into the hands of him that was clothed with linen: who took it, and went out. And there appeared in the cherubims the form of a man's hand under their wings. And when I looked, behold the four wheels by the cherubims, one wheel by one cherub, and another wheel by another cherub: and the appearance of the wheels was as the colour of a beryl stone. And as for their appearances, they four had one likeness, as if a wheel had been in the midst of a wheel. When they went, they went upon their four sides; they turned not as they went, but to the place whither the head looked they followed it; they turned not as they went. And their whole body, and their backs, and their hands, and their wings, and the wheels, were full of eyes round about, even the wheels that they four had. As for the wheels, it was cried unto them in my hearing, O wheel. And every one had four faces: the first face was the face of a cherub, and the second face was the face of a man, and the third the face of a lion, and the fourth the face of an eagle. And the cherubims were lifted up. This is the living creature that I saw by the river of Chebar. And when the cherubims went, the wheels went by them: and when the cherubims lifted up their wings to mount up from the earth, the same wheels also turned not from beside them. When they stood, these stood; and when they were lifted up, these lifted up themselves also: for the spirit of the living creature was in them. (Ezekiel 10:1-17)

The Arrival of God's Moveable Throne and its Appearance (1-17): God's moveable throne now arrives for the departure of the glory of the Lord from the temple. This throne of God was discussed in chapter one, and its appearance is now described again in verses 8-15 of this chapter.

The Man Clothed in Linen Sanctifying the City: The Lord again commissions the man clothed in linen to take coals from beneath the chariot of God, between the wheels and the cherubim, and scatter them throughout the city. This is another act that needs to transpire before

EZEKIEL'S VISION OF SOLOMON'S TEMPLE IN CHAPTERS 9 & 10

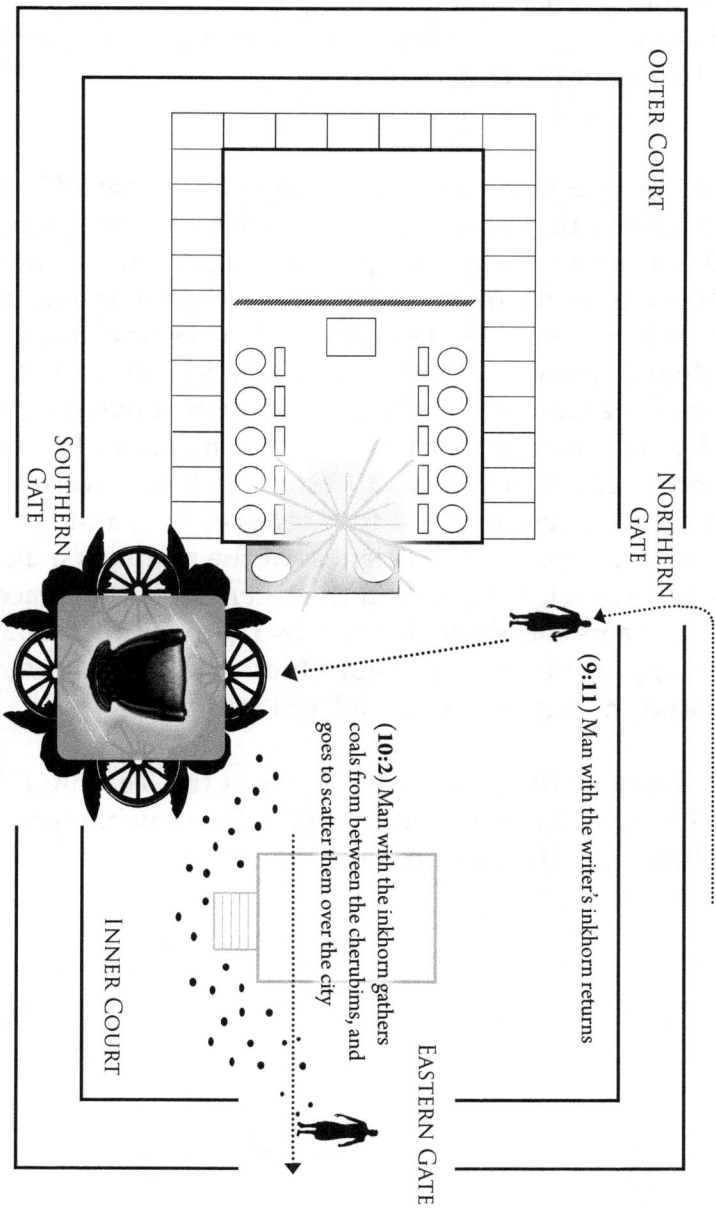

OUTER COURT

SOUTHERN GATE

NORTHERN GATE

(9:11) Man with the writer's inkhorn returns

(10:2) Man with the inkhorn gathers coals from between the cherubims, and goes to scatter them over the city

INNER COURT

EASTERN GATE

the glory of the Lord can depart from the city. This act is the sanctifying of the temple and the city, so the holiness of God is not compromised by the killing of the inhabitants of the temple and the city.

Then the glory of the LORD departed from off the threshold of the house, and stood over the cherubims. And the cherubims lifted up their wings, and mounted up from the earth in my sight: when they went out, the wheels also were beside them, and every one stood at the door of the east gate of the LORD'S house; and the glory of the God of Israel was over them above. This is the living creature that I saw under the God of Israel by the river of Chebar; and I knew that they were the cherubims. Every one had four faces apiece, and every one four wings; and the likeness of the hands of a man was under their wings. And the likeness of their faces was the same faces which I saw by the river of Chebar, their appearances and themselves: they went every one straight forward. (Ezekiel 10:18-22)

The Glory of the Lord Now Departs the Temple (18-22): The glory of the Lord mounts His movable throne and heads east to the door of the inner gate.

MOVEMENT OF GOD'S THRONE SEEN BY EZEKIEL
CHAPTER 10

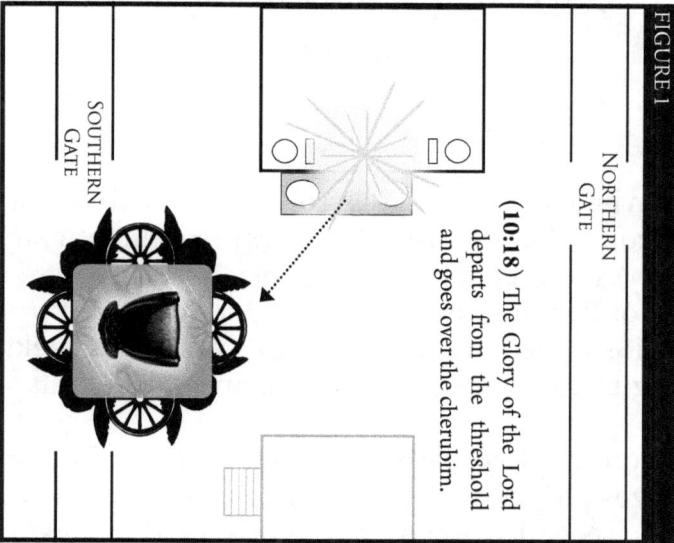

FIGURE 1

NORTHERN
GATE

SOUTHERN
GATE

(10:18) The Glory of the Lord departs from the threshold and goes over the cherubim.

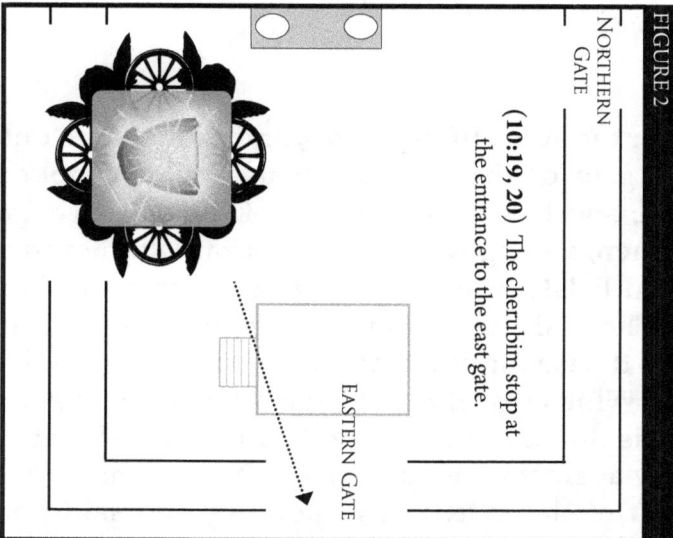

FIGURE 2

NORTHERN
GATE

(10:19, 20) The cherubim stop at the entrance to the east gate.

EASTERN GATE

CHAPTER 11

The Departure of the Glory of the Lord from the Land

Jerusalem had not yet been destroyed. Zedekiah was still on the throne. Not only were the rulers in rebellion against God, they were in rebellion against Nebuchadnezzar the king of Babylon. Before God's glory departed from the city, it stopped at the eastern gate and gave Ezekiel another glimpse of the sin of Jerusalem's inhabitants.

Ezekiel receives two messages from the Lord: The first emphasizes judgment on the people in Jerusalem (vss. 1-15). The second emphasizes the promised restoration of the people who were in captivity (vss. 16-21). Then Ezekiel recorded the final departure of God's glory (vss. 22-25).

Moreover the spirit lifted me up, and brought me unto the east gate of the LORD'S house, which looketh eastward: and behold at the door of the gate five and twenty men; among whom I saw Jaazaniah the son of Azur, and Pelatiah the son of Benaiah, princes of the people. Then said he unto me, Son of man, these are the men that devise mischief, and give wicked counsel in this city: Which say, It is not near; let us build houses: this city is the caldron, and we be the flesh. Therefore prophesy against them, prophesy, O son of man. And the Spirit of the LORD fell upon me, and said unto me, Speak; Thus saith the LORD; Thus have ye said, O house of Israel: for I know the things that come into

your mind, every one of them. Ye have multiplied your slain in this city, and ye have filled the streets thereof with the slain. Therefore thus saith the Lord GOD; Your slain whom ye have laid in the midst of it, they are the flesh, and this city is the caldron: but I will bring you forth out of the midst of it. Ye have feared the sword; and I will bring a sword upon you, saith the Lord GOD. And I will bring you out of the midst thereof, and deliver you into the hands of strangers, and will execute judgments among you. Ye shall fall by the sword; I will judge you in the border of Israel; and ye shall know that I am the LORD. This city shall not be your caldron, neither shall ye be the flesh in the midst thereof; but I will judge you in the border of Israel: And ye shall know that I am the LORD: for ye have not walked in my statutes, neither executed my judgments, but have done after the manners of the heathen that are round about you. (Ezekiel 11:1-12)

Ezekiel and the Wicked Counselors (1-12): Ezekiel is told to prophesy against the wicked counselors (2-4). These men had counseled that the nation should revolt against Babylon and form an alliance with Egypt (Ezek. 17). This was contrary to God's command (Jer. 28:16) and in violation of the oath Zedekiah made to the Chaldean monarch (2 Chron. 36:13). The elders were urging the people to build houses, for they were safe as meat in a pot (3). However they were not safe, and God would see to it. They were to be scattered out of the city and fall by the sword (7-12).

And it came to pass, when I prophesied, that Pelatiah the son of Benaiah died. Then fell I down upon my face, and cried with a loud voice, and said, Ah Lord

Movement of God's Throne seen by Ezekiel
Chapters 10 & 11

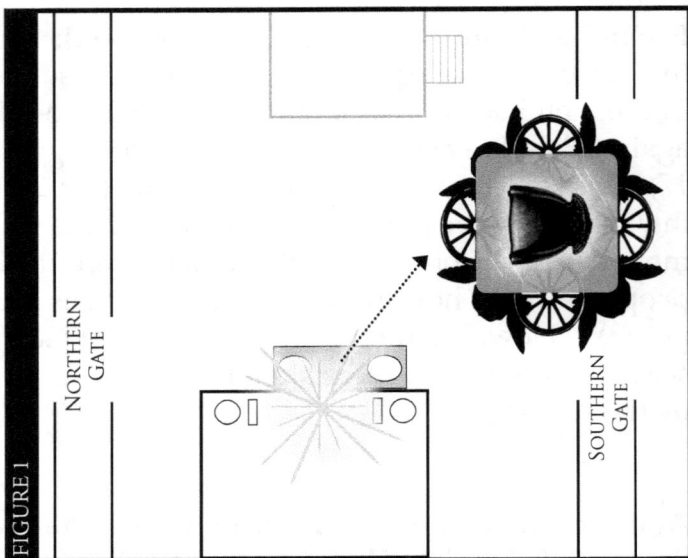

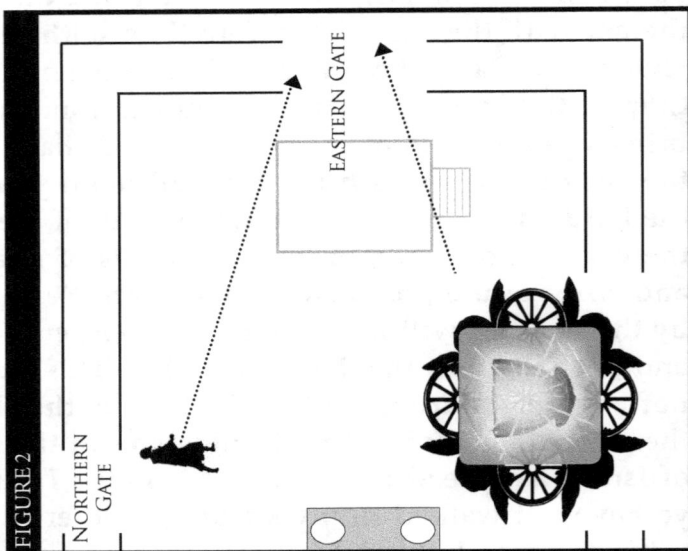

FIGURE 1

NORTHERN GATE

SOUTHERN GATE

FIGURE 2

NORTHERN GATE

EASTERN GATE

FIGURE 1

- The Glory of the Lord departs from the threshold and goes over the cherubim. (**10:18**)

FIGURE 2

- The cherubim stop at the entrance to the east gate. (**10:19, 20**)

- Ezekiel is taken to the east gate and given a prophecy. (**11:1-4**)

FIGURE 3

- Glory of the Lord leaves the temple and stands above the Mount of Olives, east of Jerusalem. (**11:23**)

FIGURE 3

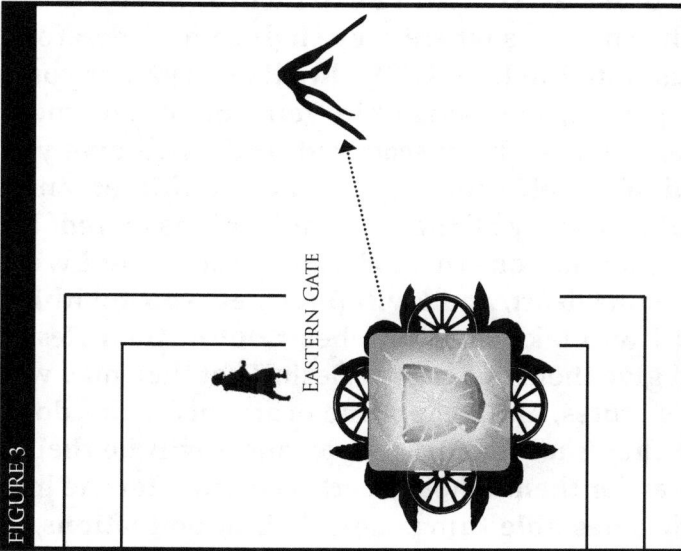

EASTERN GATE

GOD! wilt thou make a full end of the remnant of Israel? (Ezekiel 11:13)

Ezekiel Cries for His People (13): Ezekiel falls upon his face and cries out to God, wondering if God will make a full end of the remnant of Israel. He had cried out to God earlier about this very thing but had not received an answer (9:8).

Again the word of the LORD came unto me, saying, Son of man, thy brethren, even thy brethren, the men of thy kindred, and all the house of Israel wholly, are they unto whom the inhabitants of Jerusalem have said, Get you far from the LORD: unto us is this land given in possession. Therefore say, Thus saith the Lord GOD; Although I have cast them far off among the heathen, and although I have scattered them among the countries, yet will I be to them as a little sanctuary in the countries where they shall come. Therefore say, Thus saith the Lord GOD; I will even gather you from the people, and assemble you out of the countries where ye have been scattered, and I will give you the land of Israel. And they shall come thither, and they shall take away all the detestable things thereof and all the abominations thereof from thence. And I will give them one heart, and I will put a new spirit within you; and I will take the stony heart out of their flesh, and will give them an heart of flesh: That they may walk in my statutes, and keep mine ordinances, and do them: and they shall be my people, and I will be their God. But as for them whose heart walketh after the heart of their detestable things and their abominations, I will recompense their way upon their own heads, saith the Lord GOD. (Ezekiel 11:14-21)

God's Promise of Restoration One Day (14-21): God promises Israel that He will gather them again into their land one day (17-18). God also promises to give them a new heart to serve the Lord (19-21). Israel's condition was that they were spiritually unfit to serve God. Under the Old Covenant they, like us, are unable to keep all the statutes and commandments. But God will establish a New Covenant one day in which they will experience the new birth as a nation, and then they will be able to walk according to all His ways (Ezek. 36, Jer. 31 cf. Heb. 8).

Then did the cherubims lift up their wings, and the wheels beside them; and the glory of the God of Israel was over them above. And the glory of the LORD went up from the midst of the city, and stood upon the mountain which is on the east side of the city. Afterwards the spirit took me up, and brought me in a vision by the Spirit of God into Chaldea, to them of the captivity. So the vision that I had seen went up from me. Then I spake unto them of the captivity all the things that the LORD had shewed me. (Ezekiel 11:22-25)

The Glory of the Lord Departs the Land (22-25): The glory of the Lord now departs from the "midst of the city" to the hill on the east of the city (Mount of Olives). It is from this location that the glory of the Lord will one day return into the temple (Ezek. 43:1-6). Ezekiel returns to himself and tells the people all that the Lord had shown him.

CHAPTER 12

Two Symbolic Representations for the Flight from the Besieged City

The word of the LORD also came unto me, saying, Son of man, thou dwellest in the midst of a rebellious house, which have eyes to see, and see not; they have ears to hear, and hear not: for they are a rebellious house. Therefore, thou son of man, prepare thee stuff for removing, and remove by day in their sight; and thou shalt remove from thy place to another place in their sight: it may be they will consider, though they be a rebellious house. Then shalt thou bring forth thy stuff by day in their sight, as stuff for removing: and thou shalt go forth at even in their sight, as they that go forth into captivity. Dig thou through the wall in their sight, and carry out thereby. In their sight shalt thou bear it upon thy shoulders, and carry it forth in the twilight: thou shalt cover thy face, that thou see not the ground: for I have set thee for a sign unto the house of Israel. And I did so as I was commanded: I brought forth my stuff by day, as stuff for captivity, and in the even I digged through the wall with mine hand; I brought it forth in the twilight, and I bare it upon my shoulder in their sight. (Ezekiel 12:1-7)

Removal of Stuff (1-7): Ezekiel is mimicking what the people of Jerusalem will encounter when their city is besieged. Ezekiel by day and by night is told to "prepare stuff for removal." He is to do this in "their sight" showing that this is a sign for the people (6). He is to depart through the wall, showing the urgency by which they will depart the city.

And in the morning came the word of the LORD unto me, saying, Son of man, hath not the house of Israel, the rebellious house, said unto thee, What doest thou? Say thou unto them, Thus saith the Lord GOD; This burden concerneth the prince in Jerusalem, and all the house of Israel that are among them. Say, I am your sign: like as I have done, so shall it be done unto them: they shall remove and go into captivity. And the prince that is among them shall bear upon his shoulder in the twilight, and shall go forth: they shall dig through the wall to carry out thereby: he shall cover his face, that he see not the ground with his eyes. My net also will I spread upon him, and he shall be taken in my snare: and I will bring him to Babylon to the land of the Chaldeans; yet shall he not see it, though he shall die there. And I will scatter toward every wind all that are about him to help him, and all his bands; and I will draw out the sword after them. And they shall know that I am the LORD, when I shall scatter them among the nations, and disperse them in the countries. But I will leave a few men of them from the sword, from the famine, and from the pestilence; that they may declare all their abominations among the heathen whither they come; and they shall know that I am the LORD. (Ezekiel 12:8-16)

This Burden is Concerning the Prince of the People (8-16): Not only are these symbolic acts for the people but for the "prince of the people." This is for Zedekiah himself. To better understand the prophetic fulfillment of this passage of Scripture lets remind ourselves of some things regarding Zedekiah.

Zedekiah was Judah's last king; the youngest son of Josiah and Hamutal (Jer. 1:3; 37:1) and brother to Jehoahaz (2 Kings 24:17,18; 23:31). He was ten years old when his father died, 21 when he ascended the throne.

Originally named Mattaniah, Nebuchadnezzar changed his name to Zedekiah when he deposed Zedekiah's nephew, Jehoiachin. This act of changing his name shows the loyalty that was entrusted to Zedekiah by Nebuchadnezzar. Zedekiah made a covenant of loyalty with Nebuchadnezzar to which Zedekiah swore by God to keep (Ezek. 17:12-16; 2 Chron. 36:13).

Zedekiah however did not keep his oath of loyalty to Nebuchadnezzar and as a result brought ruin on his country and on himself.

And the prince that is among them shall bear upon his shoulder in the twilight, and shall go forth: they shall dig through the wall to carry out thereby: he shall cover his face, that he see not the ground with his eyes. My net also will I spread upon him, and he shall be taken in my snare: and I will bring him to Babylon to the land of the Chaldeans; yet shall he not see it, though he shall die there. (Ezekiel 12:12-13)

Prophetic Verses Fulfilled (12-13): In these verses Zedekiah, the prince of the people, is in view. Verse 12 refers to Zedekiah disguising himself and exiting Jerusalem through an exit in the palace: **And it came**

to pass, that when Zedekiah the king of Judah saw them, and all the men of war, then they fled, and went forth out of the city by night, by the way of the king's garden, by the gate betwixt the two walls: and he went out the way of the plain. (Jeremiah 39:4)

In verse 13, there is an amazing fulfillment of prophecy concerning Zedekiah. Verse 13 plainly states that Zedekiah will be taken into Babylon, the land of the Chaldeans, yet he shall not see it, though he shall die there:

My net also will I spread upon him, and he shall be taken in my snare: and I will bring him to Babylon to the land of the Chaldeans; yet shall he not see it, though he shall die there. (Ezekiel 12:13)

Ezekiel sends this prophecy to Jerusalem where Zedekiah sees an apparent discrepancy in the prophecy of Jeremiah, who wrote: And Zedekiah king of Judah shall not escape out of the hand of the Chaldeans, but shall surely be delivered into the hand of the king of Babylon, and shall speak with him mouth to mouth, and his eyes shall behold his eyes; And he shall lead Zedekiah to Babylon, and there shall he be until I visit him, saith the LORD: though ye fight with the Chaldeans, ye shall not prosper. (Jeremiah 32:4-5 cf. 34:3)

The amazing fulfillment of these passages is seen through the writings of the historian Josephus, in which he records the following:

Flavius Josephus, Antiquities, book 10 chapter 7

Now Zedekiah was twenty-and-one years old when he took the government and has the same mother with his brother Jehoiachin, but was a despiser of justice and of his duty, for truly those of the same age with him were wicked about him and the whole multitude did what unjust and insolent things they pleased.

... for which reason the prophet Jeremiah came often to him, and protested to him, and insisted that he must leave off his impieties and transgressions and take care of what was right, neither giver ear to the rulers (among whom were wicked men) nor give credit to their false prophets who deluded them, as if the king of Babylon would make no more war against him, and as if the Egyptians would make war against him, and conquer him, since what they said was not true; and the events would not prove such.

Now as Zedekiah himself, while he heard the prophet speak, he believed him, and agreed to everything as true, and supposed it was for his advantage; but then his friends perverted him, and dissuaded him from what the prophet advised, and obliged him to do what they pleased.

Ezekiel also foretold in Babylon what calamities were coming upon, which when he heard he sent accounts of them unto Jerusalem; but Zedekiah did not believe their prophecies, for the reason following – it happed that the two prophets agreed with one another in what they said as in all other things, that the city should be taken, and Zedekiah himself should be taken captive; but Ezekiel disagreed with him, and said that Zedekiah should not see Babylon; while Jeremiah said to him, that the king of Babylon should carry him away thither in bonds.

... and because they did not both say the same thing as to this circumstance, he disbelieved what they both appeared to agree in, and condemned them as not speaking truth therein, although all the things foretold him did come to pass according to their prophecies, as we shall show upon a fitter opportunity.

Flavius Josephus, Antiquities, book 10 chapter 8

Now the city was taken on the ninth day of the fourth month, in the eleventh year of the reign of Zedekiah. They were indeed only generals of the king of Babylon, to whom Nebuchadnezzar committed the care of the siege, for he abode himself in the city of Ribliah.

… and when the city was taken about midnight, and the enemy's generals were entered into the temple, and when Zedekiah was sensible of it, he took his wives and children, and his captains and friends and with them fled out of the city; through the fortified ditch and through the desert;

… and when certain of the deserters had informed the Babylonians of this at break of day, they made haste to pursue after Zedekiah, and overtook him not far from Jericho, and encamped him about. But for those friends and captains of Zedekiah who had fled out of the city with him, when they saw their enemies near them they left him and dispersed themselves, some one way and some another, and everyone resolved to save themselves.

… so the enemy took Zedekiah alive, when he was deserted by all but a few, with his children and his wives, and brought him to the king. When he was come, Nebuchadnezzar began to call him a wicked wretch, and convent-breaker, and one that had forgotten his former words, when he promised to keep the country for him.

He also reproached him for his ingratitude, that when he had received the kingdom from him, who had taken it from Jehoiachin, and given it him, he had made use of the power he gave him against him that gave it: "but" said he, "God is great, who hateth that conduct of thine, hath brought thee under us"

And when he had used these words to Zedekiah, he commanded his sons and his friends to be slain, while Zedekiah and the rest of the captains looked on; after which he put out the eyes of Zedekiah, and bound him and carried him to Babylon.

And these things happened to him, as Jeremiah and Ezekiel had foretold to him, that he should be caught, and brought before the king of Babylon, and should speak to him face to face, and should see his eyes with his own eyes; and thus far did Jeremiah prophecy. But he was also made blind, and brought to Babylon but did not see it, according to the prediction of Ezekiel.

Thus, the amazing fulfilment of this seeming discrepancy is that upon Zedekiah's fleeing from the Babylonian armies invading Jerusalem he is captured by Nebuchadnezzar's armies. At the city of Riblah Nebuchadnezzar slew the sons of Zedekiah and then took out the eyes of Zedekiah. Zedekiah was then taken into Babylon fulfilling both prophecies: **But the Chaldeans' army pursued after them, and overtook Zedekiah in the plains of Jericho: and when they had taken him, they brought him up to Nebuchadnezzar king of Babylon to Riblah in the land of Hamath, where he gave judgment upon him. Then the king of Babylon slew the sons of Zedekiah in Riblah before his eyes: also the king of Babylon slew all the nobles of Judah. Moreover he put out Zedekiah's eyes, and bound him with chains, to carry him to Babylon. (Jeremiah 39:5 – 7)**

Moreover the word of the LORD came to me, saying, Son of man, eat thy bread with quaking, and drink thy water with trembling and with carefulness; And say unto the people of the land, Thus saith the Lord GOD of the inhabitants of Jerusalem, and of the land of Israel; They shall eat their bread with carefulness, and drink their water with astonishment, that her land may be desolate from all that is therein, because of the violence of all them that dwell therein. And the cities that are inhabited shall be laid waste, and the

land shall be desolate; and ye shall know that I am the LORD. (Ezekiel 12:17-20)

Another Symbolic Act of the Violence About to Ensue (17-20): Ezekiel is to eat his bread with quaking, and drink his water with trembling and carefulness (18). This is to show the fearfulness that the people of Jerusalem will experience upon seeing the violence that the Babylonian armies will employ in taking the city, as well as the rationing of water during the siege.

And the word of the LORD came unto me, saying, Son of man, what is that proverb that ye have in the land of Israel, saying, The days are prolonged, and every vision faileth? Tell them therefore, Thus saith the Lord GOD; I will make this proverb to cease, and they shall no more use it as a proverb in Israel; but say unto them, The days are at hand, and the effect of every vision. For there shall be no more any vain vision nor flattering divination within the house of Israel. For I am the LORD: I will speak, and the word that I shall speak shall come to pass; it shall be no more prolonged: for in your days, O rebellious house, will I say the word, and will perform it, saith the Lord GOD. Again the word of the LORD came to me, saying, Son of man, behold, they of the house of Israel say, The vision that he seeth is for many days to come, and he prophesieth of the times that are far off. Therefore say unto them, Thus saith the Lord GOD; There shall none of my words be prolonged any more, but the word which I have spoken shall be done, saith the Lord GOD. (Ezekiel 12:21-28)

A Proverb in Israel (21-28): "The days are prolonged

and every vision faileth", this was the proverb that was propagated through Jerusalem. The proverb was stating that the days of judgment against Jerusalem would not come to pass in their day, and that the visions of God's prophets have failed. God however states that He will cause this proverb to cease by bringing His prophecies to pass in their day (23-25). This issue will be elaborated on in the following chapter, as we will see that it was the false prophets in the land of Jerusalem that devised this proverb out of their own hearts (13:1-3).

CHAPTER 13

Repudiation of the False Prophets

And the word of the LORD came unto me, saying, Son of man, prophesy against the prophets of Israel that prophesy, and say thou unto them that prophesy out of their own hearts, Hear ye the word of the LORD; Thus saith the Lord GOD; Woe unto the foolish prophets, that follow their own spirit, and have seen nothing! O Israel, thy prophets are like the foxes in the deserts. Ye have not gone up into the gaps, neither made up the hedge for the house of Israel to stand in the battle in the day of the LORD. They have seen vanity and lying divination, saying, The LORD saith: and the LORD hath not sent them: and they have made others to hope that they would confirm the word. Have ye not seen a vain vision, and have ye not spoken a lying divination, whereas ye say, The LORD saith it; albeit I have not spoken? Therefore thus saith the Lord GOD; Because ye have spoken vanity, and seen lies, therefore, behold, I am against you, saith the Lord GOD. And mine hand shall be upon the prophets that see vanity, and that divine lies: they shall not be in the assembly of my people, neither shall they be written in the writing of the house of Israel, neither shall they enter into the land of Israel; and ye shall know that I am the Lord GOD. (Ezekiel 13:1-9)

The Charge Against the False Prophets (1-9): The false prophets are charged by God for prophesying lies out of their own heart. They would say, *"thus saith the Lord"* when God hath not spoken by them (vs. 6, 7). The false prophets are likened to foxes in the deserts. The fox in Scripture is cunning (Luke 13:32). It spoils the vine and its fruit (Song 2:15). It burrows among the ruins (Neh. 4:3; Lam. 5:18). Thus the false prophets were crafty, laid waste the vineyard of the Lord of hosts (Isaiah 5:7), made their profit out of the ruin of Israel and made that ruin worse. Therefore the Lord is against them!

Because, even because they have seduced my people, saying, Peace; and there was no peace; and one built up a wall, and, lo, others daubed it with untempered morter: Say unto them which daub it with untempered morter, that it shall fall: there shall be an overflowing shower; and ye, O great hailstones, shall fall; and a stormy wind shall rend it. Lo, when the wall is fallen, shall it not be said unto you, Where is the daubing wherewith ye have daubed it? Therefore thus saith the Lord GOD; I will even rend it with a stormy wind in my fury; and there shall be an overflowing shower in mine anger, and great hailstones in my fury to consume it. So will I break down the wall that ye have daubed with untempered morter, and bring it down to the ground, so that the foundation thereof shall be discovered, and it shall fall, and ye shall be consumed in the midst thereof: and ye shall know that I am the LORD. Thus will I accomplish my wrath upon the wall, and upon them that have daubed it with untempered morter, and will say unto you, The wall is no more, neither they that daubed it; To wit, the prophets of Israel which prophesy concerning Jerusalem, and which see visions of peace for her, and there is no peace, saith the Lord GOD. (Ezekiel 13:10-16)

Visions of the False Prophets (10-16): These false prophets

are within the walls of Jerusalem and are prophesying that Babylon will not penetrate the walls, that peace is on the horizon. God however is prophesying 'No Peace" (vs. 10, cf. 16). The idea then behind this portion of Scripture is that the false prophets are proclaiming peace and safety within the walls of Jerusalem but God is going to treat the walls of Jerusalem as untempered mortar that it shall fall, down to its very foundation (10-11, 14).

Some of the strongest rebuking against these false prophets is done by Jeremiah who opposed them on moral, personal and political grounds *(Jer. 23:9-23 see also the opposition of Hananiah Jer. 28)*. It is an interesting note to study the false prophets that will arise in the "last days" of Israel's history *(Matt. 24:11,24; 2 Peter 2; I John 4:1)*.

Likewise, thou son of man, set thy face against the daughters of thy people, which prophesy out of their own heart; and prophesy thou against them, And say, Thus saith the Lord GOD; Woe to the women that sew pillows to all armholes, and make kerchiefs upon the head of every stature to hunt souls! Will ye hunt the souls of my people, and will ye save the souls alive that come unto you? And will ye pollute me among my people for handfuls of barley and for pieces of bread, to slay the souls that should not die, and to save the souls alive that should not live, by your lying to my people that hear your lies? Wherefore thus saith the Lord GOD; Behold, I am against your pillows, wherewith ye there hunt the souls to make them fly, and I will tear them from your arms, and will let the souls go, even the souls that ye hunt to make them fly. Your kerchiefs

also will I tear, and deliver my people out of your hand, and they shall be no more in your hand to be hunted; and ye shall know that I am the LORD. Because with lies ye have made the heart of the righteous sad, whom I have not made sad; and strengthened the hands of the wicked, that he should not return from his wicked way, by promising him life: Therefore ye shall see no more vanity, nor divine divinations: for I will deliver my people out of your hand: and ye shall know that I am the LORD. (Ezekiel 13:17-23)

False Prophetess (17-23): The gift of prophecy was not given exclusively to men, for several prophetesses are named in Scripture: *Miriam (Ex. 15:20), Deborah (Jud. 4:4-5), the wife of Isaiah (Isa. 8:3), Hulda (2 Kings 22:14), and the daughters of Philip the evangelist (Acts 21:8-9).* These prophetesses spoken of in Ezekiel 13 were sorceresses, counterparts of the false prophets, forerunner to the modern palmist, fortune-tellers, and mediums.

CHAPTER 14

Three Righteous Men Unable to Deliver the People

Then came certain of the elders of Israel unto me, and sat before me. And the word of the LORD came unto me, saying, Son of man, these men have set up their idols in their heart, and put the stumblingblock of their iniquity before their face: should I be inquired of at all by them? Therefore speak unto them, and say unto them, Thus saith the Lord GOD; Every man of the house of Israel that setteth up his idols in his heart, and putteth the stumblingblock of his iniquity before his face, and cometh to the prophet; I the LORD will answer him that cometh according to the multitude of his idols; That I may take the house of Israel in their own heart, because they are all estranged from me through their idols. Therefore say unto the house of Israel, Thus saith the Lord GOD; Repent, and turn yourselves from your idols; and turn away your faces from all your abominations. For every one of the house of Israel, or of the stranger that sojourneth in Israel, which separateth himself from me, and setteth up his idols in his heart, and putteth the stumblingblock of his iniquity before his face, and cometh to a prophet to inquire of him concerning me; I the LORD will answer him by myself: And I will set my face against that man, and will make him a sign and a proverb, and I will cut him off from the midst of my people; and ye shall know that I am the LORD. And if the prophet be deceived when he hath spoken a thing, I the LORD have deceived that prophet, and I will stretch out my hand upon him, and will destroy him from the midst of my people Israel. And they shall bear the punishment of their iniquity: the punishment of the prophet shall be even as the punishment of him that seeketh unto him; That the house of Israel may go no more astray from me, neither be polluted any more with all their transgressions; but that they may be my people, and I may be their God, saith the Lord GOD. (Ezekiel 14:1-11)

The False Prophets and Those that Follow (1-11): The leaders come before Ezekiel probably in response to their perplexity over Ezekiel's condemnation of the false prophets. In this first section the Lord lays emphasis that judgment is upon both the false prophet and those who harken to them (vs. 4 cf. vss. 7-10).

The word of the LORD came again to me, saying, Son of man, when the land sinneth against me by trespassing grievously, then will I stretch out mine hand upon it, and will break the staff of the bread thereof, and will send famine upon it, and will cut off man and beast from it: Though these three men, Noah, Daniel, and Job, were in it, they should deliver but their own souls by their righteousness, saith the Lord GOD. If I cause noisome beasts to pass through the land, and they spoil it, so that it be desolate, that no man may pass through because of the beasts: Though these three men were in it, as I live, saith the Lord GOD, they shall deliver neither sons nor daughters; they only shall be delivered, but the land shall be desolate. Or if I bring a sword upon that land, and say, Sword, go through the land; so that I cut off man and beast from it: Though these three men were in it, as I live, saith the Lord GOD, they shall deliver neither sons nor daughters, but they only shall be delivered themselves. Or if I send a pestilence into that land, and pour out my fury upon it in blood, to cut off from it man and beast: Though Noah, Daniel, and Job, were in it, as I live, saith the Lord GOD, they shall deliver neither son nor daughter; they shall but deliver their own souls by their righteousness. For thus saith the Lord GOD; How much more when I send my four sore judgments upon Jerusalem, the sword, and the famine, and the noisome beast, and the pestilence, to cut off from it man and beast? (Ezekiel 14:12-21)

Four Judgments and Three Men (12-21):
The Four Judgments: The prophet declares that when the land sinneth, God sends one of His four judgments against it (vs. 21): Famine vss. 12-14, Noisome Beasts vss. 15-16, Sword and war vss. 17-18 and Pestilence vss. 19-20. These Judgments were Foretold in Leviticus 26: Slain *(sword)* Lev. 26:17, Land shall not increase "famine" Lev. 26:20, Wild Beasts Lev. 26:22 and Plague *(pestilence)* Lev. 26:25.

The Three Men: Ezekiel chooses three men well known among the people for their saintly qualities and yet were powerless to deliver the generation in which they lived: Noah, Job and Daniel. Noah was unable to save the evil race from the flood. Job could not deliver his family **and** Daniel, though high in the king's favor had not been able to influence Nebuchadnezzar to spare the people of Judah and Jerusalem.

Ezekiel is doing the same thing that Jeremiah had done. Jeremiah had stated that even if Moses & Samuel were present in the land they would not be able to save the people (Jeremiah 15:1-3). Though the righteous ancients,

Noah, Daniel and Job were in the land, they could deliver only themselves.

Ezekiel's focus here was that Jerusalem was not going to be spared, and that even if Noah, Daniel, and Job could be there, they would be saved but not those around them. The thrust of this passage is that Jerusalem is not going to be spared.

It is interesting to contrast the judgments here with the judgments of Sodom and Gomorrah in Genesis 18. Abraham asked God if there were 10 righteous there would he spare the city. Ten were not found, only one, Lot. Lot therefore had to be removed before the judgment could be laid against Sodom. Abraham asks the question, *"shall not the judge of all the earth do right?"* - The answer is yes he will spare the righteous, but the righteous shall not prevent the judgment of God from coming.

Yet, behold, therein shall be left a remnant that shall be brought forth, both sons and daughters: behold, they shall come forth unto you, and ye shall see their way and their doings: and ye shall be comforted concerning the evil that I have brought upon Jerusalem, even concerning all that I have brought upon it. And they shall comfort you, when ye see their ways and their doings: and ye shall know that I have not done without cause all that I have done in it, saith the Lord GOD. (Ezekiel 14:22-23)

The Promised Remnant (22-23): This section has been stated and repeated throughout Ezekiel, God will not utterly destroy the people of God.

CHAPTER 15
Israel the Useless Vine

There are at least four metaphors for Israel: The Olive Tree; The Fig Tree; The Vine; and, The Bramble Bush. All these metaphors are used extensively throughout Scripture but they are used all together in Judges 9, in the parable of Jotham (Judges 9:7-15): The **Olive Tree** as a metaphor of the covenant relationship between God and Israel (Rom 11 & Jer 11). The **Fig Tree** is a common metaphor which speaks of Israel in a national sense (Mt 24:32). The **Vine** is a metaphor that speaks of the Spiritual relationship between God and Israel (Isa 5 & Hos 10). The **Bramble Bush** is a metaphor of Israel in terms of their failure (Judges 9:14,15).

And the word of the LORD came unto me, saying, Son of man, What is the vine tree more than any tree, or than a branch which is among the trees of the forest? Shall wood be taken thereof to do any work? or will men take a pin of it to hang any vessel thereon? Behold, it is cast into the fire for fuel; the fire devoureth both the ends of it, and the midst of it is burned. Is it meet for any work? Behold, when it was whole, it was meet for no work: how much less shall it be meet yet for any work, when the fire hath devoured it, and it is burned? (Ezekiel 15:1-5)

The Vine and its Purpose (1-5): The vine is one of the symbols of the nation Israel. "For the vineyard of the Lord of hosts is the house of Israel ..." *(Isa 5:7; cf. Gen*

49:22; Deut. 32:32; Hos 10:1; Isa 5:1-7; Jer. 2:21; Ezek. 17:6; Ps. 80:8-16). What is the purpose of a vine? A vine is not used to construct furniture; its purpose is either to produce fruit, or it is burnt up as fuel for the fire.

Therefore thus saith the Lord GOD; As the vine tree among the trees of the forest, which I have given to the fire for fuel, so will I give the inhabitants of Jerusalem. And I will set my face against them; they shall go out from one fire, and another fire shall devour them; and ye shall know that I am the LORD, when I set my face against them. And I will make the land desolate, because they have committed a trespass, saith the Lord GOD. (Ezekiel 15:6-8)

As the Vine so the Inhabitants of Jerusalem (6-8): The conclusion is, just as the vine is fit for the fire so the inhabitants of Jerusalem are fit for the consuming fire of God's flames.

CHAPTER 16
The long History of Israel, the Unfaithful Wife

This parable is of finding a dirty and filthy little child for whom it would seem there is nothing that can be done. This allegory like that in Chapter 23, depicts the connection between the Lord and his people in terms of a husband-wife relationship (cf. Hos. 2; Jer. 2:1-3; 3:1-5). The finding of a child of questionable origin, Jerusalem. This child is found by the roadside to die. But she is rescued by the Lord to become her benefactor. Having grown up a beautiful maidenhood, she is taken in marriage by her benefactor and becomes His royal bride, the queen. The proud queen however proves to be utterly unfaithful and plays the harlot with other gods. Therefore she is punished and put away. Nevertheless the Lord makes a glorious promise of restoration through an everlasting covenant.

This is the summary of the truth of the parable of chapter 16. God and his unfaithful wife, the people of Jerusalem.

Again the word of the LORD came unto me, saying, Son of man, cause Jerusalem to know her abominations, And say, Thus saith the Lord GOD unto Jerusalem; Thy birth and thy nativity is of the land of Canaan; thy father was an Amorite, and thy mother an Hittite. And as for thy nativity, in the day thou wast born thy

navel was not cut, neither wast thou washed in water to supple thee; thou wast not salted at all, nor swaddled at all. None eye pitied thee, to do any of these unto thee, to have compassion upon thee; but thou wast cast out in the open field, to the lothing of thy person, in the day that thou wast born. And when I passed by thee, and saw thee polluted in thine own blood, I said unto thee when thou wast in thy blood, Live; yea, I said unto thee when thou wast in thy blood, Live. I have caused thee to multiply as the bud of the field, and thou hast increased and waxen great, and thou art come to excellent ornaments: thy breasts are fashioned, and thine hair is grown, whereas thou wast naked and bare. Now when I passed by thee, and looked upon thee, behold, thy time was the time of love; and I spread my skirt over thee, and covered thy nakedness: yea, I sware unto thee, and entered into a covenant with thee, saith the Lord GOD, and thou becamest mine. Then washed I thee with water; yea, I throughly washed away thy blood from thee, and I anointed thee with oil. I clothed thee also with broidered work, and shod thee with badgers' skin, and I girded thee about with fine linen, and I covered thee with silk. I decked thee also with ornaments, and I put bracelets upon thy hands, and a chain on thy neck. And I put a jewel on thy forehead, and earrings in thine ears, and a beautiful crown upon thine head. Thus wast thou decked with gold and silver; and thy raiment was of fine linen, and silk, and broidered work; thou didst eat fine flour, and honey, and oil: and thou wast exceeding beautiful, and thou didst prosper into a kingdom. And thy renown went forth among the heathen for thy beauty: for it was perfect through my comeliness, which I had put upon thee, saith the Lord GOD. (Ezekiel 16:1-14)

Jerusalem and its Humble Origins to its Exalted Position (1-14): The history of Jerusalem is that it was in the land of Canaan with the inhabitants of the Amorite and the Hittite. Thus, this city was not of royal lineage but nonetheless God found favor in her and cleaned her up anointing her with oil and blessed her abundantly: Clothed her with beautiful garments (vs. 10), decked her with an array of costly ornaments, bracelets, jewels and a crown upon her head, ornaments of gold and silver. (11-13a) and blessed her with abundance of fine foods (vs. 13b). The result was that she became a mighty kingdom in the eyes of all the nations around her (vs. 14).

But thou didst trust in thine own beauty, and playedst the harlot because of thy renown, and pouredst out thy fornications on every one that passed by; his it was. And of thy garments thou didst take, and deckedst thy high places with divers colours, and playedst the harlot thereupon: the like things shall not come, neither shall it be so. Thou hast also taken thy fair jewels of my gold and of my silver, which I had given thee, and madest to thyself images of men, and didst commit whoredom with them, And tookest thy broidered garments, and coveredst them: and thou hast set mine oil and mine incense before them. My meat also which I gave thee, fine flour, and oil, and honey, wherewith I fed thee, thou hast even set it before them for a sweet savour: and thus it was, saith the Lord GOD. Moreover thou hast taken thy sons and thy daughters, whom thou hast borne unto me, and these hast thou sacrificed unto them to be devoured. Is this of thy whoredoms a small matter, That thou hast slain my children, and delivered them to cause them to pass through the fire for them?

And in all thine abominations and thy whoredoms thou hast not remembered the days of thy youth, when thou wast naked and bare, and wast polluted in thy blood. And it came to pass after all thy wickedness, (woe, woe unto thee! saith the Lord GOD;) That thou hast also built unto thee an eminent place, and hast made thee an high place in every street. Thou hast built thy high place at every head of the way, and hast made thy beauty to be abhorred, and hast opened thy feet to every one that passed by, and multiplied thy whoredoms. Thou hast also committed fornication with the Egyptians thy neighbours, great of flesh; and hast increased thy whoredoms, to provoke me to anger. Behold, therefore I have stretched out my hand over thee, and have diminished thine ordinary food, and delivered thee unto the will of them that hate thee, the daughters of the Philistines, which are ashamed of thy lewd way. Thou hast played the whore also with the Assyrians, because thou wast unsatiable; yea, thou hast played the harlot with them, and yet couldest not be satisfied. Thou hast moreover multiplied thy fornication in the land of Canaan unto Chaldea; and yet thou wast not satisfied herewith. How weak is thine heart, saith the Lord GOD, seeing thou doest all these things, the work of an imperious whorish woman; In that thou buildest thine eminent place in the head of every way, and makest thine high place in every street; and hast not been as an harlot, in that thou scornest hire; But as a wife that committeth adultery, which taketh strangers instead of her husband! They give gifts to all whores: but thou givest thy gifts to all thy lovers, and hirest them, that they may come unto thee on every side for thy whoredom. And the contrary is in thee from other women in thy whoredoms, whereas none followeth thee to commit whoredoms: and in that thou givest a reward, and no reward is given unto thee, therefore thou art contrary. (Ezekiel 16:15-34)

The Squandering of Jerusalem's Blessings and What Jerusalem had Become (15-34): Jerusalem had taken all the blessing that God had given her and played the harlot, offering the blessings upon the altar of gods (vs. 15):
- With her beautiful garments she decked the high places (vs. 16)
- With her costly jewels of gold and silver, she made images (vs. 17)
- Her blessing of fine foods she offered to her idols (vs. 19)

As if all this was not enough God says, "moreover":
- The fruit of the womb that was born unto Him did they offer in sacrifice to their gods (vs. 20-21)

As if offering the abundant blessings of God to their idols was not enough, they committed spiritual fornication with the countries round about her by making alliances with those countries:
- Egypt vs. 26 (2 Kings 18:21)
- Philistines vs. 27 (2 Chronicles 21:16-17)
- Assyrians vs. 28 The conduct of Ahaz stripping the temple of its gold and silver to pay tribute to Assyria gives apt illustration of what the prophet means (2 Kings 16:8).
- Chaldea vs. 29 Babylon

Thus, Jerusalem plays the harlot (see vss. 32-34) and is judged accordingly.

Wherefore, O harlot, hear the word of the LORD: Thus saith the Lord GOD; Because thy filthiness was poured out, and thy nakedness discovered through thy whoredoms with thy lovers, and with all the idols of thy abominations, and by the blood of thy children, which thou didst give unto them; Behold, therefore I will gather all thy lovers, with whom thou hast taken pleasure, and all them that thou hast loved, with all them that thou hast hated; I will even gather them round about against thee, and will discover thy nakedness unto them, that they may see all thy nakedness. And I will judge thee, as women that break wedlock and shed blood are judged; and I will give thee blood in fury and jealousy. And I will also give thee into their hand, and they shall throw down thine eminent place, and shall break down thy high places: they shall strip thee also of thy clothes, and shall take thy fair jewels, and leave thee naked and bare. They shall also bring up a company against thee, and they shall stone thee with stones, and thrust thee through with their swords. And they shall burn thine houses with fire, and execute judgments upon thee in the sight of many women: and I will cause thee to cease from playing the harlot, and thou also shalt give no hire any more. So will I make my fury toward thee to rest, and my jealousy shall depart from thee, and I will be quiet, and will be no more angry. Because thou hast not remembered the days of thy youth, but hast fretted me in all these things; behold, therefore I also will recompense thy way upon thine head, saith the Lord GOD: and thou shalt not commit this lewdness above all thine abominations. (Ezekiel 16:35-43)

The Judgment upon the Unfaithful Wife (35-43): Because of all the things previously mentioned Jerusalem is worthy of all that befalls her (vs. 36). All the nations she has committed spiritual fornication with by making alliances with them will now be turned against her (vss. 37-41).

Behold, every one that useth proverbs shall use this proverb against thee, saying, As is the mother, so is her daughter. Thou art thy mother's daughter, that lotheth her husband and her children; and thou art the sister of thy sisters, which lothed their husbands and their children: your mother was an Hittite, and your father an Amorite. And thine elder sister is Samaria, she and her daughters that dwell at thy left hand: and thy younger sister, that dwelleth at thy right hand, is Sodom and her daughters. Yet hast thou not walked after their ways, nor done after their abominations: but, as if that were a very little thing, thou wast corrupted more than they in all thy ways. As I live, saith the Lord GOD, Sodom thy sister hath not done, she nor her daughters, as thou hast done, thou and thy daughters. Behold, this was the iniquity of thy sister Sodom, pride, fulness of bread, and abundance of idleness was in her and in her daughters, neither did she strengthen the hand of the poor and needy. And they were haughty, and committed abomination before me: therefore I took them away as I saw good. Neither hath Samaria committed half of thy sins; but thou hast multiplied thine abominations more than they, and hast justified thy sisters in all thine abominations which thou hast done. Thou also, which hast judged thy sisters, bear thine own shame for thy sins that thou hast committed more abominable than they: they are more righteous than thou: yea, be thou confounded also, and bear thy shame, in that thou hast justified thy sisters. When I

shall bring again their captivity, the captivity of Sodom and her daughters, and the captivity of Samaria and her daughters, then will I bring again the captivity of thy captives in the midst of them: That thou mayest bear thine own shame, and mayest be confounded in all that thou hast done, in that thou art a comfort unto them. When thy sisters, Sodom and her daughters, shall return to their former estate, and Samaria and her daughters shall return to their former estate, then thou and thy daughters shall return to your former estate. For thy sister Sodom was not mentioned by thy mouth in the day of thy pride, Before thy wickedness was discovered, as at the time of thy reproach of the daughters of Syria, and all that are round about her, the daughters of the Philistines, which despise thee round about. Thou hast borne thy lewdness and thine abominations, saith the LORD. For thus saith the Lord GOD; I will even deal with thee as thou hast done, which hast despised the oath in breaking the covenant. (Ezekiel 16:44-59)

The Proverb against Jerusalem (44-59): The proverb put forth is "as is the mother so is her daughter". The idea is that this generation is as the previous one, they loth their husband and their children (45). Then God likens the two neighboring cities, Samaria and Sodom as sisters to Jerusalem (vs. 46) saying that Jerusalem has committed more abominations than her sisters (vss. 47-59).

Nevertheless I will remember my covenant with thee in the days of thy youth, and I will establish unto thee an everlasting covenant. Then thou shalt remember thy ways, and be ashamed, when thou shalt receive thy sisters, thine elder and thy younger: and I will give them unto thee for daughters, but not by thy covenant. And I will establish my covenant with thee; and thou shalt know that I am the LORD: That thou mayest remember, and be confounded, and never open thy mouth any more because of thy shame, when I am pacified toward thee for all that thou hast done, saith the Lord GOD. (Ezekiel 16:60-63)

The Unfaithful Wife will be Restored (60-63): God reconfirms that though Jerusalem is being put away at this time *(Loammi — ye are not my people Hos. 1:9)* they will be brought back to God (cf. Hosea 1:10).

Break not an Oath: A Parable about Zedekiah, Babylon and Egypt

Judah, Babylon and Egypt are the three in the riddle and the parable of Chapter 17: it will be stated in Ezekiel 17:3-10 and explained in Ezekiel 17:11-21.

Background to Consider: Backing up to Jehoiakim, king of Judah who reigned at 25 years of age. He reigned 11 years and did that which was evil in the sight of the Lord (2 Kings 23:36, 37) so the Lord removed him (2 Kings 24:1-5). Following Jehoiakim reigned Jehoiachin his son (2 Kings 24:6). Jehoiachin, *also called Jeconiah & Coniah* was 18 years old when he began to reign (2 Kings 24:8). He did that which was evil in the sight of the Lord (2 Kings 24:9), so the Lord removed him by Nebuchadnezzar bringing the second siege against Jerusalem (2 Kings 10:16). Jehoiachin would be the last of his descendant to sit on the thrown of David. God declares that none of Jehoiachin's seed would rule any more in Judah:
Is this man Coniah a despised broken idol? is he a vessel wherein is no pleasure? wherefore are they cast out, he and his seed, and are cast into a land which they know not? O earth, earth, earth, hear the word of the LORD. Thus saith the LORD, Write ye this man childless, a man that shall not prosper in his days: for no man of his seed shall prosper, sitting upon the throne of David, and ruling any more in Judah. (Jeremiah 22:28-30)

So then God allows something interesting to take place:

He allows Nebuchadnezzar to take the youngest son of Josiah, Mattaniah and put him on the throne as a vassal king, renaming him Zedekiah (2 Kings 24:17 cf. Jeremiah 37:1). Thus, Zedekiah is Jehoiachin's uncle. *(Josiah's sons: Jehoiakim who bore Jehoiachin and Zedekiah (Mattaniah)*

In doing this Nebuchadnezzar made Zedekiah to swear by an oath before the Lord to be loyal to Nebuchadnezzar (2 Chronicles 36:13). However Zedekiah broke this oath making alliance with Egypt (Jer. 37:7, 44:30). Ezekiel, Jeremiah and Isaiah all warned against aligning with Egypt (Isaiah 30:1-7). It is because of this alliance that the final siege against Jerusalem takes place.

And the word of the LORD came unto me, saying, Son of man, put forth a riddle, and speak a parable unto the house of Israel; And say, Thus saith the Lord GOD; A great eagle with great wings, longwinged, full of feathers, which had divers colours, came unto Lebanon, and took the highest branch of the cedar: He cropped off the top of his young twigs, and carried it into a land of traffick; he set it in a city of merchants. He took also of the seed of the land, and planted it in a fruitful field; he placed it by great waters, and set it as a willow tree. And it grew, and became a spreading vine of low stature, whose branches turned toward him, and the roots thereof were under him: so it became a vine, and brought forth branches, and shot forth sprigs. There was also another great eagle with great wings and many feathers: and, behold, this vine did bend her roots toward him, and shot forth her branches toward him, that he might water it by the furrows of her plantation. It was planted in a good soil by great waters, that it might bring forth branches,

and that it might bear fruit, that it might be a goodly vine. Say thou, Thus saith the Lord GOD; Shall it prosper? shall he not pull up the roots thereof, and cut off the fruit thereof, that it wither? it shall wither in all the leaves of her spring, even without great power or many people to pluck it up by the roots thereof. Yea, behold, being planted, shall it prosper? shall it not utterly wither, when the east wind toucheth it? it shall wither in the furrows where it grew. Moreover the word of the LORD came unto me, saying, Say now to the rebellious house, Know ye not what these things mean? tell them, Behold, the king of Babylon is come to Jerusalem, and hath taken the king thereof, and the princes thereof, and led them with him to Babylon; And hath taken of the king's seed, and made a covenant with him, and hath taken an oath of him: he hath also taken the mighty of the land: That the kingdom might be base, that it might not lift itself up, but that by keeping of his covenant it might stand. But he rebelled against him in sending his ambassadors into Egypt, that they might give him horses and much people. Shall he prosper? shall he escape that doeth such things? or shall he break the covenant, and be delivered? As I live, saith the Lord GOD, surely in the place where the king dwelleth that made him king, whose oath he despised, and whose covenant he brake, even with him in the midst of Babylon he shall die. Neither shall Pharaoh with his mighty army and great company make for him in the war, by casting up mounts, and building forts, to cut off many persons: Seeing he despised the oath by breaking the covenant, when, lo, he had given his hand, and hath done all these things, he shall not escape. Therefore thus saith the Lord GOD; As I live, surely mine oath that he hath despised, and my covenant that he hath broken, even it will I recompense upon his own head. And I will spread my net upon him, and he shall be taken in my snare, and I will bring him to Babylon, and will plead with him there for his trespass that he hath trespassed against me. And all his fugitives with all his bands shall fall by the sword, and they that remain shall be scattered toward all winds: and ye shall know that I the LORD have spoken it. (Ezekiel 17:1-21)

The Parable and its Interpretation (1-21):
- **A Great Eagle (vs. 3)** — Babylon, Nebuchadnezzar (vs. 12)
- **Lebanon (vs. 3)** — Jerusalem (vs. 12). The Temple at Jerusalem: called "Lebanon" by the Jews because its woodwork was wholly of cedars of Lebanon.
- **Highest Branch (vs. 3)** — The Davidic line, specifically Jehoiachin (vs. 12) also called Jeconiah & Coniah.
- **Young Twigs (vs. 4)** — The royal family of Jehoiachin (vs. 13) which was taken with Jehoiachin cf. 2 Kings 24:15.
- **The Land of Traffick a City of Merchants (vs. 4)** - Babylon (vs. 12). (Matt. 13:45)
- **Seed of the Land (vs. 5)** — Zedekiah (vs. 13). Zedekiah was the seed of the land not a foreigner. He was the son of Josiah brother of Jehoiachim and uncle to Jehoiachin.
- **Fruitful Field by Great Waters (vs. 5)** — The land of Israel known for its many brooks of water and fountains (Deut. 8:7).
- **Vine of Low Stature with Branches Turned Toward Him (vs. 6)** — Zedekiah and his submissiveness to Nebuchadnezzar by taking of the oath (vs. 13).
- **Another Great Eagle (vs. 7)** — Egypt (vs. 15), Pharohhopra (Jer. 44:30) who Zedekiah made

alliance with in opposition to Nebuchadnezzar.
- **It was Planted in Good Soil (vs. 8-10)** — If Zedekiah had remained loyal to Nebuchadnezzar he would have blossomed, but instead judgment (vss. 15-17). Ezekiel, like his contemporary Jeremiah (Jer. 37:7) and his predecessor Isaiah (Isa. 30:1-7), was against this policy of an Egyptian alliance.

Thus saith the Lord GOD; I will also take of the highest branch of the high cedar, and will set it; I will crop off from the top of his young twigs a tender one, and will plant it upon an high mountain and eminent: In the mountain of the height of Israel will I plant it: and it shall bring forth boughs, and bear fruit, and be a goodly cedar: and under it shall dwell all fowl of every wing; in the shadow of the branches thereof shall they dwell. And all the trees of the field shall know that I the LORD have brought down the high tree, have exalted the low tree, have dried up the green tree, and have made the dry tree to flourish: I the LORD have spoken and have done it. (Ezekiel 17:22-24)

The Interpretation (22-24): The King of the Davidic Line. Ezekiel chapters 17 & 18 are two chapters dealing with the end of the Dynasty of David, the succession of kings in Judah. However in the middle of these two chapters God promises the most important King of the Davidic line, the Messiah.

God proclaims He will also take of the "highest branch of the high cedar": God will "also" take of the Davidic line. He shall be a tender one whom God shall plant upon an high mountain, namely Zion; and it is through this tender plant on a high mountain that shall grow into a goodly cedar that all shall find shade and protection. Jesus Christ is the seed of David (2 Tim. 2:8; Rom. 1:3; John 7:42) planted in the land of Israel (Isaiah 60:21). He is as a root out of the dry ground a tender plant (Isa. 53:2). His Kingdom shall grow and prosper until it becomes a great mountain (Dan. 2:35, 45) and all shall see and find protection (Isaiah 11:1-9).

CHAPTER 18

Understanding Judgment from God

Chapter 18 is all about personal accountability for sins. God holds each individual personally accountable for their own sins. God does not judge the sons for the sins of the father.

The word of the LORD came unto me again, saying, What mean ye, that ye use this proverb concerning the land of Israel, saying, The fathers have eaten sour grapes, and the children's teeth are set on edge? As I live, saith the Lord GOD, ye shall not have occasion any more to use this proverb in Israel. Behold, all souls are mine; as the soul of the father, so also the soul of the son is mine: the soul that sinneth, it shall die. (Ezekiel 18:1-4)

A Proverb in the Land (1-4): The children of Israel had a common proverb that showed their ideology when it comes to their suffering. The proverb was *"the fathers have eaten sour grapes and the children's teeth are set on edge"* (vs.2). The idea being that the children are only suffering for the sins of their fathers; God was judging them for the sins that their fathers committed. (See: Jer. 31:29; Lam. 5:7)

However God says they will not have any occasion any more to use this proverb in Israel (vs.3). Why? Because all souls are God's, whether it be the fathers or the sons and *"the soul that sinnith it shall die"*; personal accountability for sins (vs. 4). These verses are not dealing with eternal life matters but a judgment in this life (Deut. 24:16).

Ezekiel now will use an illustration of a *grandfather* who lives justly, a *son* that lives ungodly and the *grandson* that lives justly again. Thus, no one is being put to death for the sins of their father, they are personally accountable for their own actions.

But if a man be just, and do that which is lawful and right, And hath not eaten upon the mountains, neither hath lifted up his eyes to the idols of the house of Israel, neither hath defiled his neighbour's wife, neither hath come near to a menstruous woman, And hath not oppressed any, but hath restored to the debtor his pledge, hath spoiled none by violence, hath given his bread to the hungry, and hath covered the naked with a garment; He that hath not given forth upon usury, neither hath taken any increase, that hath withdrawn his hand from iniquity, hath executed true judgment between man and man, Hath walked in my statutes, and hath kept my judgments, to deal truly; he is just, he shall surely live, saith the Lord GOD. (Ezekiel 18:5-9)

The Just Grandfather (5-9): God is showing that for walking justly, doing that which is right the man is just and will live (6). Because this man has walked according to God's statutes, judgments and dealt truly he will be blessed in this life.

If he beget a son that is a robber, a shedder of blood, and that doeth the like to any one of these things, And that doeth not any of those duties, but even hath eaten

upon the mountains, and defiled his neighbour's wife, Hath oppressed the poor and needy, hath spoiled by violence, hath not restored the pledge, and hath lifted up his eyes to the idols, hath committed abomination, Hath given forth upon usury, and hath taken increase: shall he then live? he shall not live: he hath done all these abominations; he shall surely die; his blood shall be upon him. (Ezekiel 18:10-13)

The Ungodly Son (10-13): This is the ungodly son who has done the opposite of his father and therefore will be judged for his sins, he shall die (13). Notice his just father could not store up merit with God for his son. No matter how good the father was his son is personally accountable for his own behavior. (Remember Ezek. 14:16-18).

Now, lo, if he beget a son, that seeth all his father's sins which he hath done, and considereth, and doeth not such like, That hath not eaten upon the mountains, neither hath lifted up his eyes to the idols of the house of Israel, hath not defiled his neighbour's wife, Neither hath oppressed any, hath not withholden the pledge, neither hath spoiled by violence, but hath given his bread to the hungry, and hath covered the naked with a garment, That hath taken off his hand from the poor, that hath not received usury nor increase, hath executed my judgments, hath walked in my statutes; he shall not die for the iniquity of his father, he shall surely live. As for his father, because he cruelly oppressed, spoiled his brother by violence, and did that which is not good among his people, lo, even he shall die in his iniquity. Yet say ye, Why? doth not the son bear the iniquity of the father? When the son hath done that which is lawful and right, and hath kept all my statutes, and hath done them, he shall surely live. (Ezekiel 18:14-19)

The First Objection to Personal Accountability (14-19): Again the son is not being judged for the sins of his wicked father (vs. 17). The Jews now argue for the very thing they were originally against; they ask, *"why, doth not the son bear the iniquity of the father?"* In other words, why can't the iniquity of the fathers fall on the son, why do we have to be personally responsible? Why do you think they secretly desired to have the sins of the fathers fall on the sons? Possibly because they did not like to be held accountable for their personal actions! Sounds like today!

The soul that sinneth, it shall die. The son shall not bear the iniquity of the father, neither shall the father bear the iniquity of the son: the righteousness of the righteous shall be upon him, and the wickedness of the wicked shall be upon him. But if the wicked will turn from all his sins that he hath committed, and keep all my statutes, and do that which is lawful and right, he shall surely live, he shall not die. All his transgressions that he hath committed, they shall not be mentioned unto him: in his righteousness that he hath done he shall live. Have I any pleasure at all that the wicked should die? saith the Lord GOD: and not that he should return from his ways, and live? But when the righteous turneth away from his righteousness, and committeth iniquity, and doeth according to all the abominations that the wicked man doeth, shall he live? All his righteousness that he hath done shall not be mentioned: in his trespass that he hath trespassed, and in his sin that he hath sinned, in them shall he die. (Ezekiel 18:20-24)

God's Declaration (20-24): God declares not only is the son not held accountable for the sins of the father but also the ungodly person that repents can have God's judgments on his life removed (21).

Why is this? God is not pleased that the wicked should die! (23). If man perishes it is because he will not turn to the Lord for salvation, for God is longsuffering not willing that any should perish (2 Pt. 3:9). In matters of eternal life thank the Lord for the eternal righteousness we have imputed to us by faith! (Philippians 3:7-9).

Yet ye say, The way of the Lord is not equal. Hear now, O house of Israel; Is not my way equal? are not your ways unequal? When a righteous man turneth away from his righteousness, and committeth iniquity, and dieth in them; for his iniquity that he hath done shall he die. Again, when the wicked man turneth away from his wickedness that he hath committed, and doeth that which is lawful and right, he shall save his soul alive. Because he considereth, and turneth away from all his transgressions that he hath committed, he shall surely live, he shall not die. Yet saith the house of Israel, The way of the Lord is not equal. O house of Israel, are not my ways equal? are not your ways unequal? Therefore I will judge you, O house of Israel, every one according to his ways, saith the Lord GOD. Repent, and turn yourselves from all your transgressions; so iniquity shall not be your ruin. (Ezekiel 18:25-30)

God's Final Declaration(25-30): Personal accountability is the greatest form of equality. God's ways are equal and when man tries to adjust that standard he will always find an unjust weight.

Cast away from you all your transgressions, whereby ye have transgressed; and make you a new heart and a new spirit: for why will ye die, O house of Israel? For I have no pleasure in the death of him that dieth, saith the Lord GOD: wherefore turn yourselves, and live ye. (Ezekiel 18:31-32)

A New Heart (31-32): The answer to all sin is a heart problem. Israel will / must have a heart transplant of which the New Covenant provides, both for Israel (Ezek. 36:26,27) and for ourselves (2 Cor. 3-6).

Conclusion: The teaching of this chapter answers the new psychology we have today, which argues that the reason a person is irresponsible is because his mother didn't treat him right but neglected him and didn't love him. You are a sinner because you are a sinner yourself! Every individual will stand before God, and he won't be able to blame his parents at that time. Ezekiel makes it very clear that the Israelite will be judged in this life on the basis of the life he lived, whether he was a believer or not.

CHAPTER 19

Lamentations Over the Princes of Judah and the Land of Judah

Moreover take thou up a lamentation for the princes of Israel, (Ezekiel 19:1)

Lamentation (1): This is a lamentation for the "princes of Israel" the rulers of the nation. God is lamenting for what they had become. Though not mentioned by name, this chapter deals with two "princes" Jehoahaz and Jehoiachin.

And say, What is thy mother? A lioness: she lay down among lions, she nourished her whelps among young lions. And she brought up one of her whelps: it became a young lion, and it learned to catch the prey; it devoured men. The nations also heard of him; he was taken in their pit, and they brought him with chains unto the land of Egypt. Now when she saw that she had waited, and her hope was lost, then she took another of her whelps, and made him a young lion. And he went up and down among the lions, he became a young lion, and learned to catch the prey, and devoured men. And he knew their desolate palaces, and he laid waste their cities; and the land was desolate, and the fulness thereof, by the noise of his roaring. Then the nations set against him on every side from the provinces, and spread their net over him: he was taken in their pit. And they put him in ward in chains, and brought him to the king of Babylon: they brought him into holds, that his

110

voice should no more be heard upon the mountains of Israel. (Ezekiel 19:2-9)

The Lioness and her Whelps (2-9): The Lioness is Israel, who is laid down among the heathen nations (lions). The lioness bears her whelps and one of them becomes a young lion who learned to catch the prey; to devour men (3-4). This is a reference to Jehoahaz who did that which was evil in the sight of the Lord and was taken away into Egypt (2 Kings 23:34). The lioness takes another of her whelps and makes him a "young lion" (5). This is Jehoiachin king of Judah. He also learned to catch the prey and devour men becoming as the heathen nations around him (6-7), thus he also is taken away into Babylonian captivity (8-9 cf. 2 Kings 24:15). Thus, this is God lamenting over the princes of Judah and what they had become.

Thy mother is like a vine in thy blood, planted by the waters: she was fruitful and full of branches by reason of many waters. And she had strong rods for the sceptres of them that bare rule, and her stature was exalted among the thick branches, and she appeared in her height with the multitude of her branches. But she was plucked up in fury, she was cast down to the ground, and the east wind dried up her fruit: her strong rods were broken and withered; the fire consumed them. And now she is planted in the wilderness, in a dry and thirsty ground. (Ezekiel 19:10-13)

The Vine that is Become Withered (10-13): The Lioness is now pictured as the vine (10) that has become withered, all of her branches or rods have become broken and are consumed by the fire; and now she is planted in the wilderness in a dry and thirsty land.

And fire is gone out of a rod of her branches, which hath devoured her fruit, so that she hath no strong rod to be a sceptre to rule. This is a lamentation, and shall be for a lamentation. (Ezekiel 19:14)

No King to Rule (14): The conclusion is that she has no more rod or prince to be the scepter in Judah, no King to rule.

With all the kings taken captive, who will rule anymore on the throne of David? Who will carry on the scepter? It has been prophesied that the scepter will not depart from Judah (Gen. 49:10) so how can this be?

Through none other than Jesus Christ, who is of the seed of David (Rom. 1:3) of the Tribe of Judah, who will sit on the throne of David (Luke 1:32).

CHAPTER 20

A History of the Rebellion of the Nation of Israel

In this chapter God will give an account of the history of Israel as seen from His point of view.

- Rebellion in Egypt   vss. 5-9

- Rebellion in the wilderness   vss. 10-17

- Rebellion of the children   vss. 18-26

- Rebellion entering Canaan   vss. 27-29

- Rebellion in Ezekiel's generation vss. 30-32

- God's forceful hand   vss. 33-39

- Kingdom Established   vss. 40-44

And it came to pass in the seventh year, in the fifth month, the tenth day of the month, that certain of the elders of Israel came to inquire of the LORD, and sat before me. Then came the word of the LORD unto me, saying, Son of man, speak unto the elders of Israel, and say unto them, Thus saith the Lord GOD; Are ye come to inquire of me? As I live, saith the Lord GOD, I will not be inquired of by you. Wilt thou judge them, son of man, wilt thou judge them? cause them to know the abominations of their fathers: (Ezekiel 20:1-4)

Inquiring of the Lord (1-4): Certain elders of Israel come to Ezekiel to inquire of the Lord. God however refuses their inquiries (3 cf. 31). God is not going to be questioned by these ungodly rulers of the nation. Notice the fervency that our Lord responds with, "As I live, saith the Lord GOD, I will not be inquired of by you."

And say unto them, Thus saith the Lord GOD; In the day when I chose Israel, and lifted up mine hand unto the seed of the house of Jacob, and made myself known unto them in the land of Egypt, when I lifted up mine hand unto them, saying, I am the LORD your God; In the day that I lifted up mine hand unto them, to bring them forth of the land of Egypt into a land that I had espied for them, flowing with milk and honey, which is the glory of all lands: Then said I unto them, Cast ye away every man the abominations of his eyes, and defile not yourselves with the idols of Egypt: I am the LORD your God. But they rebelled against me, and would not hearken unto me: they did not every man cast away the abominations of their eyes, neither did they forsake the idols of Egypt: then I said, I will pour out my fury upon them, to accomplish my anger against them in the midst of the land of Egypt. But I wrought for my name's sake, that it should not be polluted before the heathen, among whom they were, in whose sight I made myself known unto them, in bringing them forth out of the land of Egypt. (Ezekiel 20:5-9)

Rebellion in Egypt (5-9): In the Land of Egypt God calls forth His people for His name's sake. God would make Israel and all the world know His name (Ex. 3:11-15 cf. 5:22-23 cf. 6:1-8 cf. Isaiah 63:12-14). Truly all the world did learn the name of the LORD GOD, for even the heathen Gentile people in the city of Jericho heard of the great God of Israel (Josh. 2:8-11).

However, Israel rebelled against God and would not harken unto Him (8). Israel did not live up to the name of their God, but lusted after their idols, the abominations of Egypt. Therefore God poured out His fury toward the idols of Egypt, delivering His people from a predicament from which they could not deliver themselves.

Wherefore I caused them to go forth out of the land of Egypt, and brought them into the wilderness. And I gave them my statutes, and shewed them my judgments, which if a man do, he shall even live in them. Moreover also I gave them my sabbaths, to be a sign between me and them, that they might know that I am the LORD that sanctify them. But the house of Israel rebelled against me in the wilderness: they walked not in my statutes, and they despised my judgments, which if a man do, he shall even live in them; and my sabbaths they greatly polluted: then I said, I would pour out my fury upon them in the wilderness, to consume them. But I wrought for my name's sake, that it should not be polluted before the heathen, in whose sight I brought them out. Yet also I lifted up my hand unto them in the wilderness, that I would not bring them into the land which I had given them, flowing with milk and honey, which is the glory of all lands; Because they despised my judgments, and walked not in my statutes, but polluted my sabbaths: for their heart went after their idols. Nevertheless mine eye spared them from destroying them, neither did I make an end of them in the wilderness. (Ezekiel 20:10-17)

Rebellion in the Wilderness (10-17): The Lord God brought His people out into the wilderness with great signs and wonders. God gave them His statutes, and showed them His judgments that His people might live in them (11). God also gave them His Sabbaths that Israel might know that it is the Lord God that sanctifies them (12). However, Israel once again is found to be a rebellious people (13). They walked not in God's statutes and despised His judgments and greatly polluted His Sabbaths. So God's fury once again was poured out against His people (14-16).

However, for God's name's sake He did not totally obliterate His people, but spared the children under the age of 20 (17 cf. **Numbers 14:11-35** cf. 32:11).

But I said unto their children in the wilderness, Walk ye not in the statutes of your fathers, neither observe their judgments, nor defile yourselves with their idols: I am the LORD your God; walk in my statutes, and keep my judgments, and do them; And hallow my sabbaths; and they shall be a sign between me and you, that ye may know that I am the LORD your God. Notwithstanding the children rebelled against me: they walked not in my statutes, neither kept my judgments to do them, which if a man do, he shall even live in them; they polluted my sabbaths: then I said, I would pour out my fury upon them, to accomplish my anger against them in the wilderness. Nevertheless I withdrew mine hand, and wrought for my name's sake, that it should not be polluted in the sight of the heathen, in whose sight I brought them forth. I lifted up mine hand unto them also in the wilderness, that I would scatter them among the heathen, and disperse them through the countries; Because they had not executed my judgments, but had despised my statutes, and had polluted my sabbaths, and their eyes were after their fathers' idols. Wherefore I gave them also statutes that were not good, and judgments whereby they should not live; And I polluted them in their own gifts, in that they caused to pass through the fire all that openeth the womb, that I might make them desolate, to the end that they might know that I am the LORD. (Ezekiel 20:18-26)

Rebellion of the Children (18-26): God now deals with the children of those that fell in the wilderness (18). The children are to keep His statutes, judgments and Sabbath days (19, 20); however, as the fathers did, so do the children (24), rebelling against the Lord God in not keeping the commandments of God (21). Thus, God would judge them by scattering them among the heathen, allowing them to be fully given to the idols they desire, to the sacrificing of their children to the flames of Moloch (25-26).

Therefore, son of man, speak unto the house of Israel, and say unto them, Thus saith the Lord GOD; Yet in this your fathers have blasphemed me, in that they have committed a trespass against me. For when I had brought them into the land, for the which I lifted up mine hand to give it to them, then they saw every high hill, and all the thick trees, and they offered there their sacrifices, and there they presented the provocation of their offering: there also they made their sweet savour, and poured out there their drink offerings. Then I said unto them, What is the high place whereunto ye go?

And the name thereof is called Bamah unto this day.
(Ezekiel 20:27-29)

Rebellion Entering Canaan (27-29): But what of those
who did enter the "promised land?" Did they follow
after God? No, for upon entering the land they saw every
high hill and every thick tree and sacrificed thereon (28),
rebelling against the sacrifices of the Lord.

Wherefore say unto the house of Israel, Thus saith
the Lord GOD; Are ye polluted after the manner of
your fathers? and commit ye whoredom after their
abominations? For when ye offer your gifts, when ye
make your sons to pass through the fire, ye pollute
yourselves with all your idols, even unto this day: and
shall I be inquired of by you, O house of Israel? As
I live, saith the Lord GOD, I will not be inquired of
by you. And that which cometh into your mind shall
not be at all, that ye say, We will be as the heathen, as
the families of the countries, to serve wood and stone.
(Ezekiel 20:30-32)

Rebellion in Ezekiel's Generation (30-32): "Even unto
this day" (Ezekiel's time) Israel is in rebellion against the
Lord their God (31), even to the offering of their children
to the fires of Moloch (31). Thus, now you understand
God's fervency in saying, *"Shall I be inquired of by you,
O house of Israel? As I live saith the Lord GOD, I will not be
inquired of by you."*

As I live, saith the Lord GOD, surely with a mighty
hand, and with a stretched out arm, and with fury

poured out, will I rule over you: And I will bring you out from the people, and will gather you out of the countries wherein ye are scattered, with a mighty hand, and with a stretched out arm, and with fury poured out. And I will bring you into the wilderness of the people, and there will I plead with you face to face. Like as I pleaded with your fathers in the wilderness of the land of Egypt, so will I plead with you, saith the Lord GOD. And I will cause you to pass under the rod, and I will bring you into the bond of the covenant: And I will purge out from among you the rebels, and them that transgress against me: I will bring them forth out of the country where they sojourn, and they shall not enter into the land of Israel: and ye shall know that I am the LORD. As for you, O house of Israel, thus saith the Lord GOD; Go ye, serve ye every one his idols, and hereafter also, if ye will not hearken unto me: but pollute ye my holy name no more with your gifts, and with your idols. (Ezekiel 20:33-39)

God's Forceful Hand (33-39): God is now going to forcefully deliver His people from the heathen nations in which they have become willful captives, captive to their gods. Much like a father that has a son addicted to drugs, goes down to the drug house and forcibly removes him and pleads with him "face to face" (Zech. 12:10), so God upon His return will gather all his people from the nations together in the wilderness and plead with them "face to face." He will cause them to pass under the rod (the rod of correction – the Tribulation) and then bring them into the bond of the covenant (God will make it so they can obey His statutes, judgments and Sabbaths – Jer. 36:25-27).

For in mine holy mountain, in the mountain of the height of Israel, saith the Lord GOD, there shall all the house of Israel, all of them in the land, serve me: there will I accept them, and there will I require your offerings, and the firstfruits of your oblations, with all your holy things. I will accept you with your sweet savour, when I bring you out from the people, and gather you out of the countries wherein ye have been scattered; and I will be sanctified in you before the heathen. And ye shall know that I am the LORD, when I shall bring you into the land of Israel, into the country for the which I lifted up mine hand to give it to your fathers. And there shall ye remember your ways, and all your doings, wherein ye have been defiled; and ye shall lothe yourselves in your own sight for all your evils that ye have committed. And ye shall know that I am the LORD, when I have wrought with you for my name's sake, not according to your wicked ways, nor according to your corrupt doings, O ye house of Israel, saith the Lord GOD. (Ezekiel 20:40-44)

The Kingdom Established (40-44): The God of Israel will bring His people into the land of their promise one day (Isaiah 60). God will do for the nation what they could not do in their own strength. And God will do all of this for His name's sake, that they and all the world might know that He is the Lord God (44).

Moreover the word of the LORD came unto me, saying, Son of man, set thy face toward the south, and drop thy word toward the south, and prophesy against the forest of the south field; And say to the forest of the south, Hear the word of the LORD; Thus saith the Lord GOD; Behold, I will kindle a fire in thee, and it shall devour every green tree in thee, and every dry tree: the flaming flame shall not be quenched, and all faces from the south to the north shall be burned therein. And all flesh shall see that I the LORD have kindled it: it shall not be quenched. Then said I, Ah Lord GOD! they say of me, Doth he not speak parables? (Ezekiel 20:45-49)

Pronouncement against the South Land (45-49): These final verses of this chapter are a pronouncement against the south, Jerusalem and its occupants. The interpretation of these verses is found in the first seven verses of chapter 21. The elders are confused saying, "Doth he not speak parables?" (vs. 49); what follows in chapter 21 is the answer to these verses. Notice the correlation in the verbiage between the two passages:

Ezekiel 20:46 -

"Set thy face toward the south"

"Drop thy word toward the south"

"Prophesy against the forest of the south field"

Ezekiel 21:2 -

"Set thy face toward Jerusalem"

"Drop thy word toward the holy places"

"Prophesy against the land of Israel"

CHAPTER 21
The Sword of Judgment

Chapter 21 is an amazingly prophetic chapter. God is going to bring the sword of Babylon and cut off the kings of Judah. Babylon will be the one to bring Zedekiah, the final king of Israel, into captivity where he will die, and from that time forth no king will sit on the throne in Israel:

And thou, profane wicked prince of Israel, whose day is come, when iniquity shall have an end, Thus saith the Lord GOD; <u>Remove the diadem, and take off the crown</u>: this shall not be the same: exalt him that is low, and abase him that is high. (Ezekiel 21:25-26)

However, within this prophetic announcement there is hope, for the verse goes on to tell of another that shall come, "whose right it is" and the throne of the house of Israel shall be given to Him:

I will overturn, overturn, overturn, it: and it shall be no more, until he come whose right it is; and I will give it him. (Ezekiel 21:27)

Of course this speaks of none other than the Lord Jesus Christ, the seed of David: **Blessed be the Lord God of Israel; for he hath visited and redeemed his people, And hath raised up an horn of salvation for us in the house of his servant David; As he spake by the mouth** of his holy prophets, which have been since the world began: (Luke 1:68-70)

And the word of the LORD came unto me, saying, Son of man, set thy face toward Jerusalem, and drop thy word toward the holy places, and prophesy against the land of Israel, And say to the land of Israel, Thus saith the LORD; Behold, I am against thee, and will draw forth my sword out of his sheath, and will cut off from thee the righteous and the wicked. Seeing then that I will cut off from thee the righteous and the wicked, therefore shall my sword go forth out of his sheath against all flesh from the south to the north: That all flesh may know that I the LORD have drawn forth my sword out of his sheath: it shall not return any more. Sigh therefore, thou son of man, with the breaking of thy loins; and with bitterness sigh before their eyes. And it shall be, when they say unto thee, Wherefore sighest thou? that thou shalt answer, For the tidings; because it cometh: and every heart shall melt, and all hands shall be feeble, and every spirit shall faint, and all knees shall be weak as water: behold, it cometh, and shall be brought to pass, saith the Lord GOD. Again the word of the LORD came unto me, saying, Son of man, prophesy, and say, Thus saith the LORD; Say, A sword, a sword is sharpened, and also furbished: It is sharpened to make a sore slaughter; it is furbished that it may glitter: should we then make mirth? it contemneth the rod of my son, as every tree. And he hath given it to be furbished, that it may be handled: this sword is sharpened, and it is furbished, to give it into the hand of the slayer. Cry and howl, son of man: for it shall be upon my people, it shall be upon all the princes of Israel: terrors by reason of the sword shall be upon my people: smite therefore upon thy thigh. Because it is a trial, and what if the sword contemn even the rod? it shall be no more, saith the Lord GOD. Thou therefore, son of man, prophesy, and smite thine hands together, and let the sword be doubled the third time, the sword of the slain: it is the sword of the great men that are slain, which entereth into their privy chambers. I have set the point of the sword against all their gates, that their heart may faint, and their ruins be multiplied: ah! it is made bright, it is wrapped up for the slaughter. Go thee one way or other, either on the right hand, or on the left, whithersoever thy face is set. I will also smite mine hands together, and I will cause my fury to rest: I the LORD have said it. (Ezekiel 21:1-17)

A Sword against Jerusalem (1-17): As before stated, the sword of God's judgment is Babylon, with Nebuchadnezzar at the helm. Notice how many times the word "sword" or words dealing with a sword are used in this chapter. Notice also that it is God's sword (vs. 3, 5); it is He who chooses to draw it. The sword will destroy God's people and the princes of God's people (vs. 12). The sword will break the line of the kings of Israel (vs. 6).

The word of the LORD came unto me again, saying, Also, thou son of man, appoint thee two ways, that the sword of the king of Babylon may come: both twain shall come forth out of one land: and choose thou a place, choose it at the head of the way to the city. Appoint a way, that the sword may come to Rabbath of the Ammonites, and to Judah in Jerusalem the defenced. For the king of Babylon stood at the parting of the way, at the head of the two ways, to use divination: he made his arrows bright, he consulted with images, he looked in the liver. At his right hand was the divination for Jerusalem, to appoint captains, to open the mouth in the slaughter, to lift up the voice with shouting, to appoint battering rams against the gates, to cast a mount, and to build a fort. And it shall be unto them as a false divination in their sight, to them that have sworn oaths: but he will call to remembrance the iniquity, that they may be taken. Therefore thus saith the Lord GOD; Because ye have made your iniquity to be remembered, in that your transgressions are discovered, so that in all your doings your sins do appear; because, I say, that ye are come to remembrance, ye shall be taken with the hand. (Ezekiel 21:18-24)

Two Paths to Judgment (18-24): God now tells Ezekiel to draw out a road that breaks into two paths. The road represents the two ways the king of Babylon would come (vs. 19). One path goes to the city Rabbath of the Ammonites, and the other path Jerusalem of Judah (20). Ammon, though enemies of Judah, had allied together against Nebuchadnezzar. Of course God will see to it that Nebuchadnezzar chooses Jerusalem first.

Nebuchadnezzar stood at the parting of the two paths and used divination to choose whom he would lay siege against first (vs. 21). He employed three means of divination:

- He made his arrows bright – He wrote the two cities to be judged on two arrows and placed them into his quiver. Whichever name was drawn first, that city would be destroyed.

- He consulted with images – communicating to idols

- Looked in the liver – He cut open an animal to read the marks on the liver.

The winner (or looser in this case) was Jerusalem, thus Nebuchadnezzar would come to Jerusalem first to destroy it (vs. 22).

And thou, profane wicked prince of Israel, whose day is come, when iniquity shall have an end, Thus saith the Lord GOD; Remove the diadem, and take off the crown: this shall not be the same: exalt him that is low, and abase him that is high. I will overturn, overturn, overturn, it: and it shall be no more, until he come whose right it is; and I will give it him. (Ezekiel 21:25-27)

Removal of the Diadem (25-27): As stated in the introduction, Ezekiel prophesies that it will be Nebuchadnezzar who will remove the royal diadem from the house of Israel. Zedekiah will be the final king to sit on the throne of David. God is allowing this to happen saying, "I will overturn, overturn, overturn it: it shall be no more" (vs. 27). However, the rest of the verse goes on to say, "Until he come whose right it is; and I will give it him." Praise the LORD, there does come a deliverer out of Zion, the offspring of David, whose right it is (Rev. 5:5).

And thou, son of man, prophesy and say, Thus saith the Lord GOD concerning the Ammonites, and

concerning their reproach; even say thou, The sword, the sword is drawn: for the slaughter it is furbished, to consume because of the glittering: Whiles they see vanity unto thee, whiles they divine a lie unto thee, to bring thee upon the necks of them that are slain, of the wicked, whose day is come, when their iniquity shall have an end. Shall I cause it to return into his sheath? I will judge thee in the place where thou wast created, in the land of thy nativity. And I will pour out mine indignation upon thee, I will blow against thee in the fire of my wrath, and deliver thee into the hand of brutish men, and skilful to destroy. Thou shalt be for fuel to the fire; thy blood shall be in the midst of the land; thou shalt be no more remembered: for I the LORD have spoken it. (Ezekiel 21:28-32)

Judgment Against Ammon (28-32): Ammon and Jerusalem were the two paths sought for judgment by God with His sword, the Babylonian army. Ammon rejoiced to see the Babylonian army go to Jerusalem and seek its destruction. However, Ezekiel prophecies: **And thou, son of man, prophesy and say, <u>Thus saith the Lord GOD concerning the Ammonites, and concerning their reproach; even say thou, The sword, the sword is drawn: for the slaughter it is furbished, to consume because of the glittering:</u> (Ezekiel 21:28)**

Ammon would not escape judgment. Five years after the destruction of Jerusalem Ammon was destroyed.

CHAPTER 22

The Bloody City

This chapter continues the same scenario as chapter 20, with the elders inquiring of God before Ezekiel (20:1-4). In chapters 20-22 God rebukes the elders for their desire to inquire of Him. In this chapter, God is zeroing in on the city of Jerusalem itself, and the inhabitants thereof. This chapter will specify the abominations of which the nation was guilty (vss. 1-12), and announce the fire of judgment upon the nation (vss. 13-22). Lastly, God is lamenting over the reality that no voice was raised against the sins of His nation (vss. 23-31).

Moreover the word of the LORD came unto me, saying, Now, thou son of man, wilt thou judge, wilt thou judge the bloody city? yea, thou shalt shew her all her abominations. Then say thou, Thus saith the Lord GOD, The city sheddeth blood in the midst of it, that her time may come, and maketh idols against herself to defile herself. Thou art become guilty in thy blood that thou hast shed; and hast defiled thyself in thine idols which thou hast made; and thou hast caused thy days to draw near, and art come even unto thy years: therefore have I made thee a reproach unto the heathen, and a mocking to all countries. Those that be near, and those that be far from thee, shall mock thee, which art infamous and much vexed. Behold, the princes of Israel, every one were in thee to their power to shed blood. In thee have they set light by father and mother: in the midst of thee have they dealt by

oppression with the stranger: in thee have they vexed the fatherless and the widow. Thou hast despised mine holy things, and hast profaned my sabbaths. In thee are men that carry tales to shed blood: and in thee they eat upon the mountains: in the midst of thee they commit lewdness. In thee have they discovered their fathers' nakedness: in thee have they humbled her that was set apart for pollution. And one hath committed abomination with his neighbour's wife; and another hath lewdly defiled his daughter in law; and another in thee hath humbled his sister, his father's daughter. In thee have they taken gifts to shed blood; thou hast taken usury and increase, and thou hast greedily gained of thy neighbours by extortion, and hast forgotten me, saith the Lord GOD. (Ezekiel 22:1-12)

The Abominations of which the Nation was Guilty (1-12): God starts off by calling Jerusalem," a "bloody city" (vs. 2) which is repeated throughout this chapter (vss. 2, 3, 4, 12). Jerusalem, which very name means, "city of peace" had become a bloody city. What does this expression mean? Is it named so because they have gone to war and killed surrounding enemies, only defending themselves? No, it is that they have killed *their own people* and slaughtered them before their idols, and *their own land* is filled with their *own* blood; notice "The city shedeth blood in the midst of it" (vs. 3).

- How is the faithful city become an harlot! It was full of judgment; righteousness lodged in it; **but now murderers.** (Isaiah 1:21)
- The Lord Jesus wept over the city and said, "O Jerusalem, Jerusalem, **which killest the prophets, and stonest them that are sent unto thee**; how often would I have gathered thy children together,

as a hen doth gather her brood under her wings, and ye would not!" (Luke 13:34)

- At the death of Christ, the crowd cried out to Pilate, "...**His blood be on us, and on our children**" (Matt. 27:25)
- It was Stephen who declared to the Jews, **"Which of the prophets have not your fathers persecuted?** And they have slain them which shewed before of the coming of the Just One; **of whom ye have been now the betrayers and murders**" (Acts 7:52)

Yes, Jerusalem has become the city of blood. This stands in contrast to the Mosaic Law which hung on two principle laws; one to love the LORD your God and the second to love your neighbor as yourself: **"And thou shalt love the Lord thy God with all thy heart, and with all thy soul, and with all thy mind, and with all thy strength: this is the first commandment. And the second is like, namely this, Thou shalt love thy neighbour as thyself. There is none other commandment greater than these. (Mark 12:30-31)**

It is the "princes" that are guilty for the conduct of the people (vs. 6) and what follows is a list of all the abominations that the princes allowed, even encouraged to take place. (Notice these verses all have the expression "in thee" associated with them, meaning in Jerusalem):

- **Lightly esteemed the father and mother (vs. 7)** The expression "set light" is to lightly esteem (see I Samuel 18:30 and 26:24 where the expression "set by" means to esteem, thus, "set light" means to lightly esteem). The Jews were commanded to honor mother and father (Ex. 20:12, Duet. 27:16) as believers are today (Ephesians 6:1-3).

- **Oppression of the stranger; vexed the fatherless (orphans) and the widows (vs. 7)** The Jews were required by law to give special consideration to these groups of people (Ex. 22:21-24; 23:9-11; Lev. 19:33-34) as believers are today (James 1:27, 2:1-13; I Tim. 5).
- **Despised mine holy things, and has profaned my Sabbaths (vs. 8)** Treating God's holy things and days as if they were just another day.
- **Men telling lies, sentencing people to death (vs. 9)** (Matt. 26:60; Acts 6:13 etc.)
- **Offering food to idols and committing lewdness before them (vs. 9)**
- **They have committed various forms of immorality against every member of the family (vss. 20, 11)**
- **They have received bribes to shed innocent blood (vs. 12)**
- **Extortion of their neighbors (vs. 12)**

All this disobedience is a result of the ending statement, "and hast forgotten me, saith the Lord God."

Behold, therefore I have smitten mine hand at thy dishonest gain which thou hast made, and at thy blood which hath been in the midst of thee. Can thine heart endure, or can thine hands be strong, in the days that I shall deal with thee? I the LORD have spoken it, and will do it. And I will scatter thee among the heathen, and disperse thee in the countries, and will consume thy filthiness out of thee. And thou shalt take thine inheritance in thyself in the sight of the heathen, and thou shalt know that I am the LORD. And the word of the LORD came unto me, saying, Son of man, the house of Israel is to me become dross: all they are brass, and tin, and iron, and lead, in the midst of the furnace; they are even the dross of silver. Therefore thus saith the Lord GOD; Because ye are all become dross, behold, therefore I will gather you into the midst of Jerusalem. As they gather silver, and brass, and iron, and lead, and tin, into the midst of the furnace, to blow the fire upon it, to melt it; so will I gather you in mine anger and in my fury, and I will leave you there, and melt you. Yea, I will gather you, and blow upon you in the fire of my wrath, and ye shall be melted in the midst thereof. As silver is melted in the midst of the furnace, so shall ye be melted in the midst thereof; and ye shall know that I the LORD have poured out my fury upon you. (Ezekiel 22:13-22)

The Fire of God's Refining Judgment (13-22): The judgment of God's wrath is coming. The allegory that is used here is that of a blacksmith, one that works metals. The house of Israel is become dross (the waste of the metal). God has placed His people in the midst of Jerusalem (the furnace) and He will bring the fire of judgment against it (Babylon) that they like the dross will be consumed (vss. 18-22).

And the word of the LORD came unto me, saying, Son of man, say unto her, Thou art the land that is not cleansed, nor rained upon in the day of indignation. There is a conspiracy of her prophets in the midst thereof, like a roaring lion ravening the prey; they have devoured souls; they have taken the treasure and precious things; they have made her many widows in the midst thereof. Her priests have violated my law, and have profaned mine holy things: they have put no difference between the holy and profane, neither have they shewed difference between the unclean and the clean, and have hid their eyes from my sabbaths, and I am profaned among them. Her princes in the midst thereof are like wolves ravening the prey, to shed blood, and to destroy souls, to get dishonest gain. And her prophets have daubed them with untempered morter, seeing vanity, and divining lies unto them, saying, Thus saith the Lord GOD, when the LORD hath not spoken. The people of the land have used oppression, and exercised robbery, and have vexed the poor and needy: yea, they have oppressed the stranger wrongfully. And I sought for a man among them, that should make up the hedge, and stand in the gap before me for the land, that I should not destroy it: but I found none. Therefore have I poured out mine indignation upon them; I have consumed them with the fire of my wrath: their own way have I recompensed upon their heads, saith the Lord GOD. (Ezekiel 22:23-31)

No Voice of Objection Against the Unrighteous Conduct of the Priests, the Princes and the Prophets (23-31): Conspiracy among the false prophets has sealed the fate of the nation. God recaps the sins of the nation:

- The **Priests** have violated my law and profaned mine holy things (vs. 26)
- The **Princes** have devoured the people through dishonest gain (vs. 27)
- The **Prophets** have divined lies and seen visions of vanity, saying, "thus saith the Lord God," when the Lord hath not spoken (vs. 28)
- The **People** have used oppression and exercised robbery, and vexed the poor, needy and the stranger (vs. 29)

Unlike the time Moses stood in the gap between God and Israel (Numbers 14:11-20) and Paul in his desire for the people of Israel (Romans 9:3), here God has found no man to stand in the gap between His judgment and the people of God. Thanks be unto Jesus Christ who stood in the gap between our sins and God the Father (2 Corinthians 5:21).

The next chapter will be the final chapter before the siege on Jerusalem begins. Then, starting in chapter 25 going through chapter 32 which transpires *during* the siege on Jerusalem, will be the judgment of the Muslim nations.

CHAPTER 23
Two Sisters

In this chapter God uses a parable of Aholah and Aholibah to unmask the loathsome nature of the unfaithfulness to God that Samaria and Jerusalem have shown. As revolting as this chapter is, it shows the awfulness of the spiritual adultery whereby the Lord's people, who are one with Him as bride and bridegroom, repudiate their union with Him and give themselves to the heathen nations around them.

The word of the LORD came again unto me, saying, Son of man, there were two women, the daughters of one mother: And they committed whoredoms in Egypt; they committed whoredoms in their youth: there were their breasts pressed, and there they bruised the teats of their virginity. And the names of them were Aholah the elder, and Aholibah her sister: and they were mine, and they bare sons and daughters. Thus were their names; Samaria is Aholah, and Jerusalem Aholibah. (Ezekiel 23:1-4)

The Two Sisters (1-4): The parable here is that of two daughters from one mother who commit whoredoms in their youth and bare sons and daughters. The names of the two sisters are Aholah and Aholibah. Aholah is Samaria and Aholibah is Jerusalem. Notice they come from one mother; a reference to the time prior to the splitting of the kingdom. Notice as well the comment in verse 4, "and they were mine" which is a reference to God the Father who bore them.

And Aholah played the harlot when she was mine; and she doted on her lovers, on the Assyrians her neighbours, Which were clothed with blue, captains and rulers, all of them desirable young men, horsemen riding upon horses. Thus she committed her whoredoms with them, with all them that were the chosen men of Assyria, and with all on whom she doted: with all their idols she defiled herself. Neither left she her whoredoms brought from Egypt: for in her youth they lay with her, and they bruised the breasts of her virginity, and poured their whoredom upon her. Wherefore I have delivered her into the hand of her lovers, into the hand of the Assyrians, upon whom she doted. These discovered her nakedness: they took her sons and her daughters, and slew her with the sword: and she became famous among women; for they had executed judgment upon her. (Ezekiel 23:5-10)

Aholah Which is Samaria (5-10): Aholah is dealt with first, for she is the eldest (vs. 4). Notice God calls her His (vs. 5). Aholah which is Samaria *(Israel - the Northern Tribes)* plays the harlot with her neighbors the Assyrians. Under the reign of King Jehu, Samaria sought alliances with the Assyrians to stem off the threat of the invading Syrian armies (2 Kings 10:32-34), thus making Israel vassal to Assyria. This alliance was Israel's undoing for when she tried to break away, she felt the wrath of the Assyrians (2 Kings 17:4). The very nation to which Samaria had turned for assistance would destroy her: *Wherefore I have delivered her into the hand of her lovers, into the hand of the Assyrians, upon whom she doted. (Ezekiel 23:9)*

And when her sister Aholibah saw this, she was more

corrupt in her inordinate love than she, and in her whoredoms more than her sister in her whoredoms. She doted upon the Assyrians her neighbours, captains and rulers clothed most gorgeously, horsemen riding upon horses, all of them desirable young men. Then I saw that she was defiled, that they took both one way, And that she increased her whoredoms: for when she saw men pourtrayed upon the wall, the images of the Chaldeans pourtrayed with vermilion, Girded with girdles upon their loins, exceeding in dyed attire upon their heads, all of them princes to look to, after the manner of the Babylonians of Chaldea, the land of their nativity: And as soon as she saw them with her eyes, she doted upon them, and sent messengers unto them into Chaldea. And the Babylonians came to her into the bed of love, and they defiled her with their whoredom, and she was polluted with them, and her mind was alienated from them. So she discovered her whoredoms, and discovered her nakedness: then my mind was alienated from her, like as my mind was alienated from her sister. Yet she multiplied her whoredoms, in calling to remembrance the days of her youth, wherein she had played the harlot in the land of Egypt. For she doted upon their paramours, whose flesh is as the flesh of asses, and whose issue is like the issue of horses. Thus thou calledst to remembrance the lewdness of thy youth, in bruising thy teats by the Egyptians for the paps of thy youth. Therefore, O Aholibah, thus saith the Lord GOD; Behold, I will raise up thy lovers against thee, from whom thy mind is alienated, and I will bring them against thee on every side; The Babylonians, and all the Chaldeans, Pekod, and Shoa, and Koa, and all the Assyrians with them: all of them desirable young men, captains and rulers, great lords and renowned, all of them riding upon horses. And they shall come against thee with chariots, wagons, and wheels, and with an assembly of people, which shall set against thee buckler and shield and helmet round about: and I will set judgment before them, and they shall judge thee according to their judgments. And I will set my jealousy against thee, and they shall deal furiously with thee: they shall take away thy nose and thine ears; and thy remnant shall fall by the sword: they shall take thy sons and thy daughters; and thy residue shall be devoured by the fire. They shall also strip thee out of thy clothes, and take away thy fair jewels. Thus will I make thy lewdness to cease from thee, and thy whoredom brought from the land of Egypt: so that thou shalt not lift up thine eyes unto them, nor remember Egypt any more. For thus saith the Lord GOD; Behold, I will deliver thee into the hand of them whom thou hatest, into the hand of them from whom thy mind is alienated: And they shall deal with thee hatefully, and shall take away all thy labour, and shall leave thee naked and bare: and the nakedness of thy whoredoms shall be discovered, both thy lewdness and thy whoredoms. I will do these things unto thee, because thou hast gone a whoring after the heathen, and because thou art polluted with their idols. Thou hast walked in the way of thy sister; therefore will I give her cup into thine hand. Thus saith the Lord GOD; Thou shalt drink of thy sister's cup deep and large: thou shalt be laughed to scorn and had in derision; it containeth much. Thou shalt be filled with drunkenness and sorrow, with the cup of astonishment and desolation, with the cup of thy sister Samaria. Thou shalt even drink it and suck it out, and thou shalt break the sherds thereof, and pluck off thine own breasts: for I have spoken it, saith the Lord GOD. Therefore thus saith the Lord GOD;

Because thou hast forgotten me, and cast me behind thy back, therefore bear thou also thy lewdness and thy whoredoms. (Ezekiel 23:11-35)

Aholibah Which is Jerusalem (11-35): Aholibah is dealt with in these verses. Aholibah is Jerusalem who has committed more lewdness than her sister (vs. 11). Enamored with the look and strength of the Babylonians (vss. 12-15) she joined herself to them, defiling herself with them and thereby alienating herself from her God (vss. 16-18). What Aholibah is doing is reminiscent of her adulterous behavior in the land of Egypt (vss. 19-22). Just as God had done to Samaria, He now allows to happen to Jerusalem: the very ones she turned to for assistance will destroy her (vss. 22-30). Aholibah has gone in the way of her sister, drinking of the cup of the judgment of God (vss. 31-35).

The LORD said moreover unto me; Son of man, wilt thou judge Aholah and Aholibah? yea, declare unto them their abominations; That they have committed adultery, and blood is in their hands, and with their idols have they committed adultery, and have also caused their sons, whom they bare unto me, to pass for them through the fire, to devour them. Moreover this they have done unto me: they have defiled my sanctuary in the same day, and have profaned my sabbaths. For when they had slain their children to their idols, then they came the same day into my sanctuary to profane it; and, lo, thus have they done in the midst of mine house. And furthermore, that ye have sent for men to come from far, unto whom a messenger was sent; and, lo, they came: for whom thou didst wash thyself, paintedst thy eyes, and deckedst thyself with ornaments, And satest upon a stately bed, and a table prepared before it, whereupon thou hast set mine incense and mine oil. And a voice of a multitude being at ease was with her: and with the men of the common sort were brought Sabeans from the wilderness, which put bracelets upon their hands, and beautiful crowns upon their heads. Then said I unto her that was old in adulteries, Will they now commit whoredoms with her, and she with them? Yet they went in unto her, as they go in unto a woman that playeth the harlot: so went they in unto Aholah and unto Aholibah, the lewd women. (Ezekiel 23:36-44)

The Abominations of the Two Sisters (36-44): God will now declare the abominations of Aholah and Aholibah that they have committed. They have committed adultery with the idols of the heathen (vs. 37). They have sacrificed their children to heathen deities (vs. 37). They have defiled God's sanctuary and profaned His Sabbaths (vs. 38-39). Moreover they have invited drunken men unto them from the heathen nations, the Sabeans from the wilderness. They have decorated themselves and played the harlot with them (40-44).

And the righteous men, they shall judge them after the manner of adulteresses, and after the manner of women that shed blood; because they are adulteresses, and blood is in their hands. For thus saith the Lord GOD; I will bring up a company upon them, and will give them to be removed and spoiled. And the company shall stone them with stones, and dispatch them with their swords; they shall slay their sons and their daughters, and burn up their houses with fire. Thus will I cause lewdness to cease out of the land, that all

140

women may be taught not to do after your lewdness. And they shall recompense your lewdness upon you, and ye shall bear the sins of your idols: and ye shall know that I am the Lord GOD. (Ezekiel 23:45-49)

Judgment upon the Two Sisters (45-49): The Lord is the one judging the two sisters. At the time of Ezekiel God had already sent judgment upon Aholah (Samaria) by the Assyrian armies. And now He is sending judgment upon Aholibah (Jerusalem) by the hand of the Babylonians, and in the very next chapter Jerusalem is surrounded by the Babylonian hordes.

CHAPTER 24
The Boiling Pot

This chapter will complete this first section concerning the judgment on Israel and Jerusalem. (*The subsequent sections – 25 to 32 will deal with the judgment of the Muslim nations, whose chapters transpire during the siege on Jerusalem.*) On the day when the siege and capture of Jerusalem began, the Lord gave the prophet a parable that he acted out concerning the siege and the capture of Jerusalem.

Ezekiel was to set a pot (*Jerusalem*) on the fire, fill it with water and pieces of flesh (*the inhabitants of Jerusalem*). He was to place fuel under it to make it boil furiously (*the siege and its severity*).

Ezekiel will also witness the sudden death of his wife, whom he was not to morn over. Ezekiel was to be a symbol of the despair the people felt at the fate of the beloved city Jerusalem.

Again in the ninth year, in the tenth month, in the tenth day of the month, the word of the LORD came unto me, saying, Son of man, write thee the name of the day, even of this same day: the king of Babylon set himself against Jerusalem this same day. (Ezekiel 24:1-2)

Babylon Arrives at Jerusalem (1-2): At this very moment the walls of Jerusalem are being surrounded by the Babylonian armies. The date given is the ninth year, in the tenth month. This date is also given in the historical account in 2 Kings 25:1, by Jeremiah in 39:1 and 52:4. All the warnings by the prophet Ezekiel in the preceding chapters have led to this very day.

And utter a parable unto the rebellious house, and say unto them, Thus saith the Lord GOD; Set on a pot, set it on, and also pour water into it: Gather the pieces thereof into it, even every good piece, the thigh, and the shoulder; fill it with the choice bones. Take the choice of the flock, and burn also the bones under it, and make it boil well, and let them seethe the bones of it therein. Wherefore thus saith the Lord GOD; Woe to the bloody city, to the pot whose scum is therein, and whose scum is not gone out of it! bring it out piece by piece; let no lot fall upon it. For her blood is in the midst of her; she set it upon the top of a rock; she poured it not upon the ground, to cover it with dust; That it might cause fury to come up to take vengeance; I have set her blood upon the top of a rock, that it should not be covered. Therefore thus saith the Lord GOD; Woe to the bloody city! I will even make the pile for fire great. Heap on wood, kindle the fire, consume the flesh, and spice it well, and let the bones be burned. Then set it empty upon the coals thereof, that the brass of it may be hot, and may burn, and that the filthiness of it may be molten in it, that the scum of it may be consumed. She hath wearied herself with lies, and her great scum went not forth out of her: her scum shall be in the fire. In thy filthiness is lewdness: because I have purged thee, and thou wast not purged, thou shalt not be purged from thy filthiness any more, till I have caused my fury to rest upon thee. I the LORD have spoken it: it shall come to pass, and I will do it; I will not go back,

neither will I spare, neither will I repent; according to thy ways, and according to thy doings, shall they judge thee, saith the Lord GOD. (Ezekiel 24:3-14)

The Boiling Pot (3-14): Ezekiel now is to act out a parable. He is to take a pot and fill it with water (vs. 3). Then he is to take pieces of flesh (vs. 4). Then he is to take bones and place them under the pot to fuel the fire to a vigorous boil (vs. 5).

The interpretation is in verses 6-14. The pot is the city of Jerusalem; the citizens are in that pot. Their sin is the scum that's in the pot. Jerusalem is called the "bloody city" (vss. 6, 9) and this is in reference to their misuse of the Levitical law of covering the blood that is spilt upon the ground. According to Leviticus 17:13 blood was to be covered by dust. Any blood not covered by dust was to be avenged. Thus God is avenging the blood they have spilt (vss. 7-8). Following the boiling of the flesh and burning of the bones, Ezekiel is told to empty the pot and place it back upon the coals to burn the residue in the midst of the pot (vss. 11-12). This is to typify that the sin of the people will be burnt up in the midst of the city, the Lord is cleansing the city from all its lewdness (vss. 13-14).

Also the word of the LORD came unto me, saying, Son of man, behold, I take away from thee the desire of thine eyes with a stroke: yet neither shalt thou mourn nor weep, neither shall thy tears run down. Forbear to cry, make no mourning for the dead, bind the tire of thine head upon thee, and put on thy shoes upon thy feet, and cover not thy lips, and eat not the bread of men. So I spake unto the people in the morning: and at even my wife died; and I did in the morning as I was commanded. And the people said unto me, Wilt thou not tell us what these things are to us, that thou doest so? Then I answered them, The word of the LORD came unto me, saying, Speak unto the house of Israel, Thus saith the Lord GOD; Behold, I will profane my sanctuary, the excellency of your strength, the desire of your eyes, and that which your soul pitieth; and your sons and your daughters whom ye have left shall fall by the sword. And ye shall do as I have done: ye shall not cover your lips, nor eat the bread of men. And your tires shall be upon your heads, and your shoes upon your feet: ye shall not mourn nor weep; but ye shall pine away for your iniquities, and mourn one toward another. Thus Ezekiel is unto you a sign: according to all that he hath done shall ye do: and when this cometh, ye shall know that I am the Lord GOD. (Ezekiel 24:15-24)

Death of Ezekiel's Wife (15-24): Ezekiel is now to lose his wife, "the desire of thine eyes" (vs. 16). He is also told that he is not to mourn over her (vss. 16-18). What follows in verses 19 through 25 is the interpretation of this event. Ezekiel and his wife are to represent Israel and the city, and all therein. God is showing that just as Ezekiel lost the "desire of his eyes" (vs. 16) so shall they lose their beloved city, the sanctuary, and the children "the desire of their eyes" (vs. 21). And as Ezekiel was not allowed to mourn for his wife, Israel will not be allowed to mourn in the usual custom, for they will be taken into captivity and "pine away."

Also, thou son of man, shall it not be in the day when I take from them their strength, the joy of their glory,

the desire of their eyes, and that whereupon they set their minds, their sons and their daughters, That he that escapeth in that day shall come unto thee, to cause thee to hear it with thine ears? In that day shall thy mouth be opened to him which is escaped, and thou shalt speak, and be no more dumb: and thou shalt be a sign unto them; and they shall know that I am the LORD. (Ezekiel 24:25-27)

Ezekiel's Silence (25-27): At the beginning of Ezekiel's ministry he was told that he would be dumb, speaking only when prophesying (Ezekiel 3: 26). Now he is told that this temporary silence would last only until one comes that has escaped from the final destruction of Jerusalem and tells of its fall (see Ezekiel 33:22-23), which marks the end of the second section of Ezekiel.

Chapters 1-24: Written **before the siege** on Jerusalem

Chapters 25- 32: Written **during the siege** and eventual fall of Jerusalem

Chapters 33-48: Written **following the destruction** of Jerusalem

Section 2
CHAPTERS 25-32

GOD'S JUDGEMENT ON SURROUNDING NATIONS

Given During the Siege of Jerusalem

CHAPTER 25
Judgment Upon the Nations

This chapter marks the second section of Ezekiel, chapters 25-32. These chapters transpire **during the siege** of Jerusalem (2 Kings 25:1-3) and contain the judgments upon the surrounding nations, Israel's hostile neighbors. As we will see these judgments extend out from Israel in all directions.
- Eastern Boundary of Judah – *Ammon, Moab, Edom*
- Western Boundary of Judah - *Philistia*
- North of Judah – *Tyrus, Zidon cities of Phoenicia*
- Southwest of Judah– *Egypt was the major power*

This section (*chapters 25-32*) is a transition from the first section (*chapters 1-24*), the judgment on Judah and Jerusalem and the last section (*chapters 33-48*) the predictions of her future restoration.
- Section One (Chapters 1-24): Judgments on Judah and Jerusalem *(to the Jew first)*
- Section Two (Chapters 25- 32): Judgment on the surrounding nations (*then the Gentiles*)
- Section Three (Chapters 33-48): Promise of future restoration

The nations mentioned in these chapters are as follows:
- Chapter 25 - *Ammon, Moab, Edom, Philistia*
- Chapters 26-28 – *Tyrus and Zidon*
- Chapters 29-32 – *Egypt*

Judgment is given upon these nations from God. He is

taking ownership for it; thus, you have the phrase "Thou shalt know that I am the LORD" (vss. 5, 7, 11, 17 etc.). It is the same phrase used in the preceding chapters (section one). This judgment upon the surrounding nations is given of God because of the nations' demeanor toward Israel (*Ezekiel 25:3, 8, 15; 26:2; 29:6*) and their ungodly pride and self-deification (*Ezekiel 28; 29:3*).

The judgments against these nations are both *historical* and *prophetical*. Though the bulk of the judgments laid against these nations transpired throughout history, we do see these nations being dealt with by God in the future (*Isaiah 63*) as they mount a union against Israel (*see Psalm 83*). So then while we will look primarily at what *has* transpired, we will also take note of what *will yet* transpire as these nations await future judgments.

The word of the LORD came again unto me, saying, Son of man, set thy face against the Ammonites, and prophesy against them; And say unto the Ammonites, Hear the word of the Lord GOD; Thus saith the Lord GOD; Because thou saidst, Aha, against my sanctuary, when it was profaned; and against the land of Israel, when it was desolate; and against the house of Judah, when they went into captivity; Behold, therefore I will deliver thee to the men of the east for a possession, and they shall set their palaces in thee, and make their dwellings in thee: they shall eat thy fruit, and they shall drink thy milk. And I will make Rabbah a stable for camels, and the Ammonites a couchingplace for flocks: and ye shall know that I am the LORD. For thus saith the Lord GOD; Because thou hast clapped thine hands, and stamped with the feet, and rejoiced in heart with all thy despite against the land of Israel; Behold,

therefore I will stretch out mine hand upon thee, and will deliver thee for a spoil to the heathen; and I will cut thee off from the people, and I will cause thee to perish out of the countries: I will destroy thee; and thou shalt know that I am the LORD. (Ezekiel 25:1-7)

Ammonites (1-7): The Ammonites sprang from Benammi, the son of Lot's younger daughter (Genesis 19:38 cf. 83:7, 8) just as the Moabites came from Moab the son of Lot's older daughter. These two peoples are mentioned in Scripture continually together. When the Israelites came into the land they were commanded to leave the Ammonites alone (Deut. 2:19), which dwelt on the east side of Jordan east of the Dead Sea (*don't confuse with Amorites*). The Ammonites' hostility toward Judah can also be seen when they joined the Chaldeans to destroy Jerusalem in the first siege (2 Kings 24:25).

The Ammonites are being judged for two reasons: Ammon is being judged *first* for their haughtiness and self-deification, *secondly* for their joyful response concerning Nebuchadnezzar and his choice to lay siege to the land of Jerusalem instead of Ammon (Ezekiel 25:3 cf. 21:18-22). Ammon chose to not come to the aid of Jerusalem when Nebuchadnezzar's armies laid siege on Jerusalem, they even gloated over the destruction of the temple and deportation of God's people (vs. 6 cf. Zeph. 2:8). Thus, God is going to give them their just reward; the men of the east will invade their land and turn it into a pasture (vss. 4, 5).

Though *historically* the Ammonite people were overtaken by the nomadic tribes of the east, *prophetically* the total fulfillment of this verse is yet to come. One day the LORD will come back and deal with this nation (see

Isaiah 11:10-16; Psalm 83:7; Zeph. 2:9; Jeremiah 9:25, 26; Jeremiah 49:1-6).

Thus saith the Lord GOD; Because that Moab and Seir do say, Behold, the house of Judah is like unto all the heathen; Therefore, behold, I will open the side of Moab from the cities, from his cities which are on his frontiers, the glory of the country, Bethjeshimoth, Baalmeon, and Kiriathaim, Unto the men of the east with the Ammonites, and will give them in possession, that the Ammonites may not be remembered among the nations. And I will execute judgments upon Moab; and they shall know that I am the LORD. (Ezekiel 25:8-11)

Moabites (8-11): The Moabites descended from Moab, the son of the eldest daughter of Lot (Genesis 19:38). The hostility between Moab and Israel began when Balak, king of Moab, tried to oppose Israel as Moses was coming into the Promised Land (Numbers 22:1-3 and all of 22-24). Throughout Israel's history, relations between Israel and Moab remained hostile; during the reign of Jehoshaphat, Jehoram sought help from Jehoshaphat in an attempt to reduce the influence of the Moabites. The Moabites suffered a great loss. Reduced to despair, the Moabite King ascended the wall of the city and there, in the sight of the allied armies, offered his first-born son a sacrifice to his god (2 Kings 3:26, 27). Moab joined Babylon in the first siege that was laid against Jerusalem (2 Kings 24:2).

The fate of Moab will be like that of Ammon (vs. 10) because of their pride against Jerusalem (Isaiah 16:6) and because they lightly esteemed Israel among the nations (vs. 8). Moab will be overtaken by the "men of the east," the nomadic tribes of the east, at the same time as Ammon (vs. 10). Moab would fall in battle, God exposing their northern flank to attack, taking the cities of Bethjeshimoth, Baalmeon and Kiriathaim (vss. 8-10). Once again however the destruction of Moab is also prophetic, awaiting a day that our LORD will ultimately deal with them (Psalms 108:9, 83:7, 8; Zeph. 2:9)

Thus saith the Lord GOD; Because that Edom hath dealt against the house of Judah by taking vengeance, and hath greatly offended, and revenged himself upon them; Therefore thus saith the Lord GOD; I will also stretch out mine hand upon Edom, and will cut off man and beast from it; and I will make it desolate from Teman; and they of Dedan shall fall by the sword. And I will lay my vengeance upon Edom by the hand of my people Israel: and they shall do in Edom according to mine anger and according to my fury; and they shall know my vengeance, saith the Lord GOD. (Ezekiel 25:12-14)

Edom (12-14): Edom is the nation that came from Esau, whose beginning is found in Genesis 25. They are the dwellers of Seir, the mountainous region (Deut. 2:22). The strife began when Edom refused to let Israel cross her territory during the time of the wilderness wanderings (Numbers 20:14-21). Thus, throughout history, the relationship between Israel and Edom has been strained at best. During the reign of Ahaz the Edomites fought against Judah with great success (2 Chronicles 28:16-17). Edom was also guilty of siding with Babylon during the assaults on Jerusalem. *Seir is the mountains that encompassed the country of Edom. Over time Seir was synonymous with Edom. Seir is mentioned here* *briefly because it is synonymous with Edom, and they will suffer the same fate as Ammon and Moab.*

The judgments against Edom are extensive. *Historically* their power as a people was removed in the inter-testament period by the Nabateans, but *prophetically* their judgment is yet on the horizon and is detailed extensively in Scripture (See Jeremiah 49:7-22; Obadiah; Isaiah 63:1-4; Psalm 83 etc.)

Thus saith the Lord GOD; Because the Philistines have dealt by revenge, and have taken vengeance with a despiteful heart, to destroy it for the old hatred; Therefore thus saith the Lord GOD; Behold, I will stretch out mine hand upon the Philistines, and I will cut off the Cherethims, and destroy the remnant of the sea coast. And I will execute great vengeance upon them with furious rebukes; and they shall know that I am the LORD, when I shall lay my vengeance upon them. (Ezekiel 25:15-17)

Philistines (15-17): The Philistines were a small group that conquered a small portion of the land that gave them their name: the land of Phillistia (Psalm 87:4). There are more Old Testament references to the Philistines than any other nation other than Israel.

The Philistines had been Israel's enemy from the time of the conquest. Israel failed to take all the Promised Land because she disobeyed God (Judges 3:1-4). The Philistines were opposed by Shamgar (Judges 3:31), Samson (Judges 13-16), and Samuel (I Samuel 7:2-17). David finally subdued the Philistines after a series of battles (2 Samuel 5:17-25; 8:1). The battles however renewed during the divided kingdom, as each country tried to control the other (2 Chron. 17:10-11; 21:16-17; 26:6-7; 28:16-18). The feud between the Philistines and Judah was halted by Babylon's intervention, Nebuchadnezzar establishing control over both countries.

The judgment against the Philistines is a result of their constant attacks upon God's chosen people as they tried to dispose Israel from the Promised Land (which continues to this day). Their final fate will be vengeance from God (vss. 16-17) which, prophetically speaking, is mentioned throughout Scripture (see Zeph. 2:1-6; Amos 1:8; Ps. 83 etc.)

CHAPTER 26
Judgment of Tyrus

The next three chapters are devoted to Tyrus. The city is also mentioned in Isaiah 23 and Jeremiah 27, however it is Ezekiel that will talk the most about Tyre. Tyre was the ancient Phoenician city located at the site of present day Lebanon.

Hyram was king during the reigns of David and Solomon. He was a devoted friend, and he helped them both prepare for, and subsequently build, the temple (2 Samuel 5; I Kings 5; I Chronicles 14:2; 2 Chronicles 2). After the days of David and Solomon however, Tyre drifted away from Israel, and it finally got so bad that the people of Tyre sold Jews as slaves to the Greeks and the Edomites (Joel 3; Amos 1).

Tyre was the capital of the great Phoenician nation which was famous for its seagoing traders, and as such was a major trading center along routes from north to south. Thus, throughout these passages in Ezekiel and others, Tyre will be known as the land of 'traffick" and of "merchants" (see chapter 27).

In these chapters we will see Tyre and Zidon being judged for two things: their treatment of Israel and their pride and self-deification regarding their kingdoms.

The prophecy regarding the destruction of Tyre is pointed to as one of the most conclusive proof texts for the veracity of Scripture.

And it came to pass in the eleventh year, in the first day of the month, that the word of the LORD came unto me, saying, Son of man, because that Tyrus hath said against Jerusalem, Aha, she is broken that was the gates of the people: she is turned unto me: I shall be replenished, now she is laid waste: Therefore thus saith the Lord GOD; Behold, I am against thee, O Tyrus, and will cause many nations to come up against thee, as the sea causeth his waves to come up. And they shall destroy the walls of Tyrus, and break down her towers: I will also scrape her dust from her, and make her like the top of a rock. It shall be a place for the spreading of nets in the midst of the sea: for I have spoken it, saith the Lord GOD: and it shall become a spoil to the nations. And her daughters which are in the field shall be slain by the sword; and they shall know that I am the LORD. For thus saith the Lord GOD; Behold, I will bring upon Tyrus Nebuchadrezzar king of Babylon, a king of kings, from the north, with horses, and with chariots, and with horsemen, and companies, and much people. He shall slay with the sword thy daughters in the field: and he shall make a fort against thee, and cast a mount against thee, and lift up the buckler against thee. And he shall set engines of war against thy walls, and with his axes he shall break down thy towers. By reason of the abundance of his horses their dust shall cover thee: thy walls shall shake at the noise of the horsemen, and of the wheels, and of the chariots, when he shall enter into thy gates, as men enter into a city wherein is made a breach. With the hoofs of his horses shall he tread down all thy streets: he shall slay thy people by the sword, and thy strong garrisons shall go down to the ground. And they shall make a spoil of thy riches, and make a prey of thy merchandise: and they shall break down thy walls, and destroy thy pleasant houses: and they shall lay thy stones and thy timber and thy dust in the midst of the water. And I will cause the noise of thy songs to cease; and the sound of thy harps shall be no more heard. And I will make thee like the top of a rock: thou shalt be a place to spread nets upon; thou shalt be built no more: for I the LORD have spoken it, saith the Lord GOD. Thus saith the Lord GOD to Tyrus; Shall not the isles shake at the sound of thy fall, when the wounded cry, when the slaughter is made in the midst of thee? Then all the princes of the sea shall come down from their thrones, and lay away their robes, and put off their broidered garments: they shall clothe themselves with trembling; they shall sit upon the ground, and shall tremble at every moment, and be astonished at thee. And they shall take up a lamentation for thee, and say to thee, How art thou destroyed, that wast inhabited of seafaring men, the renowned city, which wast strong in the sea, she and her inhabitants, which cause their terror to be on all that haunt it! Now shall the isles tremble in the day of thy fall; yea, the isles that are in the sea shall be troubled at thy departure. For thus saith the Lord GOD; When I shall make thee a desolate city, like the cities that are not inhabited; when I shall bring up the deep upon thee, and great waters shall cover thee; When I shall bring thee down with them that descend into the pit, with the people of old time, and shall set thee in the low parts of the earth, in places desolate of old, with them that go down to the pit, that thou be not inhabited; and I shall set glory in the land of the living; I will make thee a terror, and thou shalt be no more: though thou be sought for, yet shalt thou never be found again, saith the Lord GOD. (Ezekiel 26:1-21)

The Prophecy of the Destruction of Jerusalem (1-21):
The prophecy here was about Nebuchadnezzar's attack of Tyre which was about to happen. But it was more than that; the Lord has more in view here than just the 13-year siege of Nebuchadnezzar and the "many nations" of which his empire consisted.

The prophetic details listed regarding the destruction of Tyrus give us the surety of the veracity of Scripture. The specific verses detailing the destruction on Tyrus are as follows:

(vs. 3) Therefore thus saith the Lord GOD; Behold, I am against thee, O Tyrus, and will cause <u>many nations to come up against thee</u>, as the sea causeth his waves to come up.

(vs. 4) And they shall destroy the walls of Tyrus, and break down her towers: <u>I will also scrape her dust from her, and make her like the top of a rock.</u>

(vs. 7) For thus saith the Lord GOD; Behold, <u>I will bring upon Tyrus Nebuchadrezzar king of Babylon,</u> a king of kings, from the north, with horses, and with chariots, and with horsemen, and companies, and much people.

(vs. 12) And they shall make a spoil of thy riches, and make a prey of thy merchandise: and they shall break down thy walls, and destroy thy pleasant houses: <u>and they shall lay thy stones and thy timber and thy dust in the midst of the water.</u>

(vs. 14) <u>And I will make thee like the top of a rock: thou shalt be a place to spread nets upon; thou shalt be built no more:</u> for I the LORD have spoken it, saith the Lord GOD.

(vs. 21) I will make thee a terror, <u>and thou shalt be no</u>

more: though thou be sought for, yet shalt thou never be found again, saith the Lord GOD.

The historical account that fulfills literally all these descriptions is as follows: Nebuchadnezzar came and laid siege on the city of Tyrus; for 13 years he cast a mount against it. Nobody could go in and nobody could go out by land. Nebuchadnezzar had Tyrus in a strangle hold as he battled against the city. However, unbeknownst to Nebuchadnezzar, the people of Tyrus had loaded their ships, taking their people and their belongings to an island a half-mile out to sea. On this island they established a new city while their old one was under siege. Finally, Nebuchadnezzar knocks down the walls and gets inside the city. He comes into Tyrus with all the nations of the world, for his army was made up of all the nations he had conquered. When Nebuchadnezzar entered the city he discovered that everyone was gone with the exception of a few people; they had reestablished themselves as the new city of Tyrus, a half-mile out to sea. There they existed for some 200 years until a conquering leader known as Alexander the Great came. It was Alexander that would fulfill the rest of Ezekiel's prophecy. Alexander, like Nebuchadnezzar, ruled the known world at this time. Concerned about the fleet of ships that Tyrus possessed, Alexander sought to destroy them. He knew that there was only one way to destroy the island of Tyrus and that was to make a land bridge out to sea to conquer the city. Alexander proceeded to take all the stones, timbers and debris from the old city of Tyrus and cast it into the water to form his land bridge. He even used the dust from the old city to make mortar for his causeway, scraping the land clean like the top of a rock. Using this land bridge Alexander conquered the city of Tyrus. In

Werner Keller's book "The Bible as History," he outlines Alexander's attack on the Phoenician city of Tyrus:

"This city well-fortified and protected by stout high walls was built on a small island which guarded the coastline. Alexander performed here a miracle of military ingenuity by building a 2,000 foot mole in the sea out to the island city. To safeguard the operations, mobile protective shields, so-called "tortoises" had to be employed. Despite this the construction of the causeway was greatly hindered by an incessant hail of missiles. Meantime his engineers were on shore building veritable monsters: "Helepoleis." These were mobile protective towers many stories high, which held the detachments of bowmen and light artillery. A drawbridge on the front of the towers enabled a surprise attack to be made on the enemy's walls. They were the highest siege towers ever used in the history of war. Each of them had twenty stories and the topmost platform towered at a height of over 160 feet far above the highest city walls.
When after seven months preparation these monsters, bristling with weapons, slowly and clumsily rolled towards Tyre, the fate of the maritime stronghold, which was considered impregnable, was sealed."

Tyrus would continue to be rebuilt until Muslims completely annihilated the city in 1290 AD, never to rise again. To this day the only thing that exists is a small fishing village where any time of the day one can see men drying their nets. As to the old city of Tyrus, nothing remains. Something was rebuilt at the same site, but it was no more the ancient city of Tyrus than it was the city of Seattle.

In recapping the fulfilled prophecies of the destruction of Tyrus:

(vs. 3) Therefore thus saith the Lord GOD; Behold, I am against thee, O Tyrus, and will cause <u>many nations to come up against thee</u>, as the sea causeth his waves to come up.

Not only was Nebuchadnezzar's army made up of these "many nations" but many nations had come up against Tyrus until it was completely destroyed in 1290AD.

(vs. 4) And they shall destroy the walls of Tyrus, and break down her towers: <u>I will also scrape her dust from her, and make her like the top of a rock.</u>

(vs. 12) And they shall make a spoil of thy riches, and make a prey of thy merchandise: and they shall break down thy walls, and destroy thy pleasant houses: <u>and they shall lay thy stones and thy timber and thy dust in the midst of the water.</u> For thus saith the Lord GOD; When I shall make thee a desolate city, like the cities that are not inhabited; when <u>I shall bring up the deep upon thee, and great waters shall cover thee;</u>

During his campaign through Asia, Alexander ordered the rubble of the old Tyrus, which had been destroyed more than 200 years before, to be cast into the sea. Nothing was left behind but barren rock. With this rubble he built a causeway to attack the "new city" of Tyrus (333 BC), which had been rebuilt on the island, thus enabling him to conquer it.

(vs. 7) For thus saith the Lord GOD; Behold, <u>I will bring upon Tyrus Nebuchadrezzar king of Babylon,</u> a king of kings, from the north, with horses, and with chariots, and with horsemen, and companies, and much people.

Nebuchadnezzar destroyed the city after a 13-year siege (585-573 BC). It was rebuilt on an island half-mile from the coast.

(vs. 14) And <u>I will make thee like the top of a rock: thou shalt be a place to spread nets upon; thou shalt be built no more:</u> for I the LORD have spoken it, saith the Lord GOD.

Even today native fishermen use this site for drying their nets. During the crusades Tyrus was finally brought to the ground by the Muslims. The old city of Tyrus was never rebuilt (1290 AD). Today the only thing remaining is a small fishing village where you can see fishermen drying their nets.

(vs. 21) I will make thee a terror, <u>and thou shalt be no more: though thou be sought for, yet shalt thou never be found again,</u> saith the Lord GOD.

The destruction of Tyrus was so complete that almost no stone was found in its original place.

CHAPTER 27
The Wealth of Tyrus

Chapter 27 is a laundry list of all the wealth of Tyrus. The wealth of Tyrus was gained through trade; one need only to read verses 5-25 to see all the merchants and their countries with which Tyrus traded. This chapter, though seemingly unimportant, is the ground work for chapter 28.

The word of the LORD came again unto me, saying, Now, thou son of man, take up a lamentation for Tyrus; And say unto Tyrus, O thou that art situate at the entry of the sea, which art a merchant of the people for many isles, Thus saith the Lord GOD; O Tyrus, thou hast said, I am of perfect beauty. Thy borders are in the midst of the seas, thy builders have perfected thy beauty. (Ezekiel 27:1-4)

Lamentation over Tyrus (1-4): in these verses God states what it was that made Tyrus fall. A couple of words associated with Tryus that are key to understanding not only this chapter but also chapter 28, are "merchant," "merchandise," "traffick" and the phrase "perfect in beauty." Tyrus was *the* trading center of the known world at the time. They were the "merchants" of the people for many isles (vs. 3). They "trafficked" in the selling of their goods whereby all the other nations that traded with her (verses 5-25) were made rich.

They have made all thy ship boards of fir trees of Senir: they have taken cedars from Lebanon to make masts for thee. Of the oaks of Bashan have they made thine oars; the company of the Ashurites have made thy benches of ivory, brought out of the isles of Chittim. Fine linen with broidered work from Egypt was that which thou spreadest forth to be thy sail; blue and purple from the isles of Elishah was that which covered thee. The inhabitants of Zidon and Arvad were thy mariners: thy wise men, O Tyrus, that were in thee, were thy pilots. The ancients of Gebal and the wise men thereof were in thee thy calkers: all the ships of the sea with their mariners were in thee to occupy thy merchandise. They of Persia and of Lud and of Phut were in thine army, thy men of war: they hanged the shield and helmet in thee; they set forth thy comeliness. The men of Arvad with thine army were upon thy walls round about, and the Gammadims were in thy towers: they hanged their shields upon thy walls round about; they have made thy beauty perfect. Tarshish was thy merchant by reason of the multitude of all kind of riches; with silver, iron, tin, and lead, they traded in thy fairs. Javan, Tubal, and Meshech, they were thy merchants: they traded the persons of men and vessels of brass in thy market. They of the house of Togarmah traded in thy fairs with horses and horsemen and mules. The men of Dedan were thy merchants; many isles were the merchandise of thine hand: they brought thee for a present horns of ivory and ebony. Syria was thy merchant by reason of the multitude of the wares of thy making: they occupied in thy fairs with emeralds, purple, and broidered work, and fine linen, and coral, and agate. Judah, and the land of Israel, they were thy merchants: they traded in thy market wheat of Minnith, and Pannag, and honey, and oil, and balm.

Damascus was thy merchant in the multitude of the wares of thy making, for the multitude of all riches; in the wine of Helbon, and white wool. Dan also and Javan going to and fro occupied in thy fairs: bright iron, cassia, and calamus, were in thy market. Dedan was thy merchant in precious clothes for chariots. Arabia, and all the princes of Kedar, they occupied with thee in lambs, and rams, and goats: in these were they thy merchants. The merchants of Sheba and Raamah, they were thy merchants: they occupied in thy fairs with chief of all spices, and with all precious stones, and gold. Haran, and Canneh, and Eden, the merchants of Sheba, Asshur, and Chilmad, were thy merchants. These were thy merchants in all sorts of things, in blue clothes, and broidered work, and in chests of rich apparel, bound with cords, and made of cedar, among thy merchandise. The ships of Tarshish did sing of thee in thy market: and thou wast replenished, and made very glorious in the midst of the seas. (Ezekiel 27:5-25)

The Merchants of Tyrus (5-25): These verses deal with the "merchants" of Tyrus that "trafficked" in their "merchandise." One need only to read over the list to see all the wealth of this great city:
- Boards of fir trees for their ships from Senir (vs. 5)
- Cedar from Lebanon for masts for their ships (vs. 5)
- Oaks from Bashan for oars (vs. 6)
- Benches of ivory made by the Ashurites (vs. 6)
- Broided linen from Egypt to make sails for their ships (vs. 7)
- Blue and purple tapestry from Elishah (vs. 7)
- Men from Zidon and Arvad were employed to be the pilots of their ships (vs. 8)

166

- Caulkers from Gebal were employed (vs. 9)
- Men from Persia and Lud and Phut were in the army (vs. 10)
- The men from Arvad carved the walls (vs. 11)
- The men from Gammadims guarded the towers (vs. 11)
- Tarshish traded in silver, iron, tin and lead (vs. 12)
- Javan, Tubal and Meshech traded men and vessels of brass (vs. 13)
- Togarmah traded horses and horsemen (vs. 14)
- Men of Dedan brought horns of ivory and ebony (vs. 15)
- Syria traded in emeralds, purple, and broidered work and fine linen and coral and agate (vs. 16)
- Judah and the land of Israel traded in wheat, pannag, honey, oil and balm (vs. 17)
- Damascus traded in wine and white wool (vs. 18)
- Dan and Javan brought iron, cassia and calamus (vs. 19)
- Dedan traded precious cloths for chariots (vs. 20)
- Arabia and Kedar traded lambs, rams and goats (vs. 21)
- Sheba and Raamah traded spices and precious stones and gold (vs. 22)
- Haran and Canneh and Eden merchants of Sheba, Asshur and Chilmad traded in blue cloths, broidered work, chest of rich apparel (vss. 23-24)

Thy rowers have brought thee into great waters: the east wind hath broken thee in the midst of the seas. Thy riches, and thy fairs, thy merchandise, thy mariners, and thy pilots, thy calkers, and the occupiers of thy merchandise, and all thy men of war, that are

in thee, and in all thy company which is in the midst of thee, shall fall into the midst of the seas in the day of thy ruin. The suburbs shall shake at the sound of the cry of thy pilots. And all that handle the oar, the mariners, and all the pilots of the sea, shall come down from their ships, they shall stand upon the land; And shall cause their voice to be heard against thee, and shall cry bitterly, and shall cast up dust upon their heads, they shall wallow themselves in the ashes: And they shall make themselves utterly bald for thee, and gird them with sackcloth, and they shall weep for thee with bitterness of heart and bitter wailing. And in their wailing they shall take up a lamentation for thee, and lament over thee, saying, What city is like Tyrus, like the destroyed in the midst of the sea? When thy wares went forth out of the seas, thou filledst many people; thou didst enrich the kings of the earth with the multitude of thy riches and of thy merchandise. In the time when thou shalt be broken by the seas in the depths of the waters thy merchandise and all thy company in the midst of thee shall fall. All the inhabitants of the isles shall be astonished at thee, and their kings shall be sore afraid, they shall be troubled in their countenance. The merchants among the people shall hiss at thee; thou shalt be a terror, and never shalt be any more. (Ezekiel 27:26-36)

Weeping over the Destruction of Tyrus (26-36): The city of Tyrus' fate is sealed, and all they that traded with this great city "wail" because of it. This weeping and lamenting over the fall of this great city is comparable to Babylon in the future. Just as Tyrus was the commercial, religious and political power of the world in its day, so Babylon will rise to be the world trading center. The correlation between these two cities is uncanny:

Tyrus Compared to Babylon *(Ezekiel 27 cf. Revelation 18):*

- She is made "perfect in beauty" by the merchants she traded with *(vss. 3, 11 cf. Rev. 17:4; 18:17)*
- Merchants of beautiful tapestries of purple and fine linens *(vss. 16, 24 cf. Rev. 18:12, 16)*
- Merchants of gold, silver and all kinds of precious metals *(vss. 12, 13, 22 cf. Rev. 18:12)*
- Merchants of all kinds of grains and spices *(vss. 17, 22, cf. Rev. 18:13)*
- Merchants of all kinds of woods and ivory *(vss. 5, 6, 15 cf. Rev. 18:12)*
- Merchants of men *(vss. 8-11 cf. Rev. 18:13)*
- Merchants of livestock *(vss. 14, 21 cf. Rev. 18:13)*
- All the "kings" of the earth were made rich by her *(vs. 33 cf. Rev. 18:3, 15)*
- All the "merchants" that traded with her will "weep" over her fall *(vss. 28-32 cf. 18:9, 11, 15)*

By comparing these two seats of world power one can see many revealing realities, the first of which is that Babylon is going to be the seat of world power in the future. Secondly, just as the Devil is associated with the city of Tyrus *(Ezekiel 28:11-19)* so the Antichrist will be associated with Babylon *(the beast of Revelation 17)*.

CHAPTER 28

Self-deification

God is now singling out the Prince of Tyrus for a special word from Him. The Prince of Tyrus is going to make the fatal mistake of looking at all his beauty and riches and think that he has done it all; he is going to place himself up as God. However, the true and living God will not share His glory with another (Isaiah 42:8), and the Prince of Tyrus will learn this in a most decisive way.

However the Prince of Tyrus is not the only one that is dealt with in this chapter; God will move from the Prince of Tyrus to the King of Tyrus, Satan himself.

The word of the LORD came again unto me, saying, Son of man, say unto the prince of Tyrus, Thus saith the Lord GOD; Because thine heart is lifted up, and thou hast said, I am a God, I sit in the seat of God, in the midst of the seas; yet thou art a man, and not God, though thou set thine heart as the heart of God: Behold, thou art wiser than Daniel; there is no secret that they can hide from thee: With thy wisdom and with thine understanding thou hast gotten thee riches, and hast gotten gold and silver into thy treasures: By thy great wisdom and by thy traffick hast thou increased thy riches, and thine heart is lifted up because of thy riches: Therefore thus saith the Lord GOD; Because thou hast set thine heart as the heart of God; Behold, therefore I will bring strangers upon thee, the terrible

of the nations: and they shall draw their swords against the beauty of thy wisdom, and they shall defile thy brightness. They shall bring thee down to the pit, and thou shalt die the deaths of them that are slain in the midst of the seas. Wilt thou yet say before him that slayeth thee, I am God? but thou shalt be a man, and no God, in the hand of him that slayeth thee. Thou shalt die the deaths of the uncircumcised by the hand of strangers: for I have spoken it, saith the Lord GOD. (Ezekiel 28:1-10)

The Prince of Tyrus (1-10): In the previous chapter all the merchants that Tyrus traded with were detailed. It was by the "trafficking" in these goods that Tyrus was made "perfect in beauty" (vss. 3, 4, 5, 11) and its prince elevated himself to God-status (vss. 2-6). However, God will not allow those rulers who set themselves up as God to stand, as the rest of the verses show. Notice other instances in the Scriptures of world leaders that have fallen to the same temptation:
- Sennacherib (2 Kings 17:33-35)
- Pharaoh (Ezek. 29:3)
- Nebuchadnezzar (Daniel 3:15; 4:30)
- Herod (Acts 12:21-23)
- The Man of Sin (2 Thess. 2:3, 4)
- Satan (Isaiah 14:13)

The Prince of Tyrus set himself up as God but will die as a man (28:7-10). The irony is that the Prince of Tyrus pictured himself as wiser than Daniel, and it is Daniel who served in the country that would ultimately defeat him.

Moreover the word of the LORD came unto me,

saying, Son of man, take up a lamentation upon the king of Tyrus, and say unto him, Thus saith the Lord GOD; Thou sealest up the sum, full of wisdom, and perfect in beauty. Thou hast been in Eden the garden of God; every precious stone was thy covering, the sardius, topaz, and the diamond, the beryl, the onyx, and the jasper, the sapphire, the emerald, and the carbuncle, and gold: the workmanship of thy tabrets and of thy pipes was prepared in thee in the day that thou wast created. Thou art the anointed cherub that covereth; and I have set thee so: thou wast upon the holy mountain of God; thou hast walked up and down in the midst of the stones of fire. Thou wast perfect in thy ways from the day that thou wast created, till iniquity was found in thee. By the multitude of thy merchandise they have filled the midst of thee with violence, and thou hast sinned: therefore I will cast thee as profane out of the mountain of God: and I will destroy thee, O covering cherub, from the midst of the stones of fire. Thine heart was lifted up because of thy beauty, thou hast corrupted thy wisdom by reason of thy brightness: I will cast thee to the ground, I will lay thee before kings, that they may behold thee. Thou hast defiled thy sanctuaries by the multitude of thine iniquities, by the iniquity of thy traffick; therefore will I bring forth a fire from the midst of thee, it shall devour thee, and I will bring thee to ashes upon the earth in the sight of all them that behold thee. All they that know thee among the people shall be astonished at thee: thou shalt be a terror, and never shalt thou be any more. (Ezekiel 28:11-19)

The King of Tyrus (11-19): Through Ezekiel God will now give a lamentation to the "king of Tyrus." It is self-evident that this lamentation goes beyond the scope of any mere mortal man, but is addressing Satan, the anointed cherub:

- Thou has been in Eden the garden of God (vs. 13)
- Anointed Cherub (vs. 14)
- He resides in the mountain of God (vs. 14)
- He was given by God the service of God's throne (vss. 13-14 "stones of fire" cf. Ex. 24:10)

No mortal man is in view; Ezekiel in this portion is looking at the person behind the earthly king of Tyrus, Satan the anointed cherub.

Discussing Satan as the anointed cherub is very fitting to the context. God has just dealt with the riches that the city of Tyrus had by the merchants that made her perfect in beauty; in fact all of chapter 27 is a detailed list of not only the merchants but the goods they traded (27: 3, 4, 11, 27 and 33). Then in 28: 1-10 God addresses the pride and self-deification of the Prince of Tyrus. Ezekiel looks into the very heart of this ruling prince of Tyrus, showing the deluded heart that would dare to say, "I am a God, I sit in the seat of God" (vs.2).

So then the ultimate embodiment of all the sin mentioned concerning the city of Tyrus and the Prince of Tyrus is Satan, the anointed cherub. He is being described here as one who, like the Prince of Tyrus, looked at his beauty by reason of the merchants and was lifted up in pride in his heart; thus he sought to be God (Isaiah 14:13 cf. 2 Thess. 2:4). This desire however did not stay in Satan's heart, but rather he "trafficked" in it; spreading it throughout the heavenly realm wherein he resided. It is at this point that the anointed cherub became Satan, the adversary of God. Spreading violence throughout the heavenly realm, Satan was cast out of the presence and service

173

of God to be consumed by the fires of eternal judgment one day (Matt. 25:41 cf. Rev. 20:10).

Satan's power over the Prince of Tyrus, and his final destruction in verses 17-19, parallels in great detail what will yet occur with the "man of sin" in the "day of the LORD"(2 Thess. 2:4). In that day Satan will be conducting himself just as is referred to here, only on a greater scale. He will directly work through another who will say, "I am a God, I sit in the seat of God." In that day he will be the source of power behind the "man of sin," just as in Ezekiel's day he is exercising his power over the "Prince of Tyrus." In the end however, Satan will be cast to the ground before the nations he deceived and there, as all those kings behold him, he will be condemned in the flames (vss. 17-19 cf. 20:7-10).

Again the word of the LORD came unto me, saying, Son of man, set thy face against Zidon, and prophesy against it, And say, Thus saith the Lord GOD; Behold, I am against thee, O Zidon; and I will be glorified in the midst of thee: and they shall know that I am the LORD, when I shall have executed judgments in her, and shall be sanctified in her. For I will send into her pestilence, and blood into her streets; and the wounded shall be judged in the midst of her by the sword upon her on every side; and they shall know that I am the LORD. (Ezekiel 28:20-23)

Judgment of Zidon (20-23): Zidon lay 25 miles north of the city of Tyrus. According to these verses the city will be judged, but not completely destroyed. Though the reason for its judgment is not mentioned in these verses, it is apparent from the judgment on all these Gentile nations that it's a result of their hostile relationship with Israel and the self-deification of their leadership.

And there shall be no more a pricking brier unto the house of Israel, nor any grieving thorn of all that are round about them, that despised them; and they shall know that I am the Lord GOD. Thus saith the Lord GOD; When I shall have gathered the house of Israel from the people among whom they are scattered, and shall be sanctified in them in the sight of the heathen, then shall they dwell in their land that I have given to my servant Jacob. And they shall dwell safely therein, and shall build houses, and plant vineyards; yea, they shall dwell with confidence, when I have executed judgments upon all those that despise them round about them; and they shall know that I am the LORD their God. (Ezekiel 28:24-26)

Israel's Restoration (24-26): This chapter ends where all prophecy will end, with Israel re-established in the land, glorified above all nations (Isaiah 65:17-25 cf. Amos 9:14, 15). The theme of all the prophets is the restoration of Israel one day (Romans 9; 10; 11).

CHAPTER 29
Judgment of Egypt

Chapters 29 – 32 are all judgments upon Egypt. Chapter 29 though, historical for us, is prophetical at the time Ezekiel is speaking. Egypt is being judged for the same two reasons all these nations in chapters 25 – 32 are being judged: self-deification by its leadership (29:3) and their dealings with Israel (29:6, 7). Egypt will be judged by Nebuchadnezzar, taken into captivity 40 years and then returned to the land as a base kingdom, never to rise to national superiority.

In the tenth year, in the tenth month, in the twelfth day of the month, the word of the LORD came unto me, saying, Son of man, set thy face against Pharaoh king of Egypt, and prophesy against him, and against all Egypt: Speak, and say, Thus saith the Lord GOD; Behold, I am against thee, Pharaoh king of Egypt, the great dragon that lieth in the midst of his rivers, which hath said, My river is mine own, and I have made it for myself. But I will put hooks in thy jaws, and I will cause the fish of thy rivers to stick unto thy scales, and I will bring thee up out of the midst of thy rivers, and all the fish of thy rivers shall stick unto thy scales. And I will leave thee thrown into the wilderness, thee and all the fish of thy rivers: thou shalt fall upon the open fields; thou shalt not be brought together, nor gathered: I have given thee for meat to the beasts of the field and to the fowls of the heaven. And all the inhabitants of Egypt shall know that I am the LORD, because they

have been a staff of reed to the house of Israel. When they took hold of thee by thy hand, thou didst break, and rend all their shoulder: and when they leaned upon thee, thou brakest, and madest all their loins to be at a stand. (Ezekiel 29:1-7)

Pharaoh the Prideful Dragon (1-7): God is against Pharaoh of Egypt, likening him to a dragon that lies in the midst of the rivers (*reference to the many rivers that shoot off the Nile river before emptying into the Mediterranean Sea*). Pharaoh had placed himself up as creator of the river itself (vs. 3). Just as a fisherman lands a fish on the shore, so God will take the dragon of the river (*Pharaoh*) and by hooks take it out of the river and cast it to the wilderness for all beasts of the field and fowls of the air to feed upon (vss. 4-5). Judgment is coming upon Egypt because they were the staff that Israel leaned upon in times of trouble (2 Kings 18:21-24 cf. Isaiah 36:6). Israel had made several alliances with Egypt for protection, and Egypt either turned on them (vs. 7), or in some cases were just ineffective. God had warned Israel through the prophets that they were not to place their trust in Egypt (Isaiah 31:1).

Therefore thus saith the Lord GOD; Behold, I will bring a sword upon thee, and cut off man and beast out of thee. And the land of Egypt shall be desolate and waste; and they shall know that I am the LORD: because he hath said, The river is mine, and I have made it. Behold, therefore I am against thee, and against thy rivers, and I will make the land of Egypt utterly waste and desolate, from the tower of Syene even unto the border of Ethiopia. No foot of man shall pass through it, nor foot of beast shall pass through it, neither shall it be inhabited forty years. And I will make the land of Egypt desolate in the midst of the countries that are desolate, and her cities among the cities that are laid waste shall be desolate forty years: and I will scatter the Egyptians among the nations, and will disperse them through the countries. (Ezekiel 29:8-12)

40 Year Captivity for Egypt (8-12): The judgment against Egypt is in response to Pharaoh's deluded statement, "The river is mine, and I have made it" (vs. 9 cf. vs. 3). Therefore God is going to make the land desolate from the rivers of Egypt to Syene (upper Egypt) bordering Ethiopia (vs. 10). God is going to bring Nebuchadnezzar against Egypt and bring them into Babylonian captivity for 40 years (vss. 11-12 cf. Jeremiah 46:25, 26) during which time the land will remain desolate.

Yet thus saith the Lord GOD; At the end of forty years will I gather the Egyptians from the people whither they were scattered: And I will bring again the captivity of Egypt, and will cause them to return into the land of Pathros, into the land of their habitation; and they shall be there a base kingdom. It shall be the basest of the kingdoms; neither shall it exalt itself any more above the nations: for I will diminish them, that they shall no more rule over the nations. And it shall be no more the confidence of the house of Israel, which bringeth their iniquity to remembrance, when they shall look after them: but they shall know that I am the Lord GOD. (Ezekiel 29:13-16)

Egyptian Captivity Returns (13-16): God promises that Egypt will return to their land (vs. 13) but will never regain their former glory. Egypt will be a base kingdom among the nations from this time forward (vss. 14, 15). God is doing this so Israel will not seek alliances with them, but rather have confidence in the LORD (vs. 16).

And it came to pass in the seven and twentieth year, in the first month, in the first day of the month, the word of the LORD came unto me, saying, Son of man, Nebuchadrezzar king of Babylon caused his army to serve a great service against Tyrus: every head was made bald, and every shoulder was peeled: yet had he no wages, nor his army, for Tyrus, for the service that he had served against it: Therefore thus saith the Lord GOD; Behold, I will give the land of Egypt unto Nebuchadrezzar king of Babylon; and he shall take her multitude, and take her spoil, and take her prey; and it shall be the wages for his army. I have given him the land of Egypt for his labour wherewith he served against it, because they wrought for me, saith the Lord GOD. (Ezekiel 29:17-20)

Egypt, the Payment of Nebuchadnezzar (17-21): When Nebuchadnezzar came against Tyrus and laid a 13 year siege against it, he received no spoils upon its fall; for unbeknownst to him Tyrus had relocated the entire city ½ mile out to sea. Because of this God is giving Egypt and all its wealth into the hands of Nebuchadnezzar as payment for punishing Tyrus. Who says God is not just!

In that day will I cause the horn of the house of Israel to bud forth, and I will give thee the opening of the mouth in the midst of them; and they shall know that I am the LORD. (Ezekiel 29:21)

179

Israel's Restoration of Power (21): As we have seen throughout this great book of Ezekiel, for all the doom and gloom of judgment God always offers hope to his people Israel. God promises that the horn of the house of Israel will bud again (Luke 1:69).

CHAPTER 30
Judgment of Egypt

This chapter and the one following are a continuation of the judgments against Egypt. In this chapter we will see these judgments have a far reaching scope, out to the "day of the LORD", the time in which the LORD will vanquish the heathen world.

The word of the LORD came again unto me, saying, Son of man, prophesy and say, Thus saith the Lord GOD; Howl ye, Woe worth the day! For the day is near, even the day of the LORD is near, a cloudy day; it shall be the time of the heathen. And the sword shall come upon Egypt, and great pain shall be in Ethiopia, when the slain shall fall in Egypt, and they shall take away her multitude, and her foundations shall be broken down. Ethiopia, and Libya, and Lydia, and all the mingled people, and Chub, and the men of the land that is in league, shall fall with them by the sword. Thus saith the LORD; They also that uphold Egypt shall fall; and the pride of her power shall come down: from the tower of Syene shall they fall in it by the sword, saith the Lord GOD. And they shall be desolate in the midst of the countries that are desolate, and her cities shall be in the midst of the cities that are wasted. And they shall know that I am the LORD, when I have set a fire in Egypt, and when all her helpers shall be destroyed. In that day shall messengers go forth from me in ships to make the careless Ethiopians afraid,

and great pain shall come upon them, as in the day of Egypt: for, lo, it cometh. Thus saith the Lord GOD; I will also make the multitude of Egypt to cease by the hand of Nebuchadrezzar king of Babylon. He and his people with him, the terrible of the nations, shall be brought to destroy the land: and they shall draw their swords against Egypt, and fill the land with the slain. And I will make the rivers dry, and sell the land into the hand of the wicked: and I will make the land waste, and all that is therein, by the hand of strangers: I the LORD have spoken it. Thus saith the Lord GOD; I will also destroy the idols, and I will cause their images to cease out of Noph; and there shall be no more a prince of the land of Egypt: and I will put a fear in the land of Egypt. And I will make Pathros desolate, and will set fire in Zoan, and will execute judgments in No. And I will pour my fury upon Sin, the strength of Egypt; and I will cut off the multitude of No. And I will set fire in Egypt: Sin shall have great pain, and No shall be rent asunder, and Noph shall have distresses daily. The young men of Aven and of Pibeseth shall fall by the sword: and these cities shall go into captivity. At Tehaphnehes also the day shall be darkened, when I shall break there the yokes of Egypt: and the pomp of her strength shall cease in her: as for her, a cloud shall cover her, and her daughters shall go into captivity. Thus will I execute judgments in Egypt: and they shall know that I am the LORD. (Ezekiel 30:1-19)

The Time of the Heathen (1-19): These verses of Scripture find their completion out in the future "Day of the LORD" (vs. 3 cf. Amos 5:18-20; Zeph. 1:7, 14; Isaiah 13:6; Joel 1:15; 2:1, 2). This could be the reason that this portion of Scripture is not dated (see. vs. 20); however, they also were fulfilled historically by the invading armies of Nebuchadnezzar (vs. 10). Thus, you have events that have a historical fulfillment (vs. 10) and that have yet to be fulfilled (vs. 12 cf. Isaiah 19:4-10). God is judging not only Egypt but all the nations that look to Egypt for help (vss. 5-8).

The destruction of the cities and people mentioned in verses 14-18 were destroyed by Nebuchadnezzar (Jeremiah 46:25-26). Pathros in upper Egypt, No the city of Thebes; Zoan in lower Egypt, Sin on the northeast boundary now completely buried in sand and Aven located seven miles northeast of Cairo. Upon the destruction of these ancient cities, over time other cities were built upon the ancient sites, changing their names. For an example of this, here is an article regarding the ancient Egyptian city of No:

*Thebes (Egypt) (Egyptian Weset or Newt), ancient city and, for many centuries, capital of ancient Egypt, on both sides of the Nile River, about 725 km (about 450 mi) south of present-day Cairo. It is partly **occupied today by the modern towns of Al Karnak and Luxor.** It was named Thebes by the Greeks, who knew it also as Diospolis ("heavenly city"); it is the city identified in the Old Testament as No ("city") or No-Amon ("city of Amon"). Scattered over the site are the remnants of numerous temples, tombs, and other ancient monuments. Of prehistoric origin, Thebes began to figure in the recorded history of Egypt during the Old Kingdom (circa 2755-2255 BC). Tombs dating from the 6th Dynasty (circa 2407-2255 BC) of Egyptian pharaohs have been discovered in the original necropolis, which is on the west side of the Nile. As the biblical name of Thebes indicates, the local deity of the city was Amon, originally the Egyptian god of the reproductive forces and, later as Amen-Ra, the "father of the gods." The ruined temple of Amon, which ranks among the best-preserved and most* *magnificent structures of Egyptian antiquity, is at Al Karnak. (Source unknown)*

And it came to pass in the eleventh year, in the first month, in the seventh day of the month, that the word of the LORD came unto me, saying, Son of man, I have broken the arm of Pharaoh king of Egypt; and, lo, it shall not be bound up to be healed, to put a roller to bind it, to make it strong to hold the sword. Therefore thus saith the Lord GOD; Behold, I am against Pharaoh king of Egypt, and will break his arms, the strong, and that which was broken; and I will cause the sword to fall out of his hand. And I will scatter the Egyptians among the nations, and will disperse them through the countries. And I will strengthen the arms of the king of Babylon, and put my sword in his hand: but I will break Pharaoh's arms, and he shall groan before him with the groanings of a deadly wounded man. But I will strengthen the arms of the king of Babylon, and the arms of Pharaoh shall fall down; and they shall know that I am the LORD, when I shall put my sword into the hand of the king of Babylon, and he shall stretch it out upon the land of Egypt. And I will scatter the Egyptians among the nations, and disperse them among the countries; and they shall know that I am the LORD. (Ezekiel 30:20-26)

The Broken Arm of Pharaoh (20-26): God is going to break the arm of Pharaoh King of Egypt (vs. 21) by God's sword in the hand of the king of Babylon (vss. 24-25).

CHAPTER 31
Judgment of Egypt

We are still on the judgments against Egypt and its allies. In this chapter Pharaoh king of Egypt and his multitude (vs. 2 cf. vs. 18) are likened to the Assyrian king that was overthrown by the Chaldeans. Though not as clear as Ezekiel 28 there are hints at Satan and his working behind the coming Assyrian king (Isaiah 10:5).

And it came to pass in the eleventh year, in the third month, in the first day of the month, that the word of the LORD came unto me, saying, Son of man, speak unto Pharaoh king of Egypt, and to his multitude; Whom art thou like in thy greatness? (Ezekiel 31:1-2)

Pharaoh's Likeness in Glory and Greatness (1-2): This portion is dated showing its historical significance of the judgments against Egypt:

- **First Declaration of Judgment**: *10th year, 10th month, 12th day (Ezekiel 29:1)* - Pharaoh is a dragon that is cast out and devoured
- **Second Declaration of Judgment**: *27th year, 1st month, 1st day (Ezekiel 29:17)* - Egypt is given to Nebuchadnezzar for his destruction of Tyrus
- **Third Declaration of Judgment**: *11th year, 1st month, 7th day (Ezekiel 30:20)* - Arm of Pharaoh will be broken by the sword of God, Nebuchadnezzar
- **Fourth Declaration of Judgment**: *11th year, 3rd*

month, 1ˢᵗ day (Ezekiel 31:1) - Pharaoh is likened to the Assyrian that will be cut down for his pride filled heart

- **Fifth Declaration of Judgment**: *12ᵗʰ year, 12ᵗʰ month, 1ˢᵗ day (Ezekiel 32:1)* - Lament over Pharaoh and his destruction by Babylon
- **Sixth Declaration of Judgment**: *12ᵗʰ year, 12ᵗʰ month, 15ᵗʰ day (Ezekiel 32:17)* - Wailing over Egypt and the nations that sided with her as they are cast down to the pit.

Pharaoh is being compared in glory and beauty to the Assyrian king. This is reminiscent of the Prince of Tyrus (Ezekiel 28:1-10); the anointed Cherub (Ezekiel 28:11-19), the king of Babylon (Daniel 4:19-37) and Lucifer (Isaiah 14:12).

Behold, the Assyrian was a cedar in Lebanon with fair branches, and with a shadowing shroud, and of an high stature; and his top was among the thick boughs. The waters made him great, the deep set him up on high with her rivers running round about his plants, and sent out her little rivers unto all the trees of the field. Therefore his height was exalted above all the trees of the field, and his boughs were multiplied, and his branches became long because of the multitude of waters, when he shot forth. All the fowls of heaven made their nests in his boughs, and under his branches did all the beasts of the field bring forth their young, and under his shadow dwelt all great nations. Thus was he fair in his greatness, in the length of his branches: for his root was by great waters. The cedars in the garden of God could not hide him: the fir trees were not like his boughs, and the chesnut trees were

not like his branches; nor any tree in the garden of God was like unto him in his beauty. I have made him fair by the multitude of his branches: so that all the trees of Eden, that were in the garden of God, envied him. (Ezekiel 31:3-9)

The Assyrian's Greatness and Glory (3-9): The Assyrian king is likened to a cedar tree (vs. 3) that flourished by the rivers making its branches long providing a lodging place for the fowls of the air and shade for the beasts of the field (vs. 6). The interpretation is that of the greatness of the kingdom of the king of Assyria, whose dominance provided safety and protection to the surrounding nations (vs. 6). Nations exalting themselves as great trees is a metaphor used in other Scripture:
- Nebuchadnezzar's kingdom (Daniel 4:1-4, 10-12, 19-22, 28-31)
- The Nation of Israel (Judges 9, Romans 11:17)
- The Kingdom of Heaven (Matthew 13:31-32)

Therefore thus saith the Lord GOD; Because thou hast lifted up thyself in height, and he hath shot up his top among the thick boughs, and his heart is lifted up in his height; I have therefore delivered him into the hand of the mighty one of the heathen; he shall surely deal with him: I have driven him out for his wickedness. And strangers, the terrible of the nations, have cut him off, and have left him: upon the mountains and in all the valleys his branches are fallen, and his boughs are broken by all the rivers of the land; and all the people of the earth are gone down from his shadow, and have left him. Upon his ruin shall all the fowls of the heaven remain, and all the beasts of the field shall be upon his branches: To the end that none of all the trees by the waters exalt themselves for their height, neither shoot up their top among the thick boughs, neither their trees stand up in their height, all that drink water: for they are all delivered unto death, to the nether parts of the earth, in the midst of the children of men, with them that go down to the pit. Thus saith the Lord GOD; In the day when he went down to the grave I caused a mourning: I covered the deep for him, and I restrained the floods thereof, and the great waters were stayed: and I caused Lebanon to mourn for him, and all the trees of the field fainted for him. I made the nations to shake at the sound of his fall, when I cast him down to hell with them that descend into the pit: and all the trees of Eden, the choice and best of Lebanon, all that drink water, shall be comforted in the nether parts of the earth. They also went down into hell with him unto them that be slain with the sword; and they that were his arm, that dwelt under his shadow in the midst of the heathen. To whom art thou thus like in glory and in greatness among the trees of Eden? yet shalt thou be brought down with the trees of Eden unto the nether parts of the earth: thou shalt lie in the midst of the uncircumcised with them that be slain by the sword. This is Pharaoh and all his multitude, saith the Lord GOD. (Ezekiel 31:10-18)

The Assyrian the High Cedar is Cut Down to Hell (10-18): The Assyrian historically was cut down by the Chaldeans around 627 BC. The destruction of the empire is because of the self-exaltation of the king of Assyria (vss. 10-11). The Assyrian king is taken and cast down to hell with them that descend into the pit. Again this has hints of a future world leader known as the Assyrian that will arise and lead all nations against Israel. However God will deal with this man and cast him into the pit of hell.

CHAPTER 32
Judgment of Egypt

This is the final judgment against the land of Egypt and Pharaoh its king. Pharaoh King of Egypt is lamented over in the first half of this chapter then in the latter verses Egypt and the multitude of the nations that were with them are judged. The sum of this chapter is that Egypt and the once powerful nations will all be condemned to the pit.

And it came to pass in the twelfth year, in the twelfth month, in the first day of the month, that the word of the LORD came unto me, saying, Son of man, take up a lamentation for Pharaoh king of Egypt, and say unto him, Thou art like a young lion of the nations, and thou art as a whale in the seas: and thou camest forth with thy rivers, and troubledst the waters with thy feet, and fouledst their rivers. Thus saith the Lord GOD; I will therefore spread out my net over thee with a company of many people; and they shall bring thee up in my net. Then will I leave thee upon the land, I will cast thee forth upon the open field, and will cause all the fowls of the heaven to remain upon thee, and I will fill the beasts of the whole earth with thee. And I will lay thy flesh upon the mountains, and fill the valleys with thy height. I will also water with thy blood the land wherein thou swimmest, even to the mountains; and the rivers shall be full of thee. And when I shall put thee out, I will cover the heaven, and make the stars thereof dark; I will cover the sun with a cloud, and the moon shall not give her light. All the bright lights of heaven will I make dark over thee, and set darkness upon thy land, saith the Lord GOD. I will also vex the hearts of many people, when I shall bring thy destruction among the nations, into the countries which thou hast not known. Yea, I will make many people amazed at thee, and their kings shall be horribly afraid for thee, when I shall brandish my sword before them; and they shall tremble at every moment, every man for his own life, in the day of thy fall. For thus saith the Lord GOD; The sword of the king of Babylon shall come upon thee. By the swords of the mighty will I cause thy multitude to fall, the terrible of the nations, all of them: and they shall spoil the pomp of Egypt, and all the multitude thereof shall be destroyed. I will destroy also all the beasts thereof from beside the great waters; neither shall the foot of man trouble them any more, nor the hoofs of beasts trouble them. Then will I make their waters deep, and cause their rivers to run like oil, saith the Lord GOD. When I shall make the land of Egypt desolate, and the country shall be destitute of that whereof it was full, when I shall smite all them that dwell therein, then shall they know that I am the LORD. This is the lamentation wherewith they shall lament her: the daughters of the nations shall lament her: they shall lament for her, even for Egypt, and for all her multitude, saith the Lord GOD. (Ezekiel 32:1-16)

Lamentation over Pharaoh King of Egypt (1-16): Pharaoh is likened to two animals, a young lion and a whale that swims in the sea (vs. 2). Using similitudes is how God teaches (Hosea 12:10). Pharaoh is likened to a young lion of the nations and a whale in the seas.

The young lion of the nations, though not developed here, is a reference to Egypt's association with the other nations who are all likened to young lions (Ezekiel 19:3, 6; 38:13) for they devour men.

Pharaoh is also likened to a whale in the sea. This similitude is used for Pharaoh King of Egypt because he resides in the midst of the great river Nile and all its rivers that lie in the Nile delta. God is looking at these nations as a whole from His vantage point in the heavens (Isaiah 40:22) as they war one against another and move against His people Israel. Thus, Pharaoh King of Egypt "troubleth the waters", he stirs up trouble among the nations. God therefore is going to come against them and the multitude that is with them. This judgment is likened to a fisherman that casts his net out into the sea to catch a great whale and as he pulls it to shore others are drawn into the net (vss. 17-32). This similitude of Pharaoh is as the one used in chapter 29 where Pharaoh is likened to a great dragon that swims in the midst of the waters who is caught by the fisherman *(only with a hook)* and cast upon the shore to be devoured by the nations *(Babylonian army)*. So then Pharaoh as the great whale is cast upon the open field to be devoured (vss. 4-11). However, as we will see, Pharaoh is not the only one that is taken in by the net of God's judgments; others will fall victim.

It came to pass also in the twelfth year, in the fifteenth day of the month, that the word of the LORD came unto me, saying, Son of man, wail for the multitude of Egypt, and cast them down, even her, and the daughters of the famous nations, unto the nether parts of the earth, with them that go down into the pit. Whom

dost thou pass in beauty? go down, and be thou laid with the uncircumcised. They shall fall in the midst of them that are slain by the sword: she is delivered to the sword: draw her and all her multitudes. The strong among the mighty shall speak to him out of the midst of hell with them that help him: they are gone down, they lie uncircumcised, slain by the sword. (Ezekiel 32:17-21)

Wailing for the Nations Condemned to the Pit (17-21): This prophetic judgment is against Pharaoh and his multitude (Ezekiel 32:32), thus in these verses you have the countries, leaders and peoples that fall in judgment along with Pharaoh King of Egypt. This section is a list of the nations that will be caught in the net of God's judgment with Egypt. They will all share in the same fate, slain and condemned to the pit (vss. 18-21).

Asshur is there and all her company: his graves are about him: all of them slain, fallen by the sword: Whose graves are set in the sides of the pit, and her company is round about her grave: all of them slain, fallen by the sword, which caused terror in the land of the living. (Ezekiel 32:22-23)

Judgment on Asshur (22-23): Asshur is Assyria and was dealt with by Ezekiel in chapter 31. They are to be slain and fallen by the sword and placed in graves in the pit.

There is Elam and all her multitude round about her grave, all of them slain, fallen by the sword, which are gone down uncircumcised into the nether parts of the earth, which caused their terror in the land of

the living; yet have they borne their shame with them that go down to the pit. They have set her a bed in the midst of the slain with all her multitude: her graves are round about him: all of them uncircumcised, slain by the sword: though their terror was caused in the land of the living, yet have they borne their shame with them that go down to the pit: he is put in the midst of them that be slain. (Ezekiel 32:24-25)

Judgment on Elam (24-25): **Elam** is located in the southwest corner of Iraq. Its judgment is to be slain by the sword and cast into the nether parts of the earth, the pit.

There is Meshech, Tubal, and all her multitude: her graves are round about him: all of them uncircumcised, slain by the sword, though they caused their terror in the land of the living. And they shall not lie with the mighty that are fallen of the uncircumcised, which are gone down to hell with their weapons of war: and they have laid their swords under their heads, but their iniquities shall be upon their bones, though they were the terror of the mighty in the land of the living. Yea, thou shalt be broken in the midst of the uncircumcised, and shalt lie with them that are slain with the sword. (Ezekiel 32:26-28)

Judgment on Meshech and Tubal (26-28): **Meshech and Tubal** are the allies of Gog (Ezekiel 38, 39). They are located in the most northern part of modern day Turkey. They will lie with the mighty that are fallen but will have a special place prepared for them in the pit.

There is Edom, her kings, and all her princes, which with their might are laid by them that were slain by the sword: they shall lie with the uncircumcised, and with them that go down to the pit. (Ezekiel 32:29)

Judgment on Edom (29): Edom or Idumea was located south of Judah and the Dead Sea. Their judgment is to be laid by them that were slain by the sword with them that go down to the pit.

There be the princes of the north, all of them, and all the Zidonians, which are gone down with the slain; with their terror they are ashamed of their might; and they lie uncircumcised with them that be slain by the sword, and bear their shame with them that go down to the pit. (Ezekiel 32:30)

Judgment on the Zidonians (30): People of Zidon located south of Tyrus along the Mediterranean Sea in the land of modern day Lebanon. Their fate also mentioned in Ezekiel 28:21-28, is the same as those that are slain.

Pharaoh shall see them, and shall be comforted over all his multitude, even Pharaoh and all his army slain by the sword, saith the Lord GOD. For I have caused my terror in the land of the living: and he shall be laid in the midst of the uncircumcised with them that are slain with the sword, even Pharaoh and all his multitude, saith the Lord GOD. (Ezekiel 32:31-32)

God's Terror in the Land of the Living (31-32): God's judgment is against Pharaoh: and all his multitude are to be slain with all the uncircumcised, slain by the sword and condemned to the pit.

—————•—————

THE FUTURE RESTORATION
OF THE JEWS
Given After the Siege of Jerusalem

CHAPTER 33
The Watchman of Israel

Ezekiel was originally called to be a watchman to the nation (Ezekiel 3:17). He was called to warn his people of the coming judgments from God; if they harkened unto the words of the LORD and turn back to God, they would live and if not they would die. Unlike the false prophets in the land prophesying peace (Ezekiel 13:16), Ezekiel told his people the truth and proved to be a faithful watchman in Israel.

Israel continued however in their rebellious ways not obeying the words of the prophet; therefore the armies of Nebuchadnezzar have besieged the city walls, the land is become desolate and all of its inhabitants are being carried into Babylonian captivity.

However this is not the end of God's people: what they were unable to do in their flesh God will accomplish by His Spirit. What remains in the upcoming chapters is the restoration and exaltation of Israel.

Again the word of the LORD came unto me, saying, Son of man, speak to the children of thy people, and say unto them, When I bring the sword upon a land, if the people of the land take a man of their coasts, and set him for their watchman: If when he seeth the sword come upon the land, he blow the trumpet, and warn the people; Then whosoever heareth the sound

of the trumpet, and taketh not warning; if the sword come, and take him away, his blood shall be upon his own head. He heard the sound of the trumpet, and took not warning; his blood shall be upon him. But he that taketh warning shall deliver his soul. But if the watchman see the sword come, and blow not the trumpet, and the people be not warned; if the sword come, and take any person from among them, he is taken away in his iniquity; but his blood will I require at the watchman's hand. (Ezekiel 33:1-6)

The Roll of the Watchman (1-6): In these verses God revisits Ezekiel's original calling, his ministry as the watchman of Israel (Ezekiel 3:17). The roll of a watchman is described in these verses; he was to warn the people of invading armies by blowing the trumpet to warn the people. The watchman was called to be faithful in fulfilling this roll; he was not accountable for the response of the people. If the people hearken to the warning of the watchman they will live. However, if they hearken not unto the watchman they will die. Israel did not listen to their watchman; now death has come upon them.

So thou, O son of man, I have set thee a watchman unto the house of Israel; therefore thou shalt hear the word at my mouth, and warn them from me. When I say unto the wicked, O wicked man, thou shalt surely die; if thou dost not speak to warn the wicked from his way, that wicked man shall die in his iniquity; but his blood will I require at thine hand. Nevertheless, if thou warn the wicked of his way to turn from it; if he do not turn from his way, he shall die in his iniquity; but thou hast delivered thy soul. Therefore, O thou son of man, speak unto the house of Israel; Thus ye speak, saying, If our transgressions and our sins be upon us, and we pine away in them, how should we then live? Say unto them, As I live, saith the Lord GOD, I have no pleasure in the death of the wicked; but that the wicked turn from his way and live: turn ye, turn ye from your evil ways; for why will ye die, O house of Israel? Therefore, thou son of man, say unto the children of thy people, The righteousness of the righteous shall not deliver him in the day of his transgression: as for the wickedness of the wicked, he shall not fall thereby in the day that he turneth from his wickedness; neither shall the righteous be able to live for his righteousness in the day that he sinneth. When I shall say to the righteous, that he shall surely live; if he trust to his own righteousness, and commit iniquity, all his righteousnesses shall not be remembered; but for his iniquity that he hath committed, he shall die for it. Again, when I say unto the wicked, Thou shalt surely die; if he turn from his sin, and do that which is lawful and right; If the wicked restore the pledge, give again that he had robbed, walk in the statutes of life, without committing iniquity; he shall surely live, he shall not die. None of his sins that he hath committed shall be mentioned unto him: he hath done that which is lawful and right; he shall surely live. Yet the children of thy people say, The way of the Lord is not equal: but as for them, their way is not equal. When the righteous turneth from his righteousness, and committeth iniquity, he shall even die thereby. But if the wicked turn from his wickedness, and do that which is lawful and right, he shall live thereby. (Ezekiel 33:7-19)

Life and Death set before the Nation (7-19): When God originally called forth His nation out of Egypt He set before them His Law; this Law, if obeyed would grant them life; they would be blessed in all their life (Deut. 28:1-14). However, if they chose not to hearken unto the commandments of the LORD, curses would follow; they would die (Deut. 28:15-68). All this was the covenant relationship that the nation of Israel had with the LORD. As Moses summarizes this idea he states, *"I call heaven and earth to record this day against you, that I have set before you life and death, blessing and cursing: therefore choose life, that both thou and thy seed may live" (Deuteronomy 30:19)*

Israel's dismal history is one of disobedience to the commandments of God. From the top of Mount Sinai, God told Israel they would be accountable for holding up their end of the covenant relationship between them (Exodus 19:1-8). Thus, God laid out the consequences for not obeying the commandments of their God (Lev. 26:14-39). Israel at the time of Ezekiel had not harkened unto the voice of God throughout their long miserable history which had now reached its end: the Babylonian Captivity and the pining away in the land of their enemies (Lev. 26:39 cf. Ezek. 33:10). Israel had merited all the curses of the Law; they chose death.

Yet ye say, The way of the Lord is not equal. O ye house of Israel, I will judge you every one after his ways. And it came to pass in the twelfth year of our captivity, in the tenth month, in the fifth day of the month, that one that had escaped out of Jerusalem came unto me, saying, The city is smitten. Now the hand of the LORD was upon me in the evening, afore he that was escaped came; and had opened my mouth, until he came to me in the morning; and my mouth was opened, and I was no more dumb. (Ezekiel 33:20-22)

Ezekiel's Dumb Status Removed (20-22): At the call of Ezekiel's ministry God had stricken him dumb, only speaking when prophesying for the LORD (Ezekiel 3:26, 27). This non-speaking state would remain until a person comes from the destruction of the city announcing the city is fallen (Ezekiel 24:27); this prophecy is now fulfilled (Ezekiel 33:21, 22).

Then the word of the LORD came unto me, saying, Son of man, they that inhabit those wastes of the land of Israel speak, saying, Abraham was one, and he inherited the land: but we are many; the land is given us for inheritance. Wherefore say unto them, Thus saith the Lord GOD; Ye eat with the blood, and lift up your eyes toward your idols, and shed blood: and shall ye possess the land? Ye stand upon your sword, ye work abomination, and ye defile every one his neighbour's wife: and shall ye possess the land? Say thou thus unto them, Thus saith the Lord GOD; As I live, surely they that are in the wastes shall fall by the sword, and him that is in the open field will I give to the beasts to be devoured, and they that be in the forts and in the caves shall die of the pestilence. For I will lay the land most desolate, and the pomp of her strength shall cease; and the mountains of Israel shall be desolate, that none shall pass through. Then shall they know that I am the LORD, when I have laid the land most desolate because of all their abominations which they have committed. Also, thou son of man, the children of thy people still are talking against thee by the walls and in the doors of the houses, and speak one to another, every one to his brother, saying, Come, I pray you, and hear what is the word that cometh forth from the LORD. And they come unto thee as the people cometh, and they sit before thee as my people, and they hear thy words, but they will not do them: for with their mouth they shew much love, but their heart goeth after their covetousness. And, lo, thou art unto them as a very lovely song of one that hath a pleasant voice, and can play well on an instrument: for they hear thy words, but they do them not. And when this cometh to pass, (lo, it will come,) then shall they know that a prophet hath been among them. (Ezekiel 33:23-33)

God's Message from Ezekiel was not Harkened unto (23-33): The people had not recognized all their ungodly disobedience, for they say "the land is given us for inheritance" (vs. 24). However, there was a great deal of difference between Abraham and the apostate nation. Abraham believed God and it was counted to him for righteousness; they however, did not obey God, and therefore they will not possess the land (vs. 25). Ezekiel was unto them as a man that sings a song unto them, a man with entertaining words; they listen and walk away unchanged (vss. 30-33).

CHAPTER 34
The Shepherds of Israel

God through Ezekiel now prophesies against the shepherds of Israel, the apostate leadership of the nation; and looks out to the day in which the LORD will bring His flock into safe pastures of the Millennial Kingdom.

And the word of the LORD came unto me, saying, Son of man, prophesy against the shepherds of Israel, prophesy, and say unto them, Thus saith the Lord GOD unto the shepherds; Woe be to the shepherds of Israel that do feed themselves! should not the shepherds feed the flocks? Ye eat the fat, and ye clothe you with the wool, ye kill them that are fed: but ye feed not the flock. The diseased have ye not strengthened, neither have ye healed that which was sick, neither have ye bound up that which was broken, neither have ye brought again that which was driven away, neither have ye sought that which was lost; but with force and with cruelty have ye ruled them. And they were scattered, because there is no shepherd: and they became meat to all the beasts of the field, when they were scattered. My sheep wandered through all the mountains, and upon every high hill: yea, my flock was scattered upon all the face of the earth, and none did search or seek after them. Therefore, ye shepherds, hear the word of the LORD; As I live, saith the Lord GOD, surely because my flock became a prey, and my flock became meat to every beast of the field, because there was no

shepherd, neither did my shepherds search for my flock, but the shepherds fed themselves, and fed not my flock; Therefore, O ye shepherds, hear the word of the LORD; Thus saith the Lord GOD; Behold, I am against the shepherds; and I will require my flock at their hand, and cause them to cease from feeding the flock; neither shall the shepherds feed themselves any more; for I will deliver my flock from their mouth, that they may not be meat for them. (Ezekiel 34:1-10)

Prophecy Against the Shepherds of Israel (1-10): Ezekiel is called to prophesy against the Shepherds of Israel, the kings and rulers both spiritual and otherwise. Apart from a ray of light most of the ruling kings over Israel and Judah were corrupt. They ceased to feed the people both physically and spiritually (*Notice what happens when King Josiah finds the book of the Law - 2 Chron. 34:14-33*). The rulership of all the house of Israel allowed the people to be devoured by the invading armies and be scattered among them. They were scattered because there was no shepherd to watch over them and care for them (vss. 3-6). Therefore God is going to cause the shepherds of Israel to cease feeding His flock (vs. 10 - Zedekiah is the last king – II Kings 24:17). This however is not to be the end of the rulers forever, for God states in the following verses that He will take the flock from the shepherds and place another shepherd over them, even David His servant (vss. 23-24).

This passage of Scripture not only deals with the kings that ruled over the nation but also deals with another group of shepherds that ruled over the nation, spiritually. Upon the return of the remnant under Ezra and Nehemiah, another ruling class emerged: the Pharisees, scribes and Sadducees. These religious leaders gained their strength in the time of the Maccabees during the inter-testament years; so that at the opening of the New Testament era they were fully entrenched in the leadership of the nation. One needs only to read over Matthew 23 to see the problems with these apostate spiritual leaders that were called to feed the people the Word of God. Thus, chapter 34 of Ezekiel gives us prophecy as to our Lord's ministry as the great Shepherd of Israel and in verses 20-22 we see these religious leaders for who they are, the bulls of Bashan (Ps. 22:12). John chapter 10:1-18 deals with this issue extensively. Our Lord came to do the very thing of which Ezekiel; He came to seek and save that which was lost (Luke 19:10), and to take from the apostate shepherds the flock of the house of Israel (Matt. 21:43, 19:28, Luke 19:10).

Lastly, this passage of Scripture also deals with an individual known as the idol shepherd that will scatter the nation. The antichrist is known as the idol shepherd (Zech. 11:15-17) that seeks to devour the sheep of the house of Israel. When the idol shepherd comes into the land to annihilate the nation of Israel, a Remnant will be scattered throughout the land. The LORD will then return to destroy all Israel's foes and gather together all the lost sheep of the house of Israel in the "cloudy and dark day" (Tribulation), and place them safely back into the land (vss. 12-16).

As a shepherd seeketh out his flock in the day that he is among his sheep that are scattered; so will I seek out my sheep, and will deliver them out of all places where they have been scattered in the cloudy and dark day. And I will bring them out from the people, and gather them from the countries, and will bring them

to their own land, and feed them upon the mountains of Israel by the rivers, and in all the inhabited places of the country. I will feed them in a good pasture, and upon the high mountains of Israel shall their fold be: there shall they lie in a good fold, and in a fat pasture shall they feed upon the mountains of Israel. I will feed my flock, and I will cause them to lie down, saith the Lord GOD. I will seek that which was lost, and bring again that which was driven away, and will bind up that which was broken, and will strengthen that which was sick: but I will destroy the fat and the strong; I will feed them with judgment. And as for you, O my flock, thus saith the Lord GOD; Behold, I judge between cattle and cattle, between the rams and the he goats. Seemeth it a small thing unto you to have eaten up the good pasture, but ye must tread down with your feet the residue of your pastures? and to have drunk of the deep waters, but ye must foul the residue with your feet? And as for my flock, they eat that which ye have trodden with your feet; and they drink that which ye have fouled with your feet. Therefore thus saith the Lord GOD unto them; Behold, I, even I, will judge between the fat cattle and between the lean cattle. Because ye have thrust with side and with shoulder, and pushed all the diseased with your horns, till ye have scattered them abroad; Therefore will I save my flock, and they shall no more be a prey; and I will judge between cattle and cattle. And I will set up one shepherd over them, and he shall feed them, even my servant David; he shall feed them, and he shall be their shepherd. And I the LORD will be their God, and my servant David a prince among them; I the LORD have spoken it. And I will make with them a covenant of peace, and will cause the evil beasts to cease out of the land: and they shall dwell safely in the wilderness, and sleep in the woods. And I will make them and the places round about my hill a blessing; and I will cause the shower to come down in his season; there shall be showers of blessing. And the tree of the field shall yield her fruit, and the earth shall yield her increase, and they shall be safe in their land, and shall know that I am the LORD, when I have broken the bands of their yoke, and delivered them out of the hand of those that served themselves of them. And they shall no more be a prey to the heathen, neither shall the beast of the land devour them; but they shall dwell safely, and none shall make them afraid. And I will raise up for them a plant of renown, and they shall be no more consumed with hunger in the land, neither bear the shame of the heathen any more. Thus shall they know that I the LORD their God am with them, and that they, even the house of Israel, are my people, saith the Lord GOD. And ye my flock, the flock of my pasture, are men, and I am your God, saith the Lord GOD. (Ezekiel 34:12-31)

The Promise of a New Shepherd Over God's Sheep (12-31): What the LORD begins in the Gospel accounts He will accomplish in the "cloudy and dark day" of the Tribulation period. When the LORD, the true Shepherd of Israel (John 10: 1-18) arrived on earth He began to call out His sheep (Matt. 10:6; 15:24; Luke 15:1-10). However what ended in Israel's rejection of the Kingdom and the ushering in of the Dispensation of Grace will find completion in the Tribulation period when the LORD, the great Shepherd of Israel comes back to gather His sheep. He will guide His sheep through the Tribulation period and lead them to feed in safe pastures of the future Kingdom (Ezekiel 34:11-14 cf. Psalm 23). Once the sheep of Israel are safely in the land of rest, the LORD will place

David as their shepherd over the flock of GOD, and the curses that they had merited for not holding to the law contract will be forever lifted (Ezekiel 34:25-31 cf. Deut. 28) dwelling in their land and having access to the house of the LORD forever (Psalm 23 cf. Ezekiel 23-31).

CHAPTER 35

Desolation of Edom

Mount Seir is the main mountain in Edom. Idumea is the Greek word for Edom (vs. 15; 36:5); with Bozrah as Edom's capital city. Edomites are the descendants of Esau (Genesis 25:30; 32:3; 36:1). Edom has a history of opposing the nation of Israel as well as being one of 10 nations that confederate against Israel in the future (Psalm 83:6). Edom will be judged for their hatred for God's people both historically and in the future day: **Because thou hast had a perpetual hatred, and hast shed the blood of the children of Israel by the force of the sword in the time of their calamity, in the time that their iniquity had an end: (Ezekiel 35:5).**
Therefore thus saith the Lord GOD; Surely in the fire of my jealousy have I spoken against the residue of the heathen, and against all Idumea, which have appointed my land into their possession with the joy of all their heart, with despiteful minds, to cast it out for a prey. (Ezekiel 36:5)

In that day when the LORD will come and deliver Israel, He will exercise a great battle in the land of Edom: **Who is this that cometh from Edom, with dyed garments from Bozrah? this that is glorious in his apparel, travelling in the greatness of his strength? I that speak in righteousness, mighty to save. (Isaiah 63:1)**
Thus saith the LORD; For three transgressions of Edom, and for four, I will not turn away the punishment thereof; because he did pursue his brother with the

sword, and did cast off all pity, and his anger did tear perpetually, and he kept his wrath for ever: But I will send a fire upon Teman, which shall devour the palaces of Bozrah. (Amos 1:11-12) (See all of Obadiah, Malachi 1:1-4).

In these chapters we see the prophetic end of Edom. In the past, Edom gloried in the destruction of Israel and in the future they will do the same. However, God will make it so they will be the ones desolate, and Israel will be the blessed in the land (see 36:6-11). In these chapters one needs to contrast these two peoples; Edom and its end (chapter 35) and Israel and its end (36:16-38).

Moreover the word of the LORD came unto me, saying, Son of man, set thy face against mount Seir, and prophesy against it, And say unto it, Thus saith the Lord GOD; Behold, O mount Seir, I am against thee, and I will stretch out mine hand against thee, and I will make thee most desolate. I will lay thy cities waste, and thou shalt be desolate, and thou shalt know that I am the LORD. Because thou hast had a perpetual hatred, and hast shed the blood of the children of Israel by the force of the sword in the time of their calamity, in the time that their iniquity had an end: Therefore, as I live, saith the Lord GOD, I will prepare thee unto blood, and blood shall pursue thee: sith thou hast not hated blood, even blood shall pursue thee. Thus will I make mount Seir most desolate, and cut off from it him that passeth out and him that returneth. And I will fill his mountains with his slain men: in thy hills, and in thy valleys, and in all thy rivers, shall they fall that are slain with the sword. I will make thee perpetual desolations, and thy cities shall not return: and ye shall know that I am the LORD. Because thou hast said, These two nations and these two countries shall be mine, and we will possess it; whereas the LORD was there: Therefore, as I live, saith the Lord GOD, I will even do according to thine anger, and according to thine envy which thou hast used out of thy hatred against them; and I will make myself known among them, when I have judged thee. And thou shalt know that I am the LORD, and that I have heard all thy blasphemies which thou hast spoken against the mountains of Israel, saying, They are laid desolate, they are given us to consume. Thus with your mouth ye have boasted against me, and have multiplied your words against me: I have heard them. Thus saith the Lord GOD; When the whole earth rejoiceth, I will make thee desolate. As thou didst rejoice at the inheritance of the house of Israel, because it was desolate, so will I do unto thee: thou shalt be desolate, O mount Seir, and all Idumea, even all of it: and they shall know that I am the LORD. (Ezekiel 35:1-15)

The Desolation of Edom (1-15): This chapter deals entirely with the desolation of Edom. The LORD will tell why it is that they are going to be judged by Him. The very thing Edom sought for themselves, the nation of Israel will receive; while the judgment they sought on Israel, Edom will receive.

The reasons for the Destruction and Desolation of Edom are:

1. Edom had a *perpetual hatred* for the children of Israel (vs. 5)
    a. Therefore God will make of Edom a *perpetual desolation* (vss. 6-9)

211

2. Edom desired the two nations of Israel and these two countries (vs. 10)
3. Edom boasted in the *desolation* of the mountains of Israel (vs. 12)
   a. Therefore God will make Edom *desolate* (vs. 14-15)

Notice the LORD in these passages is doing to Edom the very thing it sought against Israel; where Edom had a perpetual hatred, God will bring them to perpetual desolation, where Edom boasted in the desolation of Israel, God will bring Edom to desolation.

CHAPTER 36
The Restoration of Israel

The Restoration of Israel and its Land: Edom's actions have provoked the fire of God's jealousy (5, 6). He will do for Israel and the land all the things Edom sought for itself. Throughout these next chapters we need to pay close attention that it is the LORD doing this for Israel. He will not be using the nations to perform His will as He had done against Israel, but rather will deliver the judgments Himself as He established His Theocratic Kingdom on the earth. In the first portion of this chapter (vss. 1-15) the LORD prophesies against the **"mountains of Israel"** (vs. 1), concerning the literal landscape of Israel (see vs. 4). In the latter portion (16-38) of this chapter God will speak concerning the house of Israel (vs. 22).

Also, thou son of man, prophesy unto the mountains of Israel, and say, Ye mountains of Israel, hear the word of the LORD: Thus saith the Lord GOD; Because the enemy hath said against you, Aha, even the ancient high places are ours in possession: Therefore prophesy and say, Thus saith the Lord GOD; Because they have made you desolate, and swallowed you up on every side, that ye might be a possession unto the residue of the heathen, and ye are taken up in the lips of talkers, and are an infamy of the people: Therefore, ye mountains of Israel, hear the word of the Lord GOD; Thus saith the Lord GOD to the mountains, and to the hills, to the rivers, and to the valleys, to the desolate wastes, and to the cities that are forsaken, which became a prey and derision to the residue of the heathen that are round about; Therefore thus saith the Lord GOD; Surely in the fire of my jealousy have I spoken against the residue of the heathen, and against all Idumea, which have appointed my land into their possession with the joy of all their heart, with despiteful minds, to cast it out for a prey. Prophesy therefore concerning the land of Israel, and say unto the mountains, and to the hills, to the rivers, and to the valleys, Thus saith the Lord GOD; Behold, I have spoken in my jealousy and in my fury, because ye have borne the shame of the heathen: Therefore thus saith the Lord GOD; I have lifted up mine hand, Surely the heathen that are about you, they shall bear their shame. (Ezekiel 36:1-7)

The Desolate Land (1-7): In these verses we see what the land of Israel had become under the hand of the heathen nations around them: **Therefore prophesy and say, Thus saith the Lord GOD; Because they have made you desolate, and swallowed you up on every side, that ye might be a possession unto the residue of the heathen, and ye are taken up in the lips of talkers, and are an infamy of the people: (Ezekiel 36:3)**

Not only had the *people* suffered tremendously under the hand of the heathen nations, but the *land* suffered greatly. Therefore the fire of God's jealously will be kindled against the heathen nations that have been instrumental in bringing about the destruction and desolation of the land and its people. Of the heathen nations that God is going to judge it is Edom that is specifically mentioned (vs. 5). Edom or Idumea has done, and will in the future do, what verse 5 is referencing: **Therefore thus saith the Lord GOD; Surely in the fire of my jealousy have I spoken against the residue of the heathen, and against all Idumea, which have appointed my land into their** possession with the joy of all their heart, with despiteful minds, to cast it out for a prey. (Ezekiel 36:5)

And because of this God will judge them accordingly: **Therefore thus saith the Lord GOD; I have lifted up mine hand, Surely the heathen that are about you, they shall bear their shame. (Ezekiel 36:7)**

But ye, O mountains of Israel, ye shall shoot forth your branches, and yield your fruit to my people of Israel; for they are at hand to come. For, behold, I am for you, and I will turn unto you, and ye shall be tilled and sown: And I will multiply men upon you, all the house of Israel, even all of it: and the cities shall be inhabited, and the wastes shall be builded: And I will multiply upon you man and beast; and they shall increase and bring fruit: and I will settle you after your old estates, and will do better unto you than at your beginnings: and ye shall know that I am the LORD. Yea, I will cause men to walk upon you, even my people Israel; and they shall possess thee, and thou shalt be their inheritance, and thou shalt no more henceforth bereave them of men. Thus saith the Lord GOD; Because they say unto you, Thou land devourest up men, and hast bereaved thy nations; Therefore thou shalt devour men no more, neither bereave thy nations any more, saith the Lord GOD. Neither will I cause men to hear in thee the shame of the heathen any more, neither shalt thou bear the reproach of the people any more, neither shalt thou cause thy nations to fall any more, saith the Lord GOD. (Ezekiel 36:8-15)

Restoration of the Land (8-15): In these verses the land takes on a personage. The Scriptures do this often *(See*

215

Isaiah 62:4 – Beulah). There is a union between the God of Israel and the land itself, and in these verses we see the restoration of the landscape of God's land. As God says in a host of other passages He will make the place of His feet glorious: **The glory of Lebanon shall come unto thee, the fir tree, the pine tree, and the box together, to beautify the place of my sanctuary; and I will make the place of my feet glorious. (Isaiah 60:13)**

The LORD will "turn" unto the land of Israel and accomplish some of the following:
- Ye shall be tilled and sown (vs. 9)
- The land will be inhabited with the men of Israel, with cities (vs. 10)
- Man and beast will multiply upon the land (vs. 11)
- The land will be more blessed than at their beginning (vs. 11)
- Israel will be the land's inheritance (vs. 12)
- The land will not bear the reproach of the nation any longer (13-15)

Just as God promises to beautify the land of Israel that it be no more the wasted among the nations, so He will restore the nation of Israel one day.

Moreover the word of the LORD came unto me, saying, Son of man, when the house of Israel dwelt in their own land, they defiled it by their own way and by their doings: their way was before me as the uncleanness of a removed woman. Wherefore I poured my fury upon them for the blood that they had shed upon the land, and for their idols wherewith they had polluted it: And I scattered them among the heathen, and they

were dispersed through the countries: according to their way and according to their doings I judged them. And when they entered unto the heathen, whither they went, they profaned my holy name, when they said to them, These are the people of the LORD, and are gone forth out of his land. (Ezekiel 36:16-20)

Israel was Scattered out of the Land (16-20): According to the covenant made with God's nation, they had committed all the abominations of the heathen nations in the land and it "spued" them out of the land: **That the land spue not you out also, when ye defile it, as it spued out the nations that were before you. (Leviticus 18:28)**
Ye shall therefore keep all my statutes, and all my judgments, and do them: that the land, whither I bring you to dwell therein, spue you not out. (Leviticus 20:22)

Thus, the nation had found themselves, and will continue to find them, in a scattered and dispersed state until the LORD gathers them back into His land. How the LORD is to accomplish this is found in the proceeding verses.

But I had pity for mine holy name, which the house of Israel had profaned among the heathen, whither they went. Therefore say unto the house of Israel, Thus saith the Lord GOD; I do not this for your sakes, O house of Israel, but for mine holy name's sake, which ye have profaned among the heathen, whither ye went. And I will sanctify my great name, which was profaned among the heathen, which ye have profaned in the midst of them; and the heathen shall know that I am the LORD, saith the Lord GOD, when I shall

be sanctified in you before their eyes. For I will take you from among the heathen, and gather you out of all countries, and will bring you into your own land. (Ezekiel 36:21-24)

For His Name's Sake (21-24): The LORD will accomplish the restoration of the land and the people of the land for HIS NAME'S SAKE. Through their abominations the nation had corrupted the name of the LORD by their actions. Therefore God will bring them back into the land by His name, to justify His name among the heathen nations. As is said throughout these verses He will "sanctify His great name" which they have profaned in the midst of the nations (22-23).

Then will I sprinkle clean water upon you, and ye shall be clean: from all your filthiness, and from all your idols, will I cleanse you. A new heart also will I give you, and a new spirit will I put within you: and I will take away the stony heart out of your flesh, and I will give you an heart of flesh. And I will put my spirit within you, and cause you to walk in my statutes, and ye shall keep my judgments, and do them. And ye shall dwell in the land that I gave to your fathers; and ye shall be my people, and I will be your God. I will also save you from all your uncleannesses: and I will call for the corn, and will increase it, and lay no famine upon you. And I will multiply the fruit of the tree, and the increase of the field, that ye shall receive no more reproach of famine among the heathen. Then shall ye remember your own evil ways, and your doings that were not good, and shall lothe yourselves in your own sight for your iniquities and for your abominations. Not for your sakes do I this, saith the Lord GOD, be it known unto you: be ashamed and confounded for your own ways, O house of Israel. Thus saith the Lord GOD; In the day that I shall have cleansed you from all your iniquities I will also cause you to dwell in the cities, and the wastes shall be builded. And the desolate land shall be tilled, whereas it lay desolate in the sight of all that passed by. And they shall say, This land that was desolate is become like the garden of Eden; and the waste and desolate and ruined cities are become fenced, and are inhabited. Then the heathen that are left round about you shall know that I the LORD build the ruined places, and plant that that was desolate: I the LORD have spoken it, and I will do it. Thus saith the Lord GOD; I will yet for this be inquired of by the house of Israel, to do it for them; I will increase them with men like a flock. As the holy flock, as the flock of Jerusalem in her solemn feasts; so shall the waste cities be filled with flocks of men: and they shall know that I am the LORD. (Ezekiel 36:25-38)

Cleansing of the Nation (25-38): Israel's restoration to the Promised Land has always been the subject of prophecy, as these verses point out. Before the nation can be placed into the land, a cleansing must first take place. The nation had become filthy from joining itself to all the abominations of the heathen. So in these verses we see the hinting at this cleansing of the nation that had to take place (25). Then the nation will have a new heart and Spirit given them (26). Once this transformation takes place Israel, as a nation, will be able to keep the law and be that "holy nation" they were called to be. (See Deut. 30:30; Jeremiah 31:31-34).

CHAPTER 37
Valley of Dry Bones

When it comes to understanding Scripture nothing should displace the clear statement of the Scriptures themselves. In this passage of Scripture Ezekiel is given the clear interpretation of both the Valley of Dry Bones and the Two Sticks so that no other interpretation needs to be applied.

The hand of the LORD was upon me, and carried me out in the spirit of the LORD, and set me down in the midst of the valley which was full of bones, And caused me to pass by them round about: and, behold, there were very many in the open valley; and, lo, they were very dry. And he said unto me, Son of man, can these bones live? And I answered, O Lord GOD, thou knowest. Again he said unto me, Prophesy upon these bones, and say unto them, O ye dry bones, hear the word of the LORD. Thus saith the Lord GOD unto these bones; Behold, I will cause breath to enter into you, and ye shall live: And I will lay sinews upon you, and will bring up flesh upon you, and cover you with skin, and put breath in you, and ye shall live; and ye shall know that I am the LORD. So I prophesied as I was commanded: and as I prophesied, there was a noise, and behold a shaking, and the bones came together, bone to his bone. And when I beheld, lo, the sinews and the flesh came up upon them, and the skin covered them above: but there was no breath in them. Then said he unto me, Prophesy unto the wind,

prophesy, son of man, and say to the wind, Thus saith the Lord GOD; Come from the four winds, O breath, and breathe upon these slain, that they may live. So I prophesied as he commanded me, and the breath came into them, and they lived, and stood up upon their feet, an exceeding great army. (Ezekiel 37:1-10)

The Valley of Dry Bones (1-10): Ezekiel is carried out in the spirit to a valley full of dried bones that come to life from the dead in a most vivid way. Ezekiel is told to prophesy from the LORD to the bones, thus through the prophet Ezekiel God tells these dried bones that He will do 3 things for them:

1. Gather the bones together
2. Cover them in sinew and flesh
3. Breath His Spirit into them

Then he said unto me, Son of man, these bones are the whole house of Israel: behold, they say, Our bones are dried, and our hope is lost: we are cut off for our parts. Therefore prophesy and say unto them, Thus saith the Lord GOD; Behold, O my people, I will open your graves, and cause you to come up out of your graves, and bring you into the land of Israel. And ye shall know that I am the LORD, when I have opened your graves, O my people, and brought you up out of your graves, And shall put my spirit in you, and ye shall live, and I shall place you in your own land: then shall ye know that I the LORD have spoken it, and performed it, saith the LORD. (Ezekiel 37:11-14)

The Interpretation of the Vision (11-14): The interpretation is given to Ezekiel as the "whole house of Israel" (vs. 11). The truth of this vision could not be any clearer, it is not the church, it is the "whole house of Israel."

There are a couple of things to take note of in the interpretation, first notice that it is clearly stated to be Israel. Israel is likened to ones coming back from the dead, the time when the LORD revives that nation once again. Paul uses this idea in Romans when dealing with the subject of the restoration of the nation of Israel: **For if the casting away of them be the reconciling of the world, what shall the receiving of them be, but life from the dead? (Romans 11:15)**

Secondly, notice the emphasis is placed on the "whole house" of Israel. In other words it is the restored northern and southern kingdoms into one nation. This is the purpose of the next illustration given with the two sticks; it is to elevate the truth that both houses of Israel, northern and southern will be one again.

So then God in this vision gives to Ezekiel the promise that He will take the whole house of Israel out of the graveyard of the nations and place them into their land one day and then He will breathe life into them that they may live.

The word of the LORD came again unto me, saying, Moreover, thou son of man, take thee one stick, and write upon it, For Judah, and for the children of Israel his companions: then take another stick, and write upon it, For Joseph, the stick of Ephraim, and for all the house of Israel his companions: And join them one to another into one stick; and they shall become one in thine hand. (Ezekiel 37:15-17)

Two Sticks Becoming One (15-17): What Ezekiel is told to do is directly related to the preceding vision of the Valley of Dry Bones; it is a continuation and addition to that vision. Ezekiel is told to take a stick and write upon it for Judah and for the children of Israel his companions. Then Ezekiel is to take another stick and write upon it for Joseph, the stick of Ephraim and for all the house of Israel his companions. So what you have is two sticks with the following names:

1. Judah – *for the children of Israel and his companions*
2. Joseph / Ephraim - *for all the house of Israel his companions.*

Then Ezekiel is told to join the two sticks into one stick.

And when the children of thy people shall speak unto thee, saying, Wilt thou not shew us what thou meanest by these? Say unto them, Thus saith the Lord GOD; Behold, I will take the stick of Joseph, which is in the hand of Ephraim, and the tribes of Israel his fellows, and will put them with him, even with the stick of Judah, and make them one stick, and they shall be one in mine hand. And the sticks whereon thou writest shall be in thine hand before their eyes. And say unto them, Thus saith the Lord GOD; Behold, I will take the children of Israel from among the heathen, whither they be gone, and will gather them on every side, and bring them into their own land: And I will make them one nation in the land upon the mountains of Israel; and one king shall be king to them all: and they shall be no more two nations, neither shall they be divided into two kingdoms any more at all: Neither shall they defile themselves any more with their idols, nor with their detestable things, nor with any of their transgressions: but I will save them out of all their

dwellingplaces, wherein they have sinned, and will cleanse them: so shall they be my people, and I will be their God. And David my servant shall be king over them; and they all shall have one shepherd: they shall also walk in my judgments, and observe my statutes, and do them. And they shall dwell in the land that I have given unto Jacob my servant, wherein your fathers have dwelt; and they shall dwell therein, even they, and their children, and their children's children for ever: and my servant David shall be their prince for ever. Moreover I will make a covenant of peace with them; it shall be an everlasting covenant with them: and I will place them, and multiply them, and will set my sanctuary in the midst of them for evermore. My tabernacle also shall be with them: yea, I will be their God, and they shall be my people. And the heathen shall know that I the LORD do sanctify Israel, when my sanctuary shall be in the midst of them for evermore. (Ezekiel 37:18-28)

Two Sticks Interpretation (18-28): The interpretation is fairly simple when taken into account with the preceding vision of the Valley of Dry Bones. The Valley of Dry Bones is the "whole house" of Israel, thus it is both the northern and southern kingdoms of the house of Israel. The illustration Ezekiel is given to perform is the reality that both kingdoms will be restored into one nation.

This is to be taken literally and not to be looked at as some figurative language used to represent the church or some other group, but is what it plainly states: **And I will make them one nation in the land upon the mountains of Israel; and one king shall be king to them all: and they shall be no more two nations, neither shall they be divided into two kingdoms any more at all: (Ezekiel 37:22)**

Summary: What we have in this chapter is the promise of God that the "whole nation" of Israel will be gathered together under one king in the land of Israel. David will be resurrected and will be placed as "prince" over the "whole nation". God in fulfillment of the New Covenant will make the nation spiritually fit to be God's people, serving in His tabernacle and functioning as the kingdom of priests to the rest of the nations (Isaiah 66:6-8; Rev. 12:1-5).

Gog and Magog Battle

Of all the chapters in the book of Ezekiel none offer more confusion than these two, thus we will comment on them together. The confusion is over **the identity of Gog of Magog** and **when this future battle takes place**. Of the two, the question of when this event takes place is the most important and most puzzling. Pick a commentary from the shelf and you will find authors placing this event in one of the three time periods:

1. At the mid-point of the Tribulation
2. At the end of the Tribulation, as the final battle before the Millennium
3. At the end of the Millennium

I bring this up to show you the confusion over this issue, and so that you will understand that while I believe one of these views has a stronger argument than the others; the others are not without some validity.

What the Scriptures Say Regarding Gog of Magog:
- Gog is a "chief prince":
  Son of man, set thy face against Gog, the land of Magog, the chief prince of Meshech and Tubal, and prophesy against him, And say, Thus saith the Lord GOD; Behold, I am against thee, O Gog, the chief prince of Meshech and Tubal: (Ezekiel 38:2-3)

  Therefore, thou son of man, prophesy against Gog, and say, Thus saith the Lord GOD; Behold, I am against thee, O Gog, the chief prince of Meshech and Tubal: (Ezekiel 39:1)

- Magog is a people group that occupy a land:
  Son of man, set thy face against Gog, <u>the land of Magog</u>, the chief prince of Meshech and Tubal, and prophesy against him, (Ezekiel 38:2)

  Gomer, and all his bands; the house of Togarmah of the north quarters, and all his bands: and <u>many people with thee</u>. (Ezekiel 38:6)

- Gog is one that the prophets have spoken of:
  Thus saith the Lord GOD; <u>Art thou he of whom I have spoken in old time by my servants the prophets of Israel,</u> which prophesied in those days many years that I would bring thee against them? (Ezekiel 38:17)
  This verse is often overlooked, for whomever this person is he is spoken of by the prophets of Israel.

- Gog comes from the north:
  Gomer, and all his bands; the house of Togarmah of the north quarters, and all his bands: and many people with thee. (Ezekiel 38:6)

  And I will turn thee back, and leave but the sixth part of thee, <u>and will cause thee to come up from the north parts</u>, and will bring thee upon the mountains of Israel: (Ezekiel 39:2)
  *Bibles have changed this to read "from the far north" (NIV) or "remote parts of the north" (NASB). This is done to support a Russian interpretation. I am not saying it is not in the location of Russia, however **I do not believe in changing the Bible to fit ideals.***

- Gog's army:
  The people involved in this army are listed in Ezekiel 38:1-6. Most of these people can be found in Genesis 10:1-2; they would consist of Gentile nations.

- Gog's battle:
  Ezekiel 38:15-16, 18-23
  <u>**And when the thousand years are expired,**</u> **Satan shall be loosed out of his prison, And shall go out to deceive the nations which are in the four quarters of the earth, Gog and Magog, to gather them together to battle: the number of whom is as the sand of the sea. (Revelation 20:7-8)**

  And they went up on the breadth of the earth, <u>and compassed the camp of the saints about, and the beloved city: and fire came down from God out of heaven, and devoured them.</u> (Revelation 20:9)
  This is not to say that this battle in Revelation is the same as Ezekiel; we are just looking at all verses mentioning Gog of Magog.

So then this is what the Bible has to say regarding the identity of Gog of Magog, and therefore one can easily see why there is so much confusion on the issue; not a lot is revealed. However if we try to understand *when* this battle takes place it might allow us to begin to speculate further on the identity of this individual.

When Does the Battle of Gog of Magog Take Place:
The Scriptures plainly state that this event takes place following the Millennial reign of Jesus Christ: **And when the thousand years are expired, Satan shall be**

loosed out of his prison, And shall go out to deceive the nations which are in the four quarters of the earth, Gog and Magog, to gather them together to battle: the number of whom is as the sand of the sea. And they went up on the breadth of the earth, and compassed the camp of the saints about, and the beloved city: and fire came down from God out of heaven, and devoured them. (Revelation 20:7-9)

Now if this is all the information we had on the issue there would be no confusion; or if all other information in Ezekiel lined up with this time period we would have no problems and all would be in agreement. However as we look at the details in Ezekiel 38 & 39 problems arise in placing both battles as one event transpiring at the end of the Millennium.

The Gog and Magog Event in Ezekiel 38 & 39 (Cf. Gen. 10:1, 2):
- Gog's great army is brought against the mountains of Israel (Ezekiel 38:1-9)
- Gog's evil thought (Ezekiel 10-17): The evil thought brought into the mind of Gog is to invade the land of Israel to take a spoil of the people and the land.
- Gog's Destruction (Ezekiel 38:19-23; 39:1-22): The wrath of the LORD God is poured out upon Gog and his armies which are depicted by climactic events on the earth:
  - Great shaking in the land of Israel (38:19, 20) *This is very depictive of the time our LORD comes back at the end of the Tribulation period (Isaiah 2:19, 21, 13:13; Joel 3:11-16).*
  - Rain, great hailstones, fire and brimstone (38:22)

This is associated with the Second Advent (Rev. 11:19, 16:21).

o The birds and beasts of the field shall devour the dead bodies of the armies of Gog (39:4, 17-20).
This is indicative of the Battle of Armageddon (Rev. 19:17, 18; Joel 3:9-16)

o Their weapons of war will be used as fuel for Israel for 7 years (39:9)

o A graveyard east of the Dead Sea will be the burying place for the armies of Gog, named Hamongog (Hordes of Gog - 39:11)

o Fulltime employment will be sought to bury the armies of Gog, it will take 7 months (39:14)

o Any passer-by that sees a bone of the bodies of Gog's armies is not to touch it but mark it so the men can come bury it (vs. 39:15)

The State of Israel at the Time of the Battle:

• It is a time after they are brought back into the land from the Gentile nations:

After many days thou shalt be visited: in the latter years <u>thou shalt come into the land that is brought back from the sword</u>, and is gathered out of many people, against the mountains of Israel, which have been always waste: but it is <u>brought forth out of the nations</u>, and they shall dwell safely all of them. (Ezekiel 38:8)

To take a spoil, and to take a prey; to turn thine hand upon the desolate places that are now inhabited, and <u>upon the people that are gathered out of the nations</u>, which have gotten cattle and goods, that dwell in the midst of the land. (Ezekiel 38:12)

We have looked at this before in previous chapters in Ezekiel and have noted that this gathering of the nation back into the land takes place sometime in the latter half of the Tribulation period, when Zion travails (Ezekiel 36:24; Isaiah 66:7, 8)

• It is a time when Israel dwells safely in the land and they are at rest:
And thou shalt say, <u>I will go up to the land of unwalled villages</u>; I will go to <u>them that are at rest, that dwell safely</u>, all of them <u>dwelling without walls, and having neither bars nor gates</u>, (Ezekiel 38:11)
This is an interesting verse for when Gog and his armies come up against the land of Israel she will be in a state of rest, dwelling safely. This would seem to point to the Millennial rest. However it could be following the signing of the peace treaty with the confederacy of the nations, during the first 3 ½ years; or it could be that once the nations are gathered back into the land at the end of the Tribulation they are at "rest" prior to the Battle of Armageddon.

• It is a time when Israel has much prosperity:
To take a spoil, and to take a prey; to turn thine hand upon the desolate places that are now inhabited, and upon the people that are gathered out of the nations, <u>which have gotten cattle and goods,</u> that dwell in the midst of the land. Sheba, and Dedan, and the merchants of Tarshish, with all the young lions thereof, shall say unto thee, Art thou come to take a spoil? hast thou gathered thy company to take a prey? <u>to carry away silver and gold, to take away cattle</u>

and goods, to take a great spoil? (Ezekiel 38:12-13)

This would seem to be indicative of the time once the Millennium period is established, once the riches of the Gentiles have been converted unto them (Isaiah 60).

Israel following the Battle:

- Israel will be gathered back into their land to dwell no more among the nations:

  Therefore thus saith the Lord GOD; Now will I bring again the captivity of Jacob, and have mercy upon the whole house of Israel, and will be jealous for my holy name; After that they have borne their shame, and all their trespasses whereby they have trespassed against me, when they dwelt safely in their land, and none made them afraid. When I have brought them again from the people, and gathered them out of their enemies' lands, and am sanctified in them in the sight of many nations; Then shall they know that I am the LORD their God, which caused them to be led into captivity among the heathen: but I have gathered them unto their own land, and have left none of them any more there. (Ezekiel 39:25-28)

  This gathering of the nation back into the land takes place sometime in the latter half of the Tribulation period, when Zion travails (Ezekiel 36:24; Isaiah 66:7, 8)

- Israel has the spirit of God poured out on them already:

  Neither will I hide my face any more from them: for I have poured out my spirit upon the house

of Israel, saith the Lord GOD. (Ezekiel 39:29)
Israel will be born in a day and part of this born issue is having His spirit pour out upon the nation which will happen at the latter half of the Tribulation period (Joel 2:28-31)

Summary

As we started out this section I mentioned that when it comes to understanding who Gog of Magog is and when this battle takes place there are scriptural arguments on several sides; there is therefore justifiable confusion on the issue. When interpreting Scripture we need to understand the difference between what the Scriptures clearly state from what is deduced or speculated. Where the Scriptures are concerned we need to be dogmatic, but what we deduce from Scripture would fall into the area of plausible reasoning, and therefore there will most likely be alternative views that are not without merit. So then the following are for you to ponder when you search out for yourselves the answers to Gog of Magog. And while there is much more evidence presented on each of the views listed below (either persuasive or not), I have tried to simplify them for clarity.

Identifying Gog of Magog:

The Russian Invasion

Most all prophecy teachers would hold to this viewpoint. It is true that Gog and his hoards come from the north (38:6, 15; 39:2). They are Gentile nations as is seen from Genesis 10:1-5, they are from Japheth. However, it should be kept in mind that to bolster this viewpoint they change Scripture; changing "chief prince" to "prince of Rosh" (NASB) and changing "north parts" or "north quarters" to "remote parts of the north" (NASB) or "far north" (NIV). Another problem is that Scripture tells us that this man is spoken about by all the prophets of Israel (Ezekiel 38:17). If this man is a Russian ruler that will rise, it would seem the Scriptures are silent on him.

The Vile Person of the North

Another understanding of the identity of Gog would be that there is a "vile person of the north" that is to come against Israel; he is the one told about in Daniel chapter 11 (11:21-45). He would be that Assyrian from the north (Joel 2:20 cf. Micah 5:5, 6 & Isaiah 10:5, 6 cf. Jer. 6:26, 27 & Zeph. 2:13). He would be the "Prince of the people" Daniel 9:25-27 and would be the "prince of the covenant" of Daniel 11:21-22. This would explain Ezekiel 38:17: *Thus saith the Lord GOD; Art thou he of whom I have spoken in old time by my servants the prophets of Israel, which prophesied in those days many years that I would bring thee against them?* There are many titles that the Antichrist holds in Scripture. Should we add the title "Gog"? However there are problems with this view as well, one of which is the fact Gog is destroyed at a time which seems to be before the Millennial reign of Christ, leaving a question in regard to Gog's return following the Millennium (Rev. 20:7-9).

The Time of the Gog Magog War:

Prior to the Millennium

The most plausible view is that the battle of Gog & Magog in Ezekiel 38 & 39 is a different event than the one described in Revelation 20:7-9. While not much information is given on the event in Revelation, it is perfectly clear the Gog and Magog event in Revelation happens following the 1,000 year reign of Christ. This is in contrast to the event described in chapters 38 & 39 of Ezekiel which seems to argue for post-Tribulation, pre-Millennium event.

The climactic events in the earth are very depictive of the time of the Second Advent (Ezekiel 38:29-20 cf. Isaiah 2:19, 21, 13:13; Joel 3:11-16 and the bulk of passages in Revelation).

The terms used concerning the judgment against Gog is similar to that of the Second Advent (Ezekiel 38:19 cf. Zeph. 1:18; 3:8).

The description of the destruction of Gog and his armies is reminiscent of Armageddon which transpires at the end of the Tribulation (Ezekiel 39:4, 17-20 cf. Rev. 19:17, 18; Joel 3:9-16).

Gog and his armies are buried in graveyards east of the Dead Sea (Ezekiel 39:11) which would not seem to fit the end of the Millennium in which Gog is burnt up by fire from God and then a New Heaven and Earth is established (Rev. 20:9; chapter 21).

CHAPTER 40

The Millennial Temple
MILLENNIAL TEMPLE COURT, THE OUTER COURT AND GATES

In the five and twentieth year of our captivity, in the beginning of the year, in the tenth day of the month, in the fourteenth year after that the city was smitten, in the selfsame day the hand of the LORD was upon me, and brought me thither. In the visions of God brought he me into the land of Israel, and set me upon a very high mountain, by which was as the frame of a city on the south. And he brought me thither, and, behold, there was a man, whose appearance was like the appearance of brass, with a line of flax in his hand, and a measuring reed; and he stood in the gate. And the man said unto me, Son of man, behold with thine eyes, and hear with thine ears, and set thine heart upon all that I shall shew thee; for to the intent that I might shew them unto thee art thou brought hither: declare all that thou seest to the house of Israel. And behold a wall on the outside of the house round about, and in the man's hand a measuring reed of six cubits long by the cubit and an hand breadth: so he measured the breadth of the building, one reed; and the height, one reed. (Ezekiel 40:1-5)

Ezekiel is Brought into the Future Millennial Temple (1-5): The remainder of these chapters covers Ezekiel's travels through the future Millennial Kingdom to come. Ezekiel is given a first-hand view of the Millennial Temple so he can declare what he sees to all the house of

THE MILLENNIAL TEMPLE

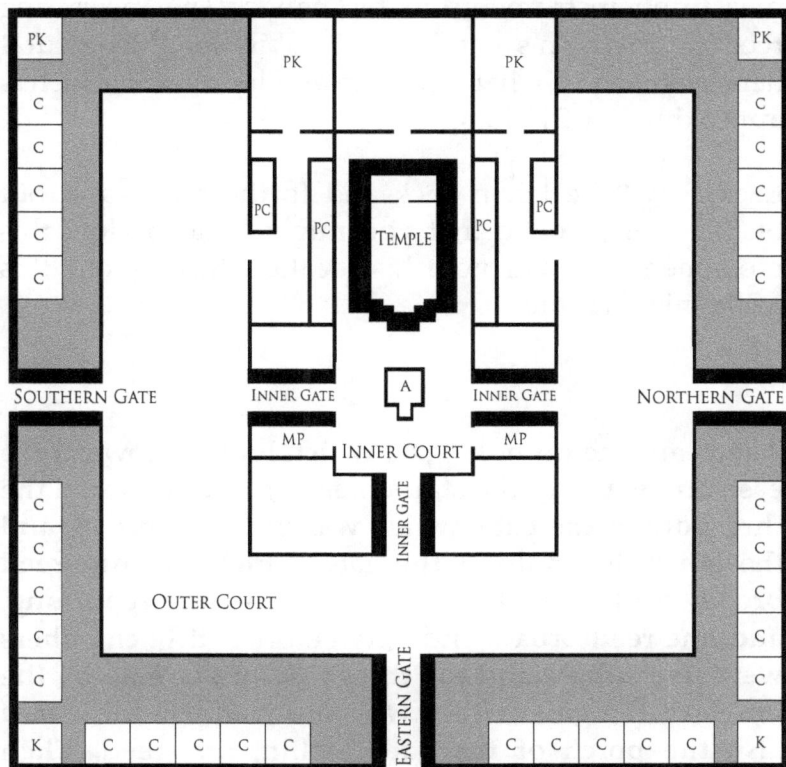

A	Altar	
C	Chambers (30 in the outer court)	
K	Kitchens for people's sacrifice	
PK	Priests' Kitchens	
PC	Priests' Chambers	
MP	Ministering Priest's Rooms	

Israel. Thus the closing chapters of the book of Ezekiel are meant to be an encouragement to the nation, who at this time is in captivity in the land of Babylon for their 25th year.

Ezekiel is brought also before a man whose appearance was like the appearance of brass, so obviously this is no ordinary man but rather an angel. This angel has measuring instruments in his hands. The measuring reed in this man's hand was 6 cubits long. The cubit here seems to be what is known as a long cubit which is approximately 21" long.

Ezekiel will be taken back and forth and in and out of this structure. So that you might better follow this movement we will note his location throughout this Millennial Temple.

Then came he unto the gate which looketh toward the east, and went up the stairs thereof, and measured the threshold of the gate, which was one reed broad; and the other threshold of the gate, which was one reed broad. And every little chamber was one reed long, and one reed broad; and between the little chambers were five cubits; and the threshold of the gate by the porch of the gate within was one reed. He measured also the porch of the gate within, one reed. Then measured he the porch of the gate, eight cubits; and the posts thereof, two cubits; and the porch of the gate was inward. And the little chambers of the gate eastward were three on this side, and three on that side; they three were of one measure: and the posts had one measure on this side and on that side. And he measured the breadth of the entry of the gate, ten cubits; and the length of the gate, thirteen cubits. The space also before the little chambers was one cubit on this side, and the space was one cubit on that side: and the little chambers were six cubits on this side, and six cubits on that side. He measured then the gate from the roof of one little chamber to the roof of another:

the breadth was five and twenty cubits, door against door. He made also posts of threescore cubits, even unto the post of the court round about the gate. And from the face of the gate of the entrance unto the face of the porch of the inner gate were fifty cubits. And there were narrow windows to the little chambers, and to their posts within the gate round about, and likewise to the arches: and windows were round about inward: and upon each post were palm trees. (Ezekiel 40:6-16)

Description of the Eastern Gate of the City (6-16): Ezekiel is taken to the Eastern Gate of the city. This gate

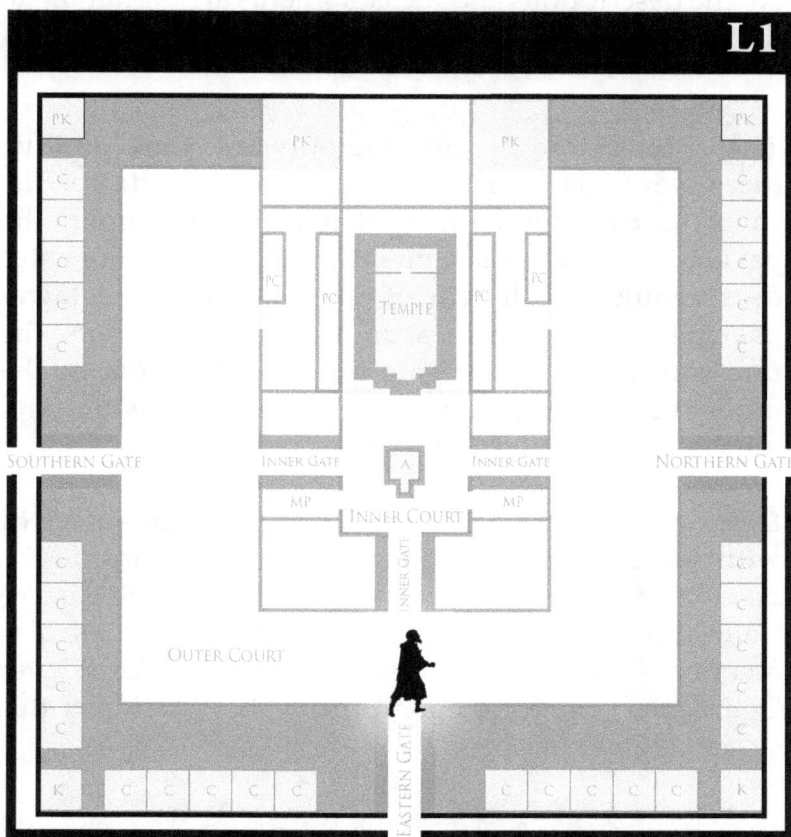

is famous in the Bible. Before the temple was destroyed, this was the most important gate of Jerusalem. This gate is the one that the glory of the LORD departed from in Ezekiel 10 & 11. This gate was also known as the "Golden Gate" and would give someone direct access to the Temple. Today, this gate in the city is sealed and a Muslim cemetery is before it. This was done by the Muslim conquerors to prevent the Messiah from coming through the gate. This is no doubt a reference to what Ezekiel will see in chapter 43 as the glory of the LORD returns through this very gate.

All the descriptions and measurements are pertaining to the Eastern Gate and its threshold area *(see map L1)*.

Then brought he me into the outward court, and, lo, there were chambers, and a pavement made for the court round about: thirty chambers were upon the pavement. And the pavement by the side of the gates over against the length of the gates was the lower pavement. Then he measured the breadth from the forefront of the lower gate unto the forefront of the inner court without, an hundred cubits eastward and northward. (Ezekiel 40:17-19)

Description of the Outward Court Pavement Area with its Chambers (17-19): Ezekiel is now inside the outer court area, giving measurements from the Eastern Gate he just went through unto the inner gate. He also mentions the 30 chambers *(see map L2)*. This Outer Court area is seven steps up from the exterior of this structure.

PK PK PK PK

C
C
C
C
C

PC PC TEMPLE PC PC

C
C
C
C
C

SOUTHERN GATE INNER GATE A INNER GATE NORTHERN GATE

MP INNER COURT MP

INNER GATE

C OUTER COURT C
C C
C C
C C
C C
K C C C C C EASTERN GATE C C C C C K

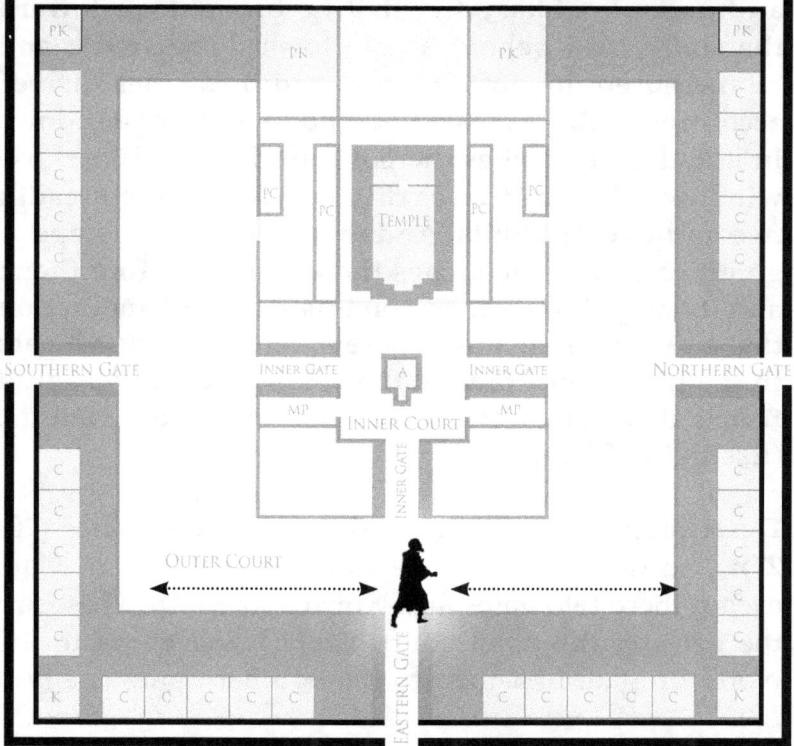

And the gate of the outward court that looked toward the north, he measured the length thereof, and the breadth thereof. And the little chambers thereof were three on this side and three on that side; and the posts thereof and the arches thereof were after the measure of the first gate: the length thereof was fifty cubits, and the breadth five and twenty cubits. And their windows, and their arches, and their palm trees, were after the measure of the gate that looketh toward the east; and they went up unto it by seven steps; and the arches thereof were before them. And the gate of the

241

inner court was over against the gate toward the north, and toward the east; and he measured from gate to gate an hundred cubits. After that he brought me toward the south, and behold a gate toward the south: and he measured the posts thereof and the arches thereof according to these measures. And there were windows in it and in the arches thereof round about, like those windows: the length was fifty cubits, and the breadth five and twenty cubits. And there were seven steps to go up to it, and the arches thereof were before them: and it had palm trees, one on this side, and another on that side, upon the posts thereof. And there was a gate in the inner court toward the south: and he measured from gate to gate toward the south an hundred cubits. (Ezekiel 40:20-27)

Description of the North and South Outer Gates (20-27): The description is the same as the Eastern Gate except these two gates face North and South. These are the gates to the outer court. Ezekiel will travel to the Northern gate first then to the Southern gate *(see map L3).*

And he brought me to the inner court by the south gate: and he measured the south gate according to these measures; And the little chambers thereof, and the posts thereof, and the arches thereof, according to these measures: and there were windows in it and in the arches thereof round about: it was fifty cubits long, and five and twenty cubits broad. And the arches round about were five and twenty cubits long, and five cubits broad. And the arches thereof were toward the utter court; and palm trees were upon the posts thereof: and the going up to it had eight steps. And he brought me

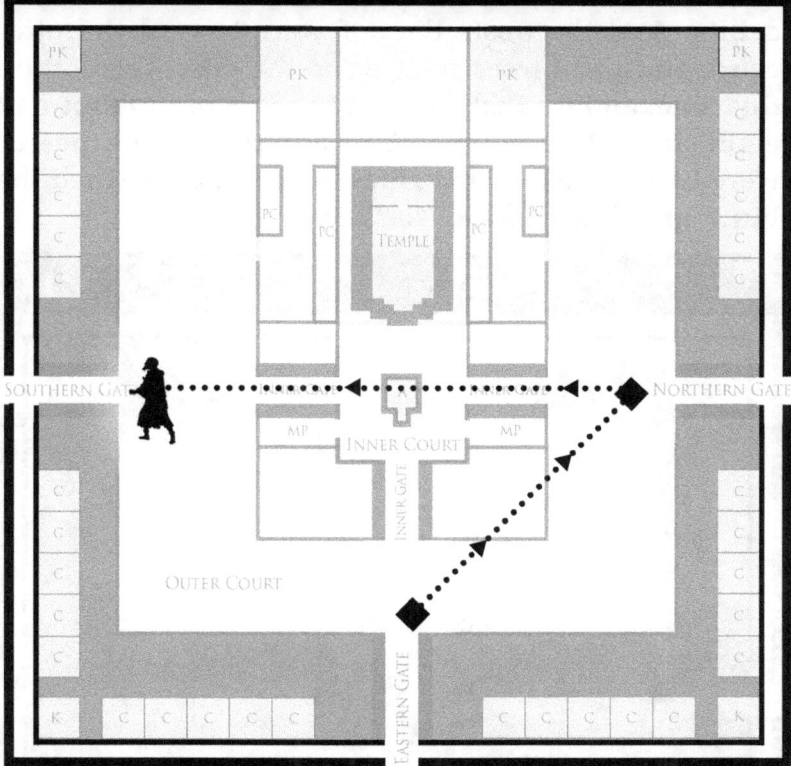

into the inner court toward the east: and he measured
the gate according to these measures. And the little
chambers thereof, and the posts thereof, and the arches
thereof, were according to these measures: and there
were windows therein and in the arches thereof round
about: it was fifty cubits long, and five and twenty
cubits broad. And the arches thereof were toward the
outward court; and palm trees were upon the posts
thereof, on this side, and on that side: and the going up
to it had eight steps. And he brought me to the north
gate, and measured it according to these measures;
The little chambers thereof, the posts thereof, and the

arches thereof, and the windows to it round about: the length was fifty cubits, and the breadth five and twenty cubits. And the posts thereof were toward the utter court; and palm trees were upon the posts thereof, on this side, and on that side: and the going up to it had eight steps. And the chambers and the entries thereof were by the posts of the gates, where they washed the burnt offering. (Ezekiel 40:28-38)

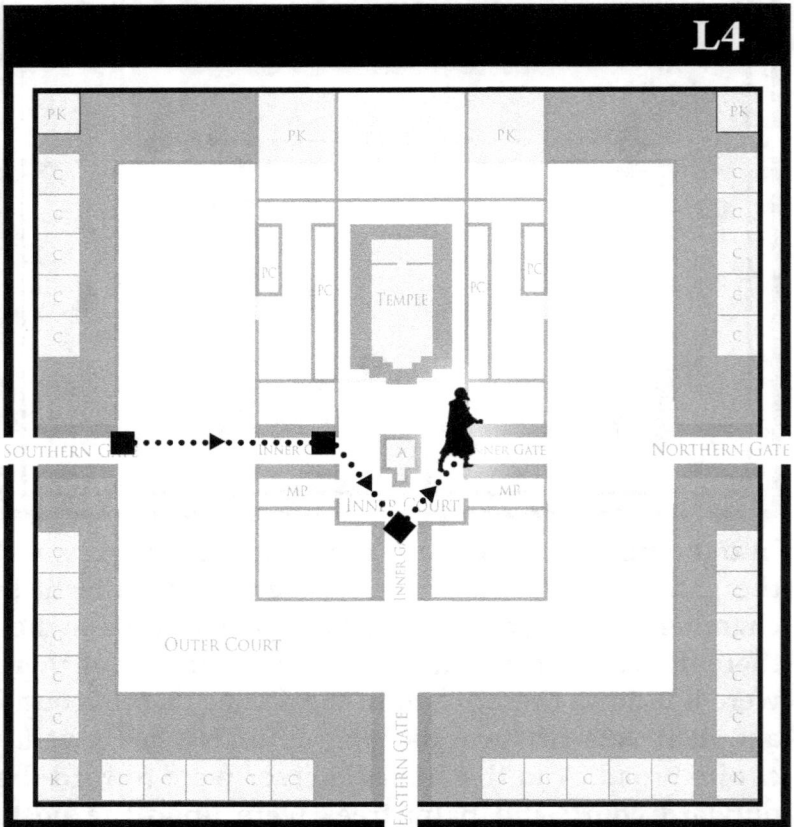

Description & Measurements of the South, East and Northern Gates of the Inner Court (28-38): Ezekiel moves from the Southern gate of the Outer Court to the Southern gate leading to the Inner Court, from here he will move to the Eastern gate of the Inner Court and then to the Northern gate of the Inner Court. The elevation from the Outer Court to the Inner Court is eight steps. At each gate Ezekiel will be given measurements of the things he sees *(see map L4)*.

And the chambers and the entries thereof were by the posts of the gates, where they washed the burnt offering. And in the porch of the gate were two tables on this side, and two tables on that side, to slay thereon the burnt offering and the sin offering and the trespass offering. And at the side without, as one goeth up to the entry of the north gate, were two tables; and on the other side, which was at the porch of the gate, were two tables. Four tables were on this side, and four tables on that side, by the side of the gate; eight tables, whereupon they slew their sacrifices. And the four tables were of hewn stone for the burnt offering, of a cubit and an half long, and a cubit and an half broad, and one cubit high: whereupon also they laid the instruments wherewith they slew the burnt offering and the sacrifice. And within were hooks, an hand broad, fastened round about: and upon the tables was the flesh of the offering. (Ezekiel 40:38-43)

Description of the Tables for Preparation of the Sacrifices (38-43): The room in the Inner Court gateway was used in connection with the sacrifices offered at the brazen altar before the Temple. The tables being described are before the entry of the North Gate of the Inner Court on either side, four tables on either side *(see map L5)*. These would have been memorial sacrifices to commemorate the work of Jesus Christ the Messiah, the Glory of the Lord, who died as the sacrifice for all

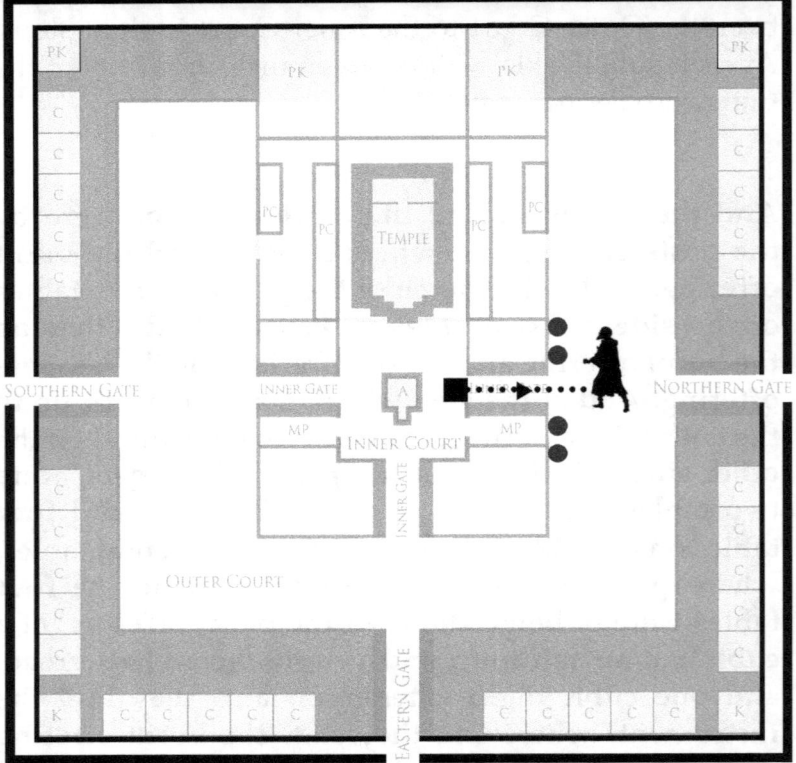

to have "faith" in Christ, and His work. The sacrifices in
the Temple are a vivid reminder of what Jesus did prior
to the Millennium.

**And without the inner gate were the chambers of the
singers in the inner court, which was at the side of the
north gate; and their prospect was toward the south:
one at the side of the east gate having the prospect
toward the north. And he said unto me, This chamber,
whose prospect is toward the south, is for the priests,**

the keepers of the charge of the house. And the chamber whose prospect is toward the north is for the priests, the keepers of the charge of the altar: these are the sons of Zadok among the sons of Levi, which come near to the LORD to minister unto him. So he measured the court, an hundred cubits long, and an hundred cubits broad, foursquare; and the altar that was before the house. (Ezekiel 40:44-47)

The Chambers for the Priests and the Singers (44-47): Ezekiel goes into the Inner Court and sees the chambers

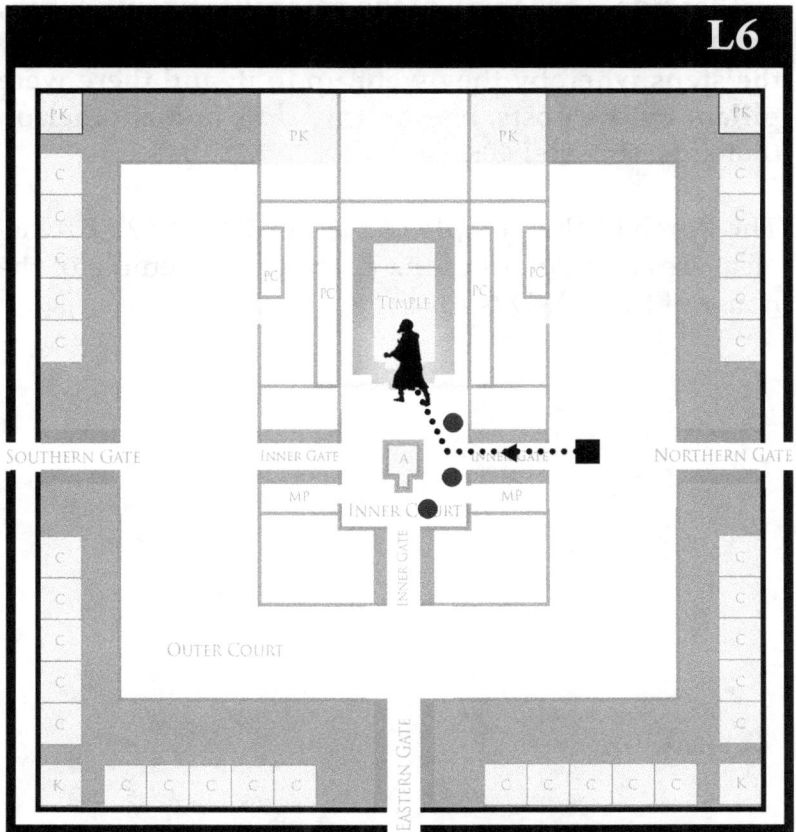

for the Priests, the sons of Zadok, which are among the sons of Levi. These chambers are located at the north side of the East Gate and on either side of the North Gate of the Inner Court *(see map above L6)*. Ezekiel sees the Altar before the porch of the *Temple (see arrow of map above L6)*.

And he brought me to the porch of the house, and measured each post of the porch, five cubits on this side, and five cubits on that side: and the breadth of the gate was three cubits on this side, and three cubits on that side. The length of the porch was twenty cubits, and the breadth eleven cubits; and he brought me by the steps whereby they went up to it: and there were pillars by the posts, one on this side, and another on that side. (Ezekiel 40:48-49)

The Porch of the Temple of the LORD (48-49): Ezekiel measures and describes the porch of the Temple of the house of the LORD *(see map L6)*.

CHAPTER 41

The Millennial Temple

THE TEMPLE & THE OUTER BUILDINGS SURROUNDING THE TEMPLE

Ezekiel is now taken into and around the exterior of the Temple itself; this would be the Sanctuary made up of the Holy Place and the Most Holy. Ezekiel will give the descriptions and the measurements of the things he sees.

Afterward he brought me to the temple, and measured the posts, six cubits broad on the one side, and six cubits broad on the other side, which was the breadth of the tabernacle. And the breadth of the door was ten cubits; and the sides of the door were five cubits on the one side, and five cubits on the other side: and he measured the length thereof, forty cubits: and the breadth, twenty cubits. Then went he inward, and measured the post of the door, two cubits; and the door, six cubits; and the breadth of the door, seven cubits. So he measured the length thereof, twenty cubits; and the breadth, twenty cubits, before the temple: and he said unto me, This is the most holy place. After he measured the wall of the house, six cubits; and the breadth of every side chamber, four cubits, round about the house on every side. And the side chambers were three, one over another, and thirty in order; and they entered into the wall which was of the house for the side chambers round about, that they might have hold, but they had not hold in the wall of the house. And there was an enlarging, and a winding about still upward to the side chambers: for the winding about of the house went still upward round about the house: therefore the breadth of the house was still upward, and so increased from the lowest chamber to the highest by the midst. I saw also the height of the house round about: the foundations of the side chambers were a full reed of six great cubits. The thickness of the wall, which was for the side chamber without, was five cubits: and that which was left was the place of the side chambers that were within. And between the chambers was the wideness of twenty cubits round about the house on every side. And the doors of the side chambers were toward the place that was left, one door toward the north, and another door toward the south: and the breadth of the place that was left was five cubits round about. (Ezekiel 41:1-11)

The Door to the Temple, the Inside Description and Measurements (1-11): Ezekiel is brought to the door and then goes inside of the Temple, or Sanctuary. Just as the Tabernacle in the Exodus and Solomon's Temple, here there is also a Holy of Holies, the "Most Holy Place." When Jesus died on the cross the curtain separating this room was torn from top to bottom, removing the wall of partition between God and man.

The Millennial Temple is to remind those who are born in the Millennium the way of salvation is through the work of Jesus. Just as we partake in communion, the events and ministry of the Temple will be to point those who are born and live in the Millennium to the work of the King, reminding them of His sacrifice. In addition to telling us the dimension of the Temple, Ezekiel also describes what he sees in the Temple, such as the carved images of Cherubim and palm trees *(see map L7)*.

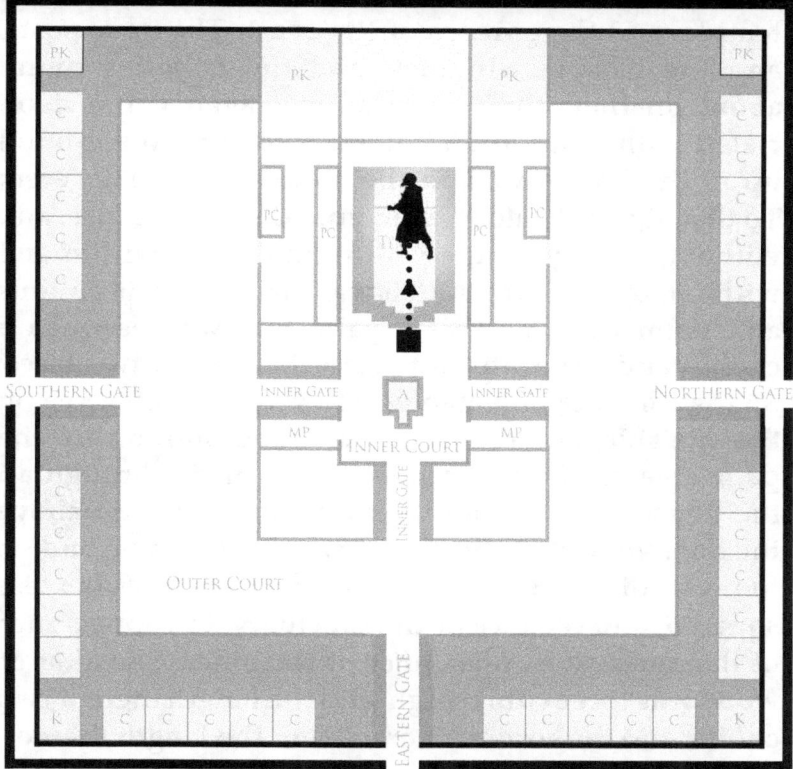

Now the building that was before the separate place at the end toward the west was seventy cubits broad; and the wall of the building was five cubits thick round about, and the length thereof ninety cubits. So he measured the house, an hundred cubits long; and the separate place, and the building, with the walls thereof, an hundred cubits long; Also the breadth of the face of the house, and of the separate place toward the east, an hundred cubits. And he measured the length of the building over against the separate place which was behind it, and the galleries thereof on the one side and on the other side, an hundred cubits, with the inner temple, and the porches of the court; The door posts, and the narrow windows, and the galleries round about on their three stories, over against the door, cieled with wood round about, and from the ground up to the windows, and the windows were covered; To that above the door, even unto the inner house, and without, and by all the wall round about within and without, by measure. And it was made with cherubims and palm trees, so that a palm tree was between a cherub and a cherub; and every cherub had two faces; So that the face of a man was toward the palm tree on the one side, and the face of a young lion toward the palm tree on the other side: it was made through all the house round about. From the ground unto above the door were cherubims and palm trees made, and on the wall of the temple. The posts of the temple were squared, and the face of the sanctuary; the appearance of the one as the appearance of the other. The altar of wood was three cubits high, and the length thereof two cubits; and the corners thereof, and the length thereof, and the walls thereof, were of wood: and he said unto me, This is the table that is before the LORD. And the temple and the sanctuary had two doors. And the doors had two leaves apiece, two turning leaves; two leaves for the one door, and two leaves for the other door. And there were made on them, on the doors of the temple, cherubims and palm trees, like as were made upon the walls; and there were thick planks upon the face of the porch without. And there were narrow windows and palm trees on the one side and on the other side, on the sides of the porch, and upon the side chambers of the house, and thick planks. (Ezekiel 41:12-26)

The Building West of the Temple and Further Descriptions and Measurements of the Buildings that Surround the Sanctuary, as well as the Sanctuary (12-26): As mentioned earlier there is no western gate; a building is placed at this location. The "separate place" mentioned in verses 12 & 13 is the Temple or Sanctuary that is in the midst of these various buildings *(see map L8).*

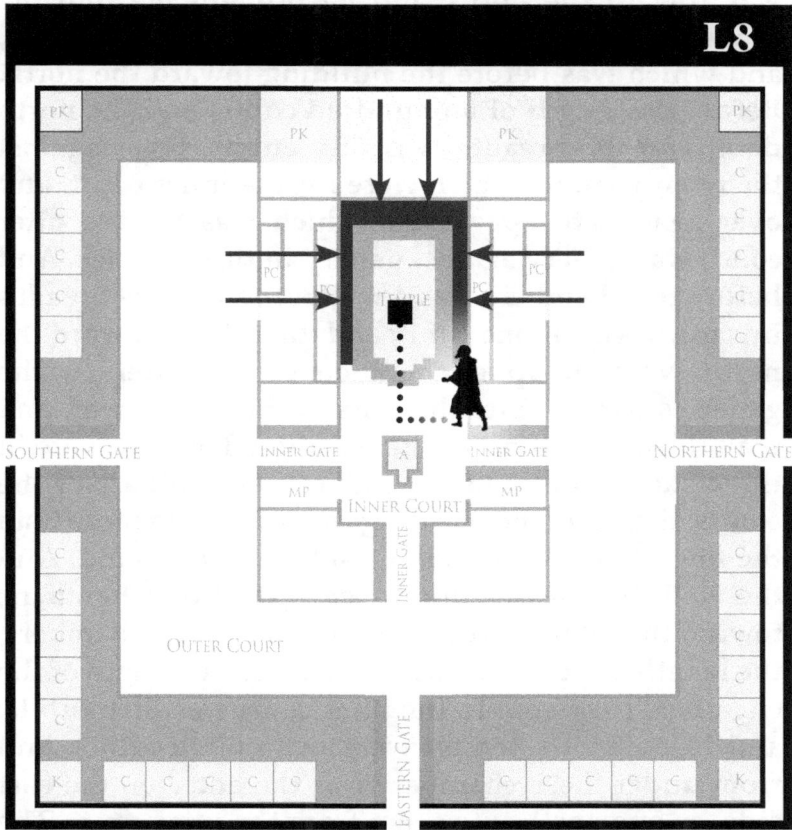

L8

CHAPTER 42

The Millennial Temple

THE CHAMBERS OF THE PRIESTS & OTHER DIMENSIONS
OF THE TEMPLE AREA

Then he brought me forth into the utter court, the way toward the north: and he brought me into the chamber that was over against the separate place, and which was before the building toward the north. Before the length of an hundred cubits was the north door, and the breadth was fifty cubits. Over against the twenty cubits which were for the inner court, and over against the pavement which was for the utter court, was gallery against gallery in three stories. And before the chambers was a walk of ten cubits breadth inward, a way of one cubit; and their doors toward the north. Now the upper chambers were shorter: for the galleries were higher than these, than the lower, and than the middlemost of the building. For they were in three stories, but had not pillars as the pillars of the courts: therefore the building was straitened more than the lowest and the middlemost from the ground. And the wall that was without over against the chambers, toward the utter court on the forepart of the chambers, the length thereof was fifty cubits. For the length of the chambers that were in the utter court was fifty cubits: and, lo, before the temple were an hundred cubits. And from under these chambers was the entry on the east side, as one goeth into them from the utter court. The chambers were in the thickness of the wall of the court toward the east, over against the separate place, and over against the building. And the way before them was like the appearance of the chambers which were toward the north, as long as they, and as broad as they: and all their goings out were both according to their fashions, and according to their doors. And according to the doors of the chambers that were toward the south was a door in the head of the way, even the way directly before the wall toward the east, as one entereth into them. Then said he unto me, The north chambers and the south chambers, which are before the separate place, they be holy chambers, where the priests that approach unto the LORD shall eat the most holy things: there shall they lay the most holy things, and the meat offering, and the sin offering, and the trespass offering; for the place is holy. When the priests enter therein, then shall they not go out of the holy place into the utter court, but there they shall lay their garments wherein they minister; for they are holy; and shall put on other garments, and shall approach to those things which are for the people. (Ezekiel 42:1-14)

The Chambers for the Priests (1-14): Ezekiel is taken through the North gate to the Outer Court (utter court) to the exterior of the Priest Chambers or holy places. These housings for the Priests are three stories tall (vs. 6) and are for the Priests' various functions of Temple Service *(see map L9)*.

Now when he had made an end of measuring the inner house, he brought me forth toward the gate whose prospect is toward the east, and measured it round about. He measured the east side with the measuring reed, five hundred reeds, with the measuring reed round about. He measured the north side, five hundred reeds, with the measuring reed round about. He

255

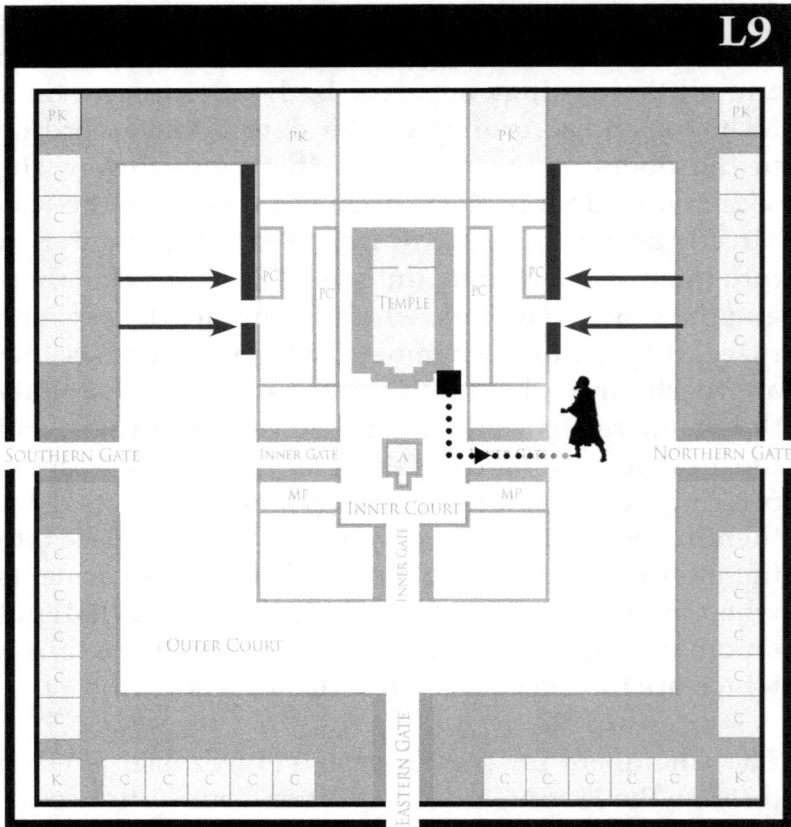

measured the south side, five hundred reeds, with the measuring reed. He turned about to the west side, and measured five hundred reeds with the measuring reed. He measured it by the four sides: it had a wall round about, five hundred reeds long, and five hundred broad, to make a separation between the sanctuary and the profane place. (Ezekiel 42:15-20)

The Dimensions of the Exterior of the City (15-20): Ezekiel is brought back out to the Eastern Gate to measure the exterior of the city walls or the Temple area as a whole *(see map L10)*.

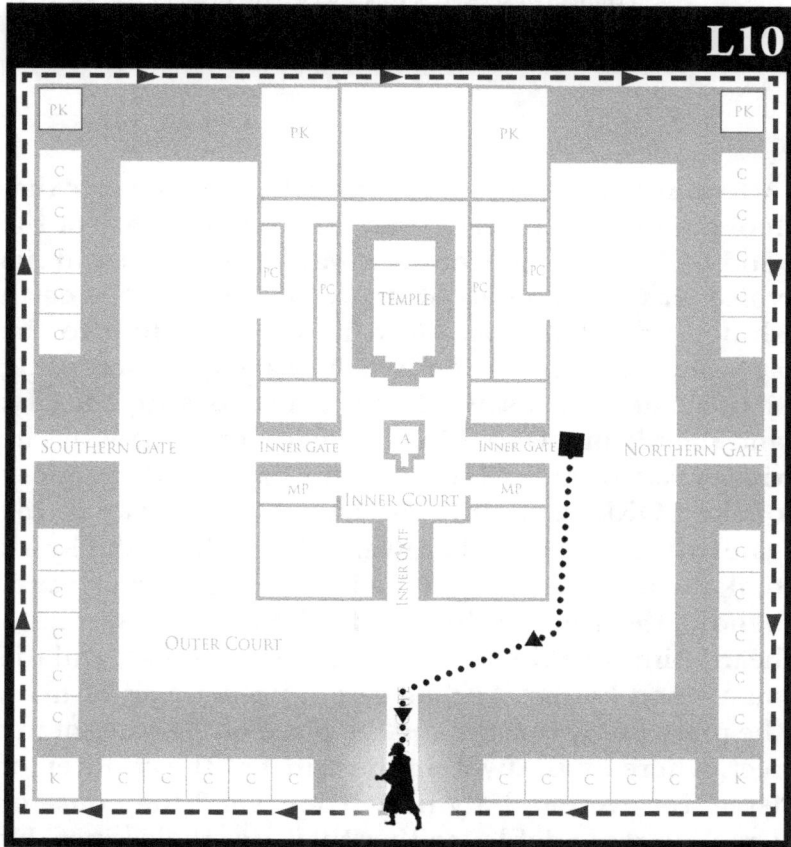

CHAPTER 43

The Millennial Temple

THE RETURN OF THE GLORY OF THE LORD,
THE ALTAR AND OFFERINGS

Afterward he brought me to the gate, even the gate that looketh toward the east: And, behold, the glory of the God of Israel came from the way of the east: and his voice was like a noise of many waters: and the earth shined with his glory. And it was according to the appearance of the vision which I saw, even according to the vision that I saw when I came to destroy the city: and the visions were like the vision that I saw by the river Chebar; and I fell upon my face. And the glory of the LORD came into the house by the way of the gate whose prospect is toward the east. So the spirit took me up, and brought me into the inner court; and, behold, the glory of the LORD filled the house. And I heard him speaking unto me out of the house; and the man stood by me. And he said unto me, Son of man, the place of my throne, and the place of the soles of my feet, where I will dwell in the midst of the children of Israel for ever, and my holy name, shall the house of Israel no more defile, neither they, nor their kings, by their whoredom, nor by the carcases of their kings in their high places. In their setting of their threshold by my thresholds, and their post by my posts, and the wall between me and them, they have even defiled my holy name by their abominations that they have committed: wherefore I have consumed them in mine anger. Now let them put away their whoredom, and the carcases of their kings, far from me, and I will dwell in the midst of them for ever. (Ezekiel 43:1-9)

The Glory of the LORD returns to the Temple (1-9): Ezekiel is brought to the Eastern Gate and sees the "Glory of the GOD of Israel" come from the way of the east. The Glory of God enters the Temple from the same direction that He departed; from the Mount of Olives, across the Kidron Valley, through the Eastern Gate (Ezekiel 10:18-19; 11:22-23). Once the Glory of the LORD enters the Temple the Eastern Gate of the city will be sealed forever (Ezekiel 44:1-2) however, the Eastern Gate of the Inner court will be closed six days a week but open on the Sabbath (Ezekiel 46:1). Ezekiel says that what he sees is the same as he saw by the river Chebar when He came to destroy the city (Ezekiel 1:3 cf. chapter 10).

Once the Glory of the LORD enters the temple Ezekiel, with the angel standing by him, hears the voice from the throne say: **And he said unto me, Son of man, the place of my throne, and the place of the soles of my feet, where I will dwell in the midst of the children of Israel for ever, and my holy name, shall the house of Israel no more defile, neither they, nor their kings, by their whoredom, nor by the carcases of their kings in their high places. In their setting of their threshold by my thresholds, and their post by my posts, and the wall between me and them, they have even defiled my holy name by their abominations that they have committed: wherefore I have consumed them in mine anger. Now let them put away their whoredom, and the carcases of their kings, far from me, and I will dwell in the midst of them for ever. (Ezekiel 43:7-9)**

The LORD declares the fulfillment of the promises of the long-awaited Kingdom.

Thou son of man, shew the house to the house of Israel, that they may be ashamed of their iniquities: and let them measure the pattern. And if they be ashamed of all that they have done, shew them the form of the house, and the fashion thereof, and the goings out thereof, and the comings in thereof, and all the forms thereof, and all the ordinances thereof, and all the forms thereof, and all the laws thereof: and write it in their sight, that they may keep the whole form thereof, and all the ordinances thereof, and do them. This is the law of the house; Upon the top of the mountain the whole limit thereof round about shall be most holy. Behold, this is the law of the house. And these are the measures of the altar after the cubits: The cubit is a cubit and an hand breadth; even the bottom shall be a cubit, and the breadth a cubit, and the border thereof by the edge thereof round about shall be a span: and this shall be the higher place of the altar. And from the bottom upon the ground even to the lower settle shall be two cubits, and the breadth one cubit; and from the lesser settle even to the greater settle shall be four cubits, and the breadth one cubit. So the altar shall be four cubits; and from the altar and upward shall be four horns. And the altar shall be twelve cubits long, twelve broad, square in the four squares thereof. And the settle shall be fourteen cubits long and fourteen broad in the four squares thereof; and the border about it shall be half a cubit; and the bottom thereof shall be a cubit about; and his stairs shall look toward the east. And he said unto me, Son of man, thus saith the Lord GOD; These are the ordinances of the altar in the day when they shall make it, to offer burnt offerings thereon, and to sprinkle blood thereon. And thou shalt give to the priests the Levites that be of the seed of Zadok, which approach unto me, to minister unto me, saith the Lord

GOD, a young bullock for a sin offering. And thou shalt take of the blood thereof, and put it on the four horns of it, and on the four corners of the settle, and upon the border round about: thus shalt thou cleanse and purge it. Thou shalt take the bullock also of the sin offering, and he shall burn it in the appointed place of the house, without the sanctuary. And on the second day thou shalt offer a kid of the goats without blemish for a sin offering; and they shall cleanse the altar, as they did cleanse it with the bullock. When thou hast made an end of cleansing it, thou shalt offer a young bullock without blemish, and a ram out of the flock without blemish. And thou shalt offer them before the LORD, and the priests shall cast salt upon them, and they shall offer them up for a burnt offering unto the LORD. Seven days shalt thou prepare every day a goat for a sin offering: they shall also prepare a young bullock, and a ram out of the flock, without blemish. Seven days shall they purge the altar and purify it; and they shall consecrate themselves. And when these days are expired, it shall be, that upon the eighth day, and so forward, the priests shall make your burnt offerings upon the altar, and your peace offerings; and I will accept you, saith the Lord GOD. (Ezekiel 43:10-27)

The Altar of the House of the LORD (10-27): Ezekiel is told to write down the ordinances, forms and the laws of the House of God, and what follows almost to the end of this book is that very thing. Ezekiel starts with the *measurements* of the Altar (13-17) and then details the *offerings* of the Altar (18-27).

CHAPTER 44

The Millennial Temple

THE ORDINANCES OF THE HOUSE OF THE LORD

In this chapter, and continuing through chapter 46, Ezekiel is given the ordinances of the temple and who may minister in the temple; the priests, Levites, and the Prince.

Then he brought me back the way of the gate of the outward sanctuary which looketh toward the east; and it was shut. Then said the LORD unto me; This gate shall be shut, it shall not be opened, and no man shall enter in by it; because the LORD, the God of Israel, hath entered in by it, therefore it shall be shut. It is for the prince; the prince, he shall sit in it to eat bread before the LORD; he shall enter by the way of the porch of that gate, and shall go out by the way of the same. (Ezekiel 44:1-3)

The Prince and the Sealing of the Outer Eastern Gate (1-3): Once the Glory of the LORD enters the Eastern Gate of the Outer Court the gate is sealed forever. The Prince is to sit at this gate in the porch thereof and eat bread before the LORD[1].

Then brought he me the way of the north gate before the house: and I looked, and, behold, the glory of the LORD filled the house of the LORD: and I fell upon

---

[1] *It is a possibility that this "prince' is David (Ezekiel 34:23-24; 37:24).*

my face. And the LORD said unto me, Son of man, mark well, and behold with thine eyes, and hear with thine ears all that I say unto thee concerning all the ordinances of the house of the LORD, and all the laws thereof; and mark well the entering in of the house, with every going forth of the sanctuary. And thou shalt say to the rebellious, even to the house of Israel, Thus saith the Lord GOD; O ye house of Israel, let it suffice you of all your abominations, In that ye have brought into my sanctuary strangers, uncircumcised in heart, and uncircumcised in flesh, to be in my sanctuary, to pollute it, even my house, when ye offer my bread, the fat and the blood, and they have broken my covenant because of all your abominations. And ye have not kept the charge of mine holy things: but ye have set keepers of my charge in my sanctuary for yourselves. Thus saith the Lord GOD; No stranger, uncircumcised in heart, nor uncircumcised in flesh, shall enter into my sanctuary, of any stranger that is among the children of Israel. And the Levites that are gone away far from me, when Israel went astray, which went astray away from me after their idols; they shall even bear their iniquity. Yet they shall be ministers in my sanctuary, having charge at the gates of the house, and ministering to the house: they shall slay the burnt offering and the sacrifice for the people, and they shall stand before them to minister unto them. Because they ministered unto them before their idols, and caused the house of Israel to fall into iniquity; therefore have I lifted up mine hand against them, saith the Lord GOD, and they shall bear their iniquity. And they shall not come near unto me, to do the office of a priest unto me, nor to come near to any of my holy things, in the most holy place: but they shall bear their shame, and their abominations which they have committed. But I will make them keepers of the charge of the house, for all the service thereof, and for all that shall be done therein. (Ezekiel 44:4-14)

The Strangers and the Levites (4-14): One of the indictments against the nation was that they permitted foreigners to enter and profane the Sanctuary, and to officiate in the Sanctuary. In verses 4-8 God is rebuking not only the nation for allowing this to take place but lays the charge of this at the feet of the Levites for corrupting the offerings of the LORD. Because of this the Levites are downgraded to only be allowed to minister in the Sanctuary as gatekeepers, slayers of the sacrifices, and to help worshipers (11). They will not be allowed to serve the LORD as priests or come near any of His holy things or offerings.

But the priests the Levites, the sons of Zadok, that kept the charge of my sanctuary when the children of Israel went astray from me, they shall come near to me to minister unto me, and they shall stand before me to offer unto me the fat and the blood, saith the Lord GOD: They shall enter into my sanctuary, and they shall come near to my table, to minister unto me, and they shall keep my charge. And it shall come to pass, that when they enter in at the gates of the inner court, they shall be clothed with linen garments; and no wool shall come upon them, whiles they minister in the gates of the inner court, and within. They shall have linen bonnets upon their heads, and shall have linen breeches upon their loins; they shall not gird themselves with any thing that causeth sweat. And when they go forth into the utter court, even into the utter court to the people, they shall put off their garments wherein they ministered, and lay them in the holy chambers, and they shall put on other garments; and they shall not sanctify the people with their garments. Neither shall they shave their heads, nor suffer their locks to grow long; they shall only poll their heads. Neither shall any priest drink wine, when they enter into the inner court. Neither shall they take for their wives a widow, nor her that is put away: but they shall take maidens of the seed of the house of Israel, or a widow that had a priest before. And they shall teach my people the difference between the holy and profane, and cause them to discern between the unclean and the clean. And in controversy they shall stand in judgment; and they shall judge it according to my judgments: and they shall keep my laws and my statutes in all mine assemblies; and they shall hallow my sabbaths. And they shall come at no dead person to defile themselves: but for father, or for mother, or for son, or for daughter, for brother, or for sister that hath had no husband, they may defile themselves. And after he is cleansed, they shall reckon unto him seven days. And in the day that he goeth into the sanctuary, unto the inner court, to minister in the sanctuary, he shall offer his sin offering, saith the Lord GOD. And it shall be unto them for an inheritance: I am their inheritance: and ye shall give them no possession in Israel: I am their possession. They shall eat the meat offering, and the sin offering, and the trespass offering; and every dedicated thing in Israel shall be theirs. And the first of all the firstfruits of all things, and every oblation of all, of every sort of your oblations, shall be the priest's: ye shall also give unto the priest the first of your dough, that he may cause the blessing to rest in thine house. The priests shall not eat of any thing that is dead of itself, or torn, whether it be fowl or beast. (Ezekiel 44:15-31)

The Priests of Zadok and various Duties of the Levites (15-31): The priesthood was entrusted to Aaron and his sons, following the death of Aaron it passed to Eleazar his oldest living son. After the death of Eleazar, the priesthood passes to Phinehas the eldest son of Eleazar. In the time of the judges the high priesthood belonged to Eli, of the line of Ithamar and at the time of David it was held conjointly by Abiathar and Zadok. In this future Millennial Temple it will be the sons of Zadok; only they will be allowed to perform the office of priest (16-17). What follows in the remaining verses of this chapter are various duties of this position.

CHAPTER 45

The Millennial Temple

THE DIVIDING OF THE HOLY PORTION OF THE LAND & VARIOUS OFFERINGS

Moreover, when ye shall divide by lot the land for inheritance, ye shall offer an oblation unto the LORD, an holy portion of the land: the length shall be the length of five and twenty thousand reeds, and the breadth shall be ten thousand. This shall be holy in all the borders thereof round about. Of this there shall be for the sanctuary five hundred in length, with five hundred in breadth, square round about; and fifty cubits round about for the suburbs thereof. And of this measure shalt thou measure the length of five and twenty thousand, and the breadth of ten thousand: and in it shall be the sanctuary and the most holy place. The holy portion of the land shall be for the priests the ministers of the sanctuary, which shall come near to minister unto the LORD: and it shall be a place for their houses, and an holy place for the sanctuary. And the five and twenty thousand of length, and the ten thousand of breadth, shall also the Levites, the ministers of the house, have for themselves, for a possession for twenty chambers. And ye shall appoint the possession of the city five thousand broad, and five and twenty thousand long, over against the oblation of the holy portion: it shall be for the whole house of Israel. And a portion shall be for the prince on the one side and on the other side of the oblation of the holy portion, and of the possession of the city, before the oblation of the holy portion, and before the possession

DIVISION OF THE LAND IN THE MILLENNIAL KINGDOM

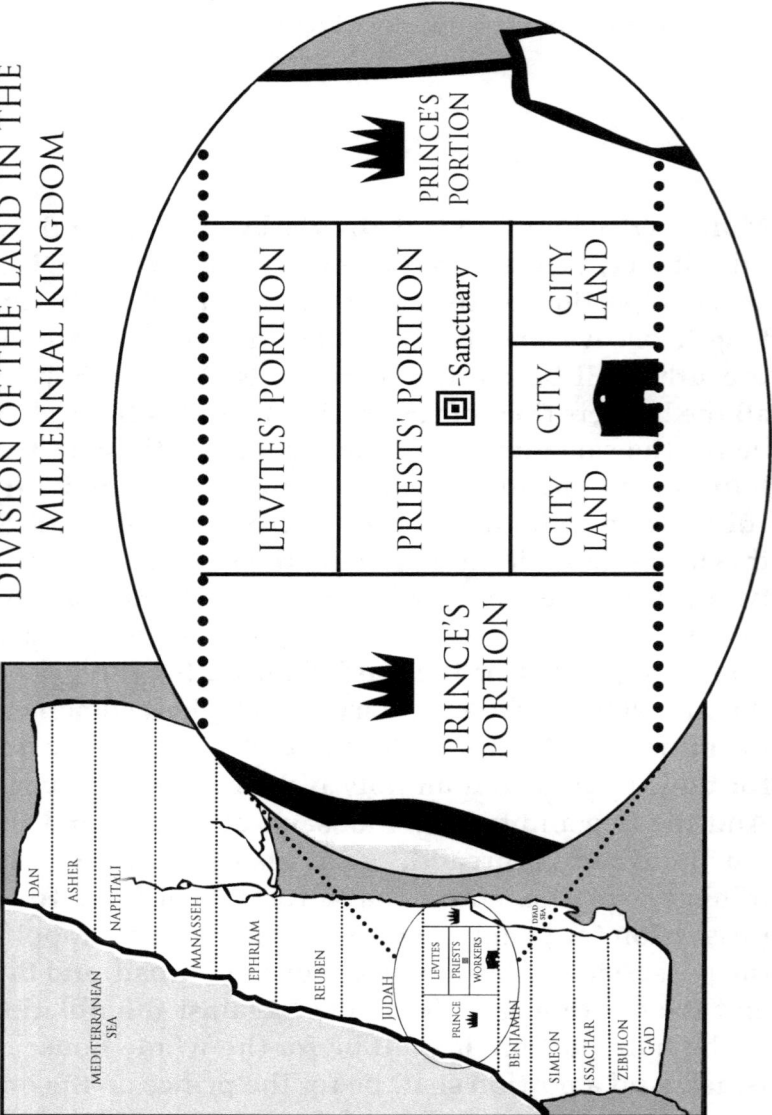

PRINCE'S PORTION

LEVITES' PORTION

PRIESTS' PORTION

□ -Sanctuary

CITY LAND

CITY

CITY LAND

PRINCE'S PORTION

PRINCE'S PORTION

DAN

ASHER

NAPHTALI

MANASSEH

EPHRIAM

REUBEN

JUDAH

MEDITERRANEAN SEA

LEVITES

PRIESTS

WORKERS

PRINCE

BENJAMIN

SIMEON

ISSACHAR

ZEBULON

GAD

DEAD SEA

of the city, from the west side westward, and from the east side eastward: and the length shall be over against one of the portions, from the west border unto the east border. (Ezekiel 45:1-7)

The Holy Portion of the Land (1-7): Ezekiel is told how the Holy District is divided, how property for the Temple, Jerusalem and the Prince is distributed. The magnified area of the map on the previous page shows the portion of the land distributed for the inheritance of those that minister in the house of the LORD as well as area for the city and temple.

In the land shall be his possession in Israel: and my princes shall no more oppress my people; and the rest of the land shall they give to the house of Israel according to their tribes. Thus saith the Lord GOD; Let it suffice you, O princes of Israel: remove violence and spoil, and execute judgment and justice, take away your exactions from my people, saith the Lord GOD. Ye shall have just balances, and a just ephah, and a just bath. The ephah and the bath shall be of one measure, that the bath may contain the tenth part of an homer, and the ephah the tenth part of an homer: the measure thereof shall be after the homer. And the shekel shall be twenty gerahs: twenty shekels, five and twenty shekels, fifteen shekels, shall be your maneh. This is the oblation that ye shall offer; the sixth part of an ephah of an homer of wheat, and ye shall give the sixth part of an ephah of an homer of barley: Concerning the ordinance of oil, the bath of oil, ye shall offer the tenth part of a bath out of the cor, which is an homer of ten baths; for ten baths are an homer: And one lamb out of the flock, out of two hundred, out of the fat pastures of

Israel; for a meat offering, and for a burnt offering, and for peace offerings, to make reconciliation for them, saith the Lord GOD. All the people of the land shall give this oblation for the prince in Israel. And it shall be the prince's part to give burnt offerings, and meat offerings, and drink offerings, in the feasts, and in the new moons, and in the sabbaths, in all solemnities of the house of Israel: he shall prepare the sin offering, and the meat offering, and the burnt offering, and the peace offerings, to make reconciliation for the house of Israel. Thus saith the Lord GOD; In the first month, in the first day of the month, thou shalt take a young bullock without blemish, and cleanse the sanctuary: And the priest shall take of the blood of the sin offering, and put it upon the posts of the house, and upon the four corners of the settle of the altar, and upon the posts of the gate of the inner court. And so thou shalt do the seventh day of the month for every one that erreth, and for him that is simple: so shall ye reconcile the house. In the first month, in the fourteenth day of the month, ye shall have the passover, a feast of seven days; unleavened bread shall be eaten. And upon that day shall the prince prepare for himself and for all the people of the land a bullock for a sin offering. And seven days of the feast he shall prepare a burnt offering to the LORD, seven bullocks and seven rams without blemish daily the seven days; and a kid of the goats daily for a sin offering. And he shall prepare a meat offering of an ephah for a bullock, and an ephah for a ram, and an hin of oil for an ephah. In the seventh month, in the fifteenth day of the month, shall he do the like in the feast of the seven days, according to the sin offering, according to the burnt offering, and according to the meat offering, and according to the oil. (Ezekiel 45:8-25)

Ordinances and Outlines (8-25): The remainder of the chapter deals with various ordinances and is outlined as such: just measurement standards (9-13), reconciliation offerings for the house of Israel (14-17), cleansing of the Sanctuary (14-20), and the sin offering for the people and the Prince (21-25).

CHAPTER 46

The Millennial Temple

SACRIFICES, OFFERINGS & ORDINANCES

Thus saith the Lord GOD; The gate of the inner court that looketh toward the east shall be shut the six working days; but on the sabbath it shall be opened, and in the day of the new moon it shall be opened. And the prince shall enter by the way of the porch of that gate without, and shall stand by the post of the gate, and the priests shall prepare his burnt offering and his peace offerings, and he shall worship at the threshold of the gate: then he shall go forth; but the gate shall not be shut until the evening. Likewise the people of the land shall worship at the door of this gate before the LORD in the sabbaths and in the new moons. And the burnt offering that the prince shall offer unto the LORD in the sabbath day shall be six lambs without blemish, and a ram without blemish. And the meat offering shall be an ephah for a ram, and the meat offering for the lambs as he shall be able to give, and an hin of oil to an ephah. And in the day of the new moon it shall be a young bullock without blemish, and six lambs, and a ram: they shall be without blemish. And he shall prepare a meat offering, an ephah for a bullock, and an ephah for a ram, and for the lambs according as his hand shall attain unto, and an hin of oil to an ephah. And when the prince shall enter, he shall go in by the way of the porch of that gate, and he shall go forth by the way thereof. But when the people of the land shall come before the LORD in the solemn feasts, he that entereth in by the way of the north gate to worship shall go out by the way of the south gate; and he that entereth by the way of the south gate shall go forth by the way of the north gate: he shall not return by the way of the gate whereby he came in, but shall go forth over against it. And the prince in the midst of them, when they go in, shall go in; and when they go forth, shall go forth. And in the feasts and in the solemnities the meat offering shall be an ephah to a bullock, and an ephah to a ram, and to the lambs as he is able to give, and an hin of oil to an ephah. (Ezekiel 46:1-11)

Sacrifices, Offerings and Ordinances (1-11): Ezekiel is given details pertaining to the sacrifices, offerings and ordinances. The Eastern Gate of the Inner Court is to be closed six days, only opened on the Sabbath day (1-2). The people of the land shall worship before the Lord at this gate (3). The Prince's offerings on the Sabbath and New Moons are described in verses 4-8. When the people of the land offer their offerings on the feast days they are to enter in the North Gate and exit the way of the South Gate, and those that enter by way of the South Gate are to exit the North Gate; they are not to exit the gate from which they entered (9-10).

Now when the prince shall prepare a voluntary burnt offering or peace offerings voluntarily unto the LORD, one shall then open him the gate that looketh toward the east, and he shall prepare his burnt offering and his peace offerings, as he did on the sabbath day: then he shall go forth; and after his going forth one shall shut the gate. Thou shalt daily prepare a burnt offering unto the LORD of a lamb of the first year without blemish: thou shalt prepare it every morning. And thou shalt prepare a meat offering for it every morning, the sixth part of an ephah, and the third part of an hin of oil, to temper with the fine flour; a meat offering continually by a perpetual ordinance unto the LORD. Thus shall they prepare the lamb, and the meat offering, and the oil, every morning for a continual burnt offering. Thus saith the Lord GOD; If the prince give a gift unto any of his sons, the inheritance thereof shall be his sons'; it shall be their possession by inheritance. But if he give a gift of his inheritance to one of his servants, then it shall be his to the year of liberty; after it shall return to the prince: but his inheritance shall be his sons' for them. Moreover the prince shall not take of the people's inheritance by oppression, to thrust them out of their possession; but he shall give his sons inheritance out of his own possession: that my people be not scattered every man from his possession. After he brought me through the entry, which was at the side of the gate, into the holy chambers of the priests, which looked toward the north: and, behold, there was a place on the two sides westward. Then said he unto me, This is the place where the priests shall boil the trespass offering and the sin offering, where they shall bake the meat offering; that they bear them not out into the utter court, to sanctify the people. Then he brought me forth into the utter court, and caused me to pass by the four corners of the court; and, behold, in every corner of the court there was a court. In the four corners of the court there were courts joined of forty cubits long and thirty broad: these four corners were of one measure. And there was a row of building round about in them, round about them four, and it was made with boiling places under the rows round about. Then said he unto me, These are the places of them that boil, where the ministers of the house shall boil the sacrifice of the people. (Ezekiel 46:12-24)

Various Things Pertaining to the Priestly Service (12-24): Daily offerings are mentioned in verses 12-15. The Prince's sons that inherit land are to remain in their possession, however if land is given to a servant it will be returned in the year of liberty or "Jubilee" (16-18).

The location, measurements and description of the priests' boiling place is mentioned in the remaining verses.

CHAPTER 47

The Millennial Temple

DETAILS AND DIVISION OF THE LAND

Afterward he brought me again unto the door of the house; and, behold, waters issued out from under the threshold of the house eastward: for the forefront of the house stood toward the east, and the waters came down from under from the right side of the house, at the south side of the altar. Then brought he me out of the way of the gate northward, and led me about the way without unto the utter gate by the way that looketh eastward; and, behold, there ran out waters on the right side. And when the man that had the line in his hand went forth eastward, he measured a thousand cubits, and he brought me through the waters; the waters were to the ancles. Again he measured a thousand, and brought me through the waters; the waters were to the knees. Again he measured a thousand, and brought me through; the waters were to the loins. Afterward he measured a thousand; and it was a river that I could not pass over: for the waters were risen, waters to swim in, a river that could not be passed over. And he said unto me, Son of man, hast thou seen this? Then he brought me, and caused me to return to the brink of the river. Now when I had returned, behold, at the bank of the river were very many trees on the one side and on the other. Then said he unto me, These waters issue out toward the east country, and go down into the desert, and go into the sea: which being brought forth into the sea, the waters shall be healed. And it shall come to pass, that every thing that liveth, which moveth, whithersoever the rivers shall come, shall live: and there shall be a very great multitude of fish, because these waters shall come thither: for they shall be healed; and every thing shall live whither the river cometh. And it shall come to pass, that the fishers shall stand upon it from Engedi even unto Eneglaim; they shall be a place to spread forth nets; their fish shall be according to their kinds, as the fish of the great sea, exceeding many. But the miry places thereof and the marishes thereof shall not be healed; they shall be given to salt. And by the river upon the bank thereof, on this side and on that side, shall grow all trees for meat, whose leaf shall not fade, neither shall the fruit thereof be consumed: it shall bring forth new fruit according to his months, because their waters they issued out of the sanctuary: and the fruit thereof shall be for meat, and the leaf thereof for medicine. (Ezekiel 47:1-12)

The River from the Temple (1-12): Ezekiel is brought back to the door of the House of the LORD where he sees water coming down from under the threshold of the door of the house of the LORD that faces east. Ezekiel goes out the Northern Gate to the Eastern Gate of the Outer Court and sees the river flowing on the right side of the Eastern Gate, flowing east. As Ezekiel is brought into the water it is first measured up to his ankles (3) however the farther along he travels the waters soon become a mighty river that cannot be crossed (4-5).

Ezekiel is then brought back to the brink of the river and sees trees on either side of the river. He is told that the river goes into the sea (Dead Sea) and the waters of the sea shall be healed (6-11). Thus the Dead Sea will be healed by the living waters that flow from the throne of God.

Ezekiel also describes the trees mentioned earlier; that they are for meat whose leaves shall be for medicine (12).

Though Ezekiel only describes the waters that flow to the Dead Sea, Zechariah tells us that the waters also flow to the Mediterranean Sea: **And it shall be in that day, that living waters shall go out from Jerusalem; half of them toward the former sea, and half of them toward the hinder sea: in summer and in winter shall it be. (Zechariah 14:8)**

All this is very reminiscent of the New Jerusalem described in Revelation, which has a river of life flowing from it and trees that are for the healing of the nations: **And he shewed me a pure river of water of life, clear as crystal, proceeding out of the throne of God and of the Lamb. In the midst of the street of it, and on either side of the river, was there the tree of life, which bare twelve manner of fruits, and yielded her fruit every month: and the leaves of the tree were for the healing of the nations. (Revelation 22:1-2)**

Thus saith the Lord GOD; This shall be the border, whereby ye shall inherit the land according to the twelve tribes of Israel: Joseph shall have two portions. And ye shall inherit it, one as well as another: concerning the which I lifted up mine hand to give it unto your fathers: and this land shall fall unto you for inheritance. And this shall be the border of the land toward the north side, from the great sea, the way

Israel in the Millennial Kingdom

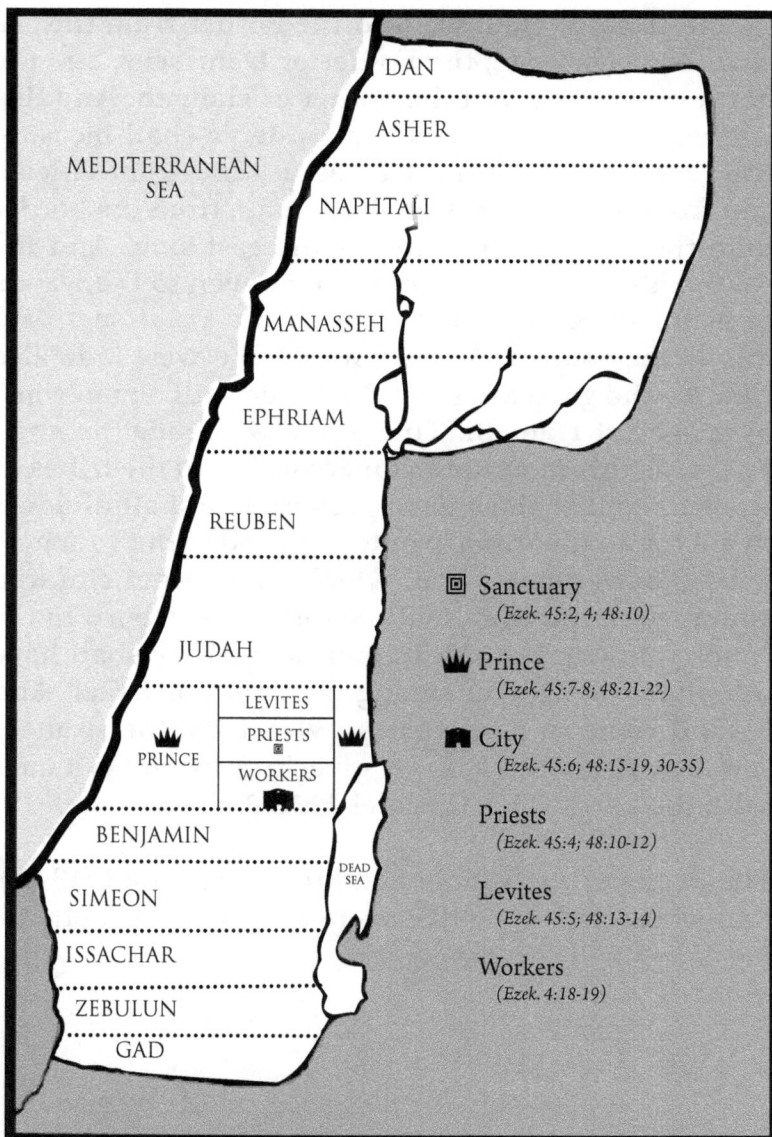

MEDITERRANEAN
SEA

DAN

ASHER

NAPHTALI

MANASSEH

EPHRIAM

REUBEN

JUDAH

LEVITES

PRIESTS

PRINCE

WORKERS

BENJAMIN

DEAD
SEA

SIMEON

ISSACHAR

ZEBULUN

GAD

▣ Sanctuary
(Ezek. 45:2, 4; 48:10)

♛ Prince
(Ezek. 45:7-8; 48:21-22)

🏰 City
(Ezek. 45:6; 48:15-19, 30-35)

Priests
(Ezek. 45:4; 48:10-12)

Levites
(Ezek. 45:5; 48:13-14)

Workers
(Ezek. 4:18-19)

of Hethlon, as men go to Zedad; Hamath, Berothah, Sibraim, which is between the border of Damascus and the border of Hamath; Hazarhatticon, which is by the coast of Hauran. And the border from the sea shall be Hazarenan, the border of Damascus, and the north northward, and the border of Hamath. And this is the north side. And the east side ye shall measure from Hauran, and from Damascus, and from Gilead, and from the land of Israel by Jordan, from the border unto the east sea. And this is the east side. And the south side southward, from Tamar even to the waters of strife in Kadesh, the river to the great sea. And this is the south side southward. The west side also shall be the great sea from the border, till a man come over against Hamath. This is the west side. So shall ye divide this land unto you according to the tribes of Israel. And it shall come to pass, that ye shall divide it by lot for an inheritance unto you, and to the strangers that sojourn among you, which shall beget children among you: and they shall be unto you as born in the country among the children of Israel; they shall have inheritance with you among the tribes of Israel. And it shall come to pass, that in what tribe the stranger sojourneth, there shall ye give him his inheritance, saith the Lord GOD. (Ezekiel 47:13-23)

The Scope of the Whole Land to be Inherited (13-23): Ezekiel has now given the overall scope of the land that the nation will occupy (*see map*).

CHAPTER 48

The Millennial Temple

DIVISION OF THE LAND

Now these are the names of the tribes. From the north end to the coast of the way of Hethlon, as one goeth to Hamath, Hazarenan, the border of Damascus northward, to the coast of Hamath; for these are his sides east and west; a portion for Dan. And by the border of Dan, from the east side unto the west side, a portion for Asher. And by the border of Asher, from the east side even unto the west side, a portion for Naphtali. And by the border of Naphtali, from the east side unto the west side, a portion for Manasseh. And by the border of Manasseh, from the east side unto the west side, a portion for Ephraim. And by the border of Ephraim, from the east side even unto the west side, a portion for Reuben. And by the border of Reuben, from the east side unto the west side, a portion for Judah. (Ezekiel 48:1-7)

The division of the Promised Land to God's people (1-7): The division of the land to God's people is the fulfillment of the land covenant promised to Abraham and his descendants. Ezekiel is told who is to occupy what territory, beginning farthest north with the tribe of Dan, then moving southward toward Jerusalem, with Asher, Naphtali, Manasseh, Ephraim and Reuben and then Judah (*see* Israel in the Millennial Kingdom *map from previous chapter*).

And by the border of Judah, from the east side unto the west side, shall be the offering which ye shall offer of five and twenty thousand reeds in breadth, and in length as one of the other parts, from the east side unto the west side: and the sanctuary shall be in the midst of it. The oblation that ye shall offer unto the LORD shall be of five and twenty thousand in length, and of ten thousand in breadth. And for them, even for the priests, shall be this holy oblation; toward the north five and twenty thousand in length, and toward the west ten thousand in breadth, and toward the east ten thousand in breadth, and toward the south five and twenty thousand in length: and the sanctuary of the LORD shall be in the midst thereof. It shall be for the priests that are sanctified of the sons of Zadok; which have kept my charge, which went not astray when the children of Israel went astray, as the Levites went astray. And this oblation of the land that is offered shall be unto them a thing most holy by the border of the Levites. And over against the border of the priests the Levites shall have five and twenty thousand in length, and ten thousand in breadth: all the length shall be five and twenty thousand, and the breadth ten thousand. And they shall not sell of it, neither exchange, nor alienate the firstfruits of the land: for it is holy unto the LORD. (Ezekiel 48:8-14)

The Portion for the Priests and Those Who Serve (8-14): Ezekiel is then given the portion for the land assigned for the priests and those who are to minister in the sanctuary.

And the five thousand, that are left in the breadth over against the five and twenty thousand, shall be a profane place for the city, for dwelling, and for suburbs: and the city shall be in the midst thereof. And these shall be the measures thereof; the north side four thousand and five hundred, and the south side four thousand and five hundred, and on the east side four thousand and five hundred, and the west side four thousand and five hundred. And the suburbs of the city shall be toward the north two hundred and fifty, and toward the south two hundred and fifty, and toward the east two hundred and fifty, and toward the west two hundred and fifty. And the residue in length over against the oblation of the holy portion shall be ten thousand eastward, and ten thousand westward: and it shall be over against the oblation of the holy portion; and the increase thereof shall be for food unto them that serve the city. And they that serve the city shall serve it out of all the tribes of Israel. All the oblation shall be five and twenty thousand by five and twenty thousand: ye shall offer the holy oblation foursquare, with the possession of the city. (Ezekiel 48:15-20)

The City of Suburbs (15-20): Over the portion assigned to the Priests and those ministering in the sanctuary is to be the profane place for suburbs, for dwelling with the city in the midst.

And the residue shall be for the prince, on the one side and on the other of the holy oblation, and of the possession of the city, over against the five and twenty thousand of the oblation toward the east border, and westward over against the five and twenty thousand toward the west border, over against the portions for the prince: and it shall be the holy oblation; and the sanctuary of the house shall be in the midst thereof.

Moreover from the possession of the Levites, and from the possession of the city, being in the midst of that which is the prince's, between the border of Judah and the border of Benjamin, shall be for the prince. (Ezekiel 48:21-22)

The Prince's Portion (21-22): The Prince's portion is described as being on either side of the holy oblation (*see* Israel in the Millennial Kingdom *map from previous chapter*).

As for the rest of the tribes, from the east side unto the west side, Benjamin shall have a portion. And by the border of Benjamin, from the east side unto the west side, Simeon shall have a portion. And by the border of Simeon, from the east side unto the west side, Issachar a portion. And by the border of Issachar, from the east side unto the west side, Zebulun a portion. And by the border of Zebulun, from the east side unto the west side, Gad a portion. And by the border of Gad, at the south side southward, the border shall be even from Tamar unto the waters of strife in Kadesh, and to the river toward the great sea. This is the land which ye shall divide by lot unto the tribes of Israel for inheritance, and these are their portions, saith the Lord GOD. (Ezekiel 48:23-29)

Occupation of the Southland (23-29): Next, Ezekiel is told the tribes that are to occupy the land south of Jerusalem starting with the tribe closest to the city, Benjamin, then heading south there will be Simeon, Issachar, Zebulun and Gad (*see* Israel in the Millennial Kingdom *map from previous chapter*).

This is the land which ye shall divide by lot unto the tribes of Israel for inheritance, and these are their portions, saith the Lord GOD. And these are the goings out of the city on the north side, four thousand and five hundred measures. And the gates of the city shall be after the names of the tribes of Israel: three gates northward; one gate of Reuben, one gate of Judah, one gate of Levi. And at the east side four thousand and five hundred: and three gates; and one gate of Joseph, one gate of Benjamin, one gate of Dan. And at the south side four thousand and five hundred measures: and three gates; one gate of Simeon, one gate of Issachar, one gate of Zebulun. At the west side four thousand and five hundred, with their three gates; one gate of Gad, one gate of Asher, one gate of Naphtali. It was round about eighteen thousand measures: and the name of the city from that day shall be, The LORD is there. (Ezekiel 48:29-35)

Names of the Gates and their Location (29-35): Lastly, Ezekiel is given the names of the gates of the city beginning with the north, the gate of Reuben, Judah and Levi, on the east side the gate Joseph, Benjamin and Dan, on the south side, the gate of Simeon, Issachar and Zebulun and on the west, the gate of Gad, Asher and Naphtali.

Ezekiel brings this vivid picture of the Millennial landscape to a close with this statement: **It was round about eighteen thousand measures: and the name of the city from that day shall be, The LORD is there. (Ezekiel 48:35)**

Conclusion

As stated in the outset of our study, the key to interpreting the book of Ezekiel is to understand the major event during the time of Ezekiel. The final destruction of Jerusalem by Babylon is the main event that drives the thought and theme of this book.

In the first portion of the great prophetic book (chapters 4-24) it would be natural for God to be communicating through Ezekiel why this judgment is coming. As a result God through Ezekiel is communicating, in various ways why they deserve the coming judgments. It is also therefore natural to see the glory of the LORD departing the temple and the land prior to the Gentiles coming in to destroy and desecrate the temple.

In the middle portion of Ezekiel (chapters 25 – 32) prophesied while the siege on Jerusalem is transpiring, the Jewish people would naturally be wondering what about us? Is no one going to deliver us from our enemies that have plagued us since we first occupied this land? The answer is yes, for God through His prophet Ezekiel is prophesying of the judgment on all the Gentile nations surrounding God's nation, Israel.

The last and final section (chapters 33- 45), Ezekiel is prophesying following the siege on Jerusalem. The Jewish people seeing their place of worship in flames and they themselves captive in the land of Babylon would naturally be wondering, has God forsaken us forever? Are all the covenant promises given to us by

God now null and void? God therefore through Ezekiel prophesies in several different ways that God is not done with His people. God will breathe life into them and they will live! They will occupy all the land they were originally promised and they will be that Nation of Priests to the rest of the world, while their God, the God of all the earth reigns with them!

Bibliography

Wiersbe, Warren W. The Bible Exposition Commentary, Prophets. Colorado Springs: Cook Communications Ministries, 2002.

Josephus, Flavius. The Works of Flavius Josephus, Volume III. Grand Rapids: Baker Book House, 1974.

Keller, Werner. The Bible As History. New York: Bantam, 1982.

Ezekiel: An Expositional Commentary. CD-ROM, 2008. Dr. Chuck Missler